A GUIDE TO CRETE

John Bowman

A Guide to CRETE

with photographs by Herbert Spencer

Pantheon Books

Text © 1962 by Helga Greene
Photographs © 1962 by Herbert Spencer
First American Edition 1963
Published by Pantheon Books, a Division of Random House, Inc.
Library of Congress Catalog Card Number: 63–7351

Printed in Great Britain by
Headley Brothers Ltd, London and Ashford, Kent

Every effort has been made to ensure that the prices and
information given in this book are accurate at the
time of publication. The publishers will however welcome
readers' suggestions for improvements, or corrections,
for subsequent editions.

Contents

Maps and Plans

Author's Acknowledgment

The author wishes to take this occasion to acknowledge the many sources and people who inevitably contribute to a book such as this. One, at least, must be singled out, and that is Mr Andreas Vlahakis of the Greek National Tourist Organization, Iraklion, Crete. Without his prompting, this guide would never have been begun; without his help, it could never have been completed.

The profile of Mount Iouktas, where Cretan myth claims Zeus is buried, is seen through the sacred horns that crown the walls of the Palace of Knossos.

This charging bull, one of many frescoes reproduced in their original locations at Knossos, conjures up visions of the Labyrinth and the Minotaur.

In the antechamber of the Throne Room of Knossos, this porphyry bowl was used by the Priest-King in the performance of certain rites.

Like giant insects at rest, these are only a few of the thousands of windmills on the Lasithi Plain, below Psykhro and the Cave of Dhikti.

Silhouetted in the dramatic light of dawn, the
remains of the Palace of Phaestos seem to evoke ghosts
from the past.

The majestic central courtyard of the Palace of Phaestos enjoys a breathtaking view across the Messara Plain and its encircling mountains: here, dimly seen to the north, is Kamares Cave, at the right of the saddle between two peaks of the Idha Range.

In the shadow of the nearby mountains, this ceremonial altar has survived at the Palace of Mallia. Seeds or crops were probably consecrated in the hollows, with prayers for continuing fertility.

A giant provision jar, one of many surviving from the
Minoan era, sits in the ruins of the Palace of Mallia.
Several feet high, such jars, or *pithoi*, were used to store
all kinds of produce.

The Law Code of Gortyne, written in an archaic
'ox-plough' script, is to be seen in its original site; dating
from about 500 BC, it is still remarkably clear.

Cretans perform most of their daily activities out-of-doors: this woman is doing her laundry by the roadside in the village of Potamies.

This roadside chapel is typical of the hundreds scattered over Crete: some hold services only a few times a year, but they are always open to wayfarers—and many have fine old frescoes.

Viewed through the churchyard portal, on the road from
Phaestos to Matala, the Byzantine Chapel of Ayios
Pavlos (right) appears like some archaic, natural
phenomenon.

This roadside memorial shrine (below) is but one of many
manifestations of the pervasive and spontaneous piety of
the Orthodox Cretans.

Cretans have always preferred to express their devotion in modest and non-monumental ways, as is testified by this icon enshrined in a wall near Knossos.

Little tin simulacra crowd the altar in the Chapel of Ayios Georgios of Selinaris. These modern votive offerings represent people and parts of the body the petitioner wants cured or protected.

Windmills help to irrigate the coastal plain near Mallia,
just above some of the finest swimming beaches on Crete.
The climate here is such that even bananas flourish.

Villages such as this, en route to Arvi, appear to be clinging precariously to the hillsides; but, like wildflowers, they are well rooted in the land.

Giant reeds—both as natural growth and as man-made fences—serve as wind-breakers for the farm plots along the coast near Ierapetra.

The forbidding bluffs of Sfakia, dropping sheer onto the sea, characterize the rugged, primeval features of Crete's southern regions.

From this point on the edge of the Omalos Plateau, near Xyloskalon, begins the steep descent through the Gorge of Samaria to Ayia Roumeli.

In the harbour of Rethymnon, two fishermen go about their work early in the morning; some Cretans fish offshore at night, using lanterns.

Centuries-old, the caves above the lovely cove of Matala still accommodate many Cretans who come to enjoy the swimming at this fine, sandy beach.

Many of the Cretan roads – this one leads down onto the coast by Khora Sfakia – were laid out centuries ago at the convenience of foot travellers and heavily laden animals.

A fisherman's boat and nets spread out on the beach near Ierapetra, the largest city on Crete's southern coast. Less than two hundred miles from here, across the Libyan Sea, lies Africa.

Introduction to Crete

Crete is not simply 'one of the Greek Islands'. Her history of independence goes back a very long way and includes recurrent and persistent insurrection against foreign rule. She did not even join the Greek nation officially until 1913 and Cretans often think of themselves as Cretans first and Greeks second. This is nothing to worry about but is something that might be borne in mind by the visitor to the island.

The Cretan People Today

Contemporary Cretans, as a whole, probably represent a mixture of many racial genes and national traits, which makes it all the more remarkable that there is a peculiar genus that can be called 'Cretan'. Physical appearances among Cretans, too, vary considerably—from the short wiry 'Mediterranean' to the tall fair 'Dorian'. This second type is only found among certain isolated communities, usually in the mountains, but you can still run into men in the villages who look and bear themselves like gods—whether it be Zeus or Pan. And once in a while you will encounter a man who has a bearing and an eye that make the most imperious Spanish grandee seem like an effeminate poseur. The traditional costume—black knee-length boots, baggy, wrap-around pantaloons, sash, embroidered jacket, black head-wrapping—is generally disappearing, although quite a number of the older generation still wear it. Among the younger village men, however, boots and riding trousers predominate, as does a black cloth for the head, with a little fringe, worn at a rakish angle.

Women on Crete are not much in evidence. In the villages you will see them lurking in doorways or behind windows, bundled up in rather graceless, timeless dresses. They often go about their work in the fields with their heads wrapped up Moslem-fashion. The wearing of black is also standard in the villages, though if you happen to arrive at some special festival, you may see women in gay traditional costume. In the cities, of course, western clothes have taken over and people dress very stylishly when promenade-time comes on Saturday night.

The old ways, it is true, are gradually dying out—but not without a good deal of delaying action and rear-guard tactics. Family ties are still strong and they serve as brakes. Young men's careers are often settled by their parents; marriages are usually arranged, to some degree. (Even the Code of Gortyne dealt, among other things, with the need to marry heiresses within the 'tribe'—to prevent the break-up of families.) The village people, too, are surrounded by rituals and formulas, traditions, superstitions, proverbial ways. And as is to be expected, the younger generation and the urban types comprise the 'modernist' element; they are strongly oriented towards America—studying the 'American language', buying American clothes, watching American films, learning American songs. Yet the dominant tone of the island is set by the conservative, orthodox groups, and the more intelligent and balanced young people do not find it necessary to turn their backs on all the old ways. They are the first to appreciate the traditional social and personal relationships; they still love to dance the old dances, sing the old songs.

Dances provide the most authentic evidence of the continuity of Crete's popular traditions and rhythms. Homer in *The Iliad* describes how 'Daedalus in Knossos once contrived/A dancing-floor for fair-haired Ariadne', and the Cretans have always been known for their dances: the *pentozalis*—a lively, swinging dance, with the arms interlocked; the *khaniotikos*—a circle dance; the *syrtos*—a sedate circle dance; and many others—the *sousta, ortzes, kastrinos, malevysiotikos, sitiakos*. A newer favourite is the tango. Today there are groups who revive and perform the traditional dances. But perhaps the really pure Cretan dance is to be seen in any village café or festival—or, for that matter, in some Iraklion taverna—when a man or several men spontaneously move into the centre of the floor and start to dance. And the young people of Iraklion can be just as proud and graceful when they circle in the old dances. It makes no difference that the old melodies are played on electric guitars, or even on a gramophone: the dancing is still performed to the old rhythms. But undoubtedly the most picturesque occasions for the traditional music and dances are at village ceremonies—weddings, baptisms, saints' days.

As for the music of Crete, it strikes the ear as one would expect: an amalgamation of all the styles and cultures that have entered Crete. Into Near Eastern music the familiar strains of European folk music intrude. If you are lucky, you will see one of the old instruments played —the *lyra*, a small, three-stringed lute-like instrument that is bowed as it is held on the knee. Or you may hear some really old ballads. Most exciting of all are the *mantinadhes*—improvized rhyming couplets that follow the inspiration of some occasion, joyful or mournful. Although traditionally improvized there is actually a repertoire of *mantinadhes* on which to draw. In Iraklion—and possibly Khania—you may also hear the *bouzouki* music: taking its name from the instrument (something like a mandolin) it has now come to stand more for the mood of the songs and the atmosphere of the places where it is played—a mood akin to jazz 'blues'. Greek music, then, traditional or otherwise, is very much alive, and it will be a long time before American hit songs —which, to be sure, often blare out from some radio—drown out the old melodies.

For the true Cretan is essentially reactionary. Many of the men have seen the benefits of American and Western European industrial society at first-hand, and they often profess to want these benefits translated to Crete. But few are really prepared to make the basic adaptations and sacrifices required—so the old ways prevail. It is safe to say that it will be some time yet before the washing machine replaces the village wash-hole.

The Koumbaros

In Greek life, family loyalties take precedence over all others. But there is one relationship in Greek social life that the foreigner may not have encountered elsewhere and that is interesting for him to know about. This is the role of the *koumbaros* (feminine: *koumbara*). Technically he is either the godfather or the 'best man' at the wedding, but the obligations and the significance of his office go far beyond anything we know in our societies. The office of *koumbaros* as best man does indeed resemble our own except that as Greeks stay closer to a small circle of intimates a best man in Greece will probably be the groom's closest friend for the whole of his life. As godfather the *koumbaros* has even more significance, and a young couple choose him very carefully. He must be a responsible person as well as a friend. During the years of a child's growing up the *koumbaros* will be consulted on all vital matters, and when the child reaches manhood he will probably still turn to his *koumbaros* for counsel. The *koumbaros* on his side will have provided aid and favours of all kinds throughout the years and is an honoured guest at family gatherings. He may be of the same social and economic status as his godchild's family or he may be considerably higher, but the links are just as strong, whatever the boundaries to be observed. A *koumbaros* may share a family's light moments, but he does not take his relationship lightly.

Hospitality

Greek hospitality is a byword among foreigners: by now everyone except the native has marvelled that the Greek word for 'stranger' is also the word for 'guest'. But this hospitality is quite complex: on the one hand it reaches out to embrace the stranger-guest, on the other it is restrained by many points of procedure and ritual. For example, when a stranger walks into a village its inhabitants will not speak until spoken to. But once the newcomer speaks he will be overwhelmed with friendly greetings.

Perhaps nowhere is Greek hospitality seen in such intensity as on Crete. There it becomes almost aggressive at times, and the traveller who really wants to understand and take part in local life must be prepared to go all the way. It is no good going into the villages and mixing with the people and then—when the going becomes a bit strenuous—discreetly retiring. If you are welcomed into a home you will be plied with drinks and sweets that must not be refused; you will be given meals that cannot be paid for except with thanks. The less they have the more they will produce for you. Food, drink, flowers, souvenirs—these are their welcome to a guest and should be gracefully accepted. You will find yourself stared at, asked personal questions; if you get the impression that everyone for miles around has been called in to 'inspect' you—that is probably exactly what has happened. The greater the number of people who are packed into a small space—whether it's the front parlour or the back seat of a car—the more successful is the hospitality.

Café Life

On Crete the café is the man's world. If you see any women in one they will most likely be foreigners—tourists. Men sit there and nurse a single drink for hours, talking, reading newspapers, watching the world go by. Two active café occupations may puzzle visitors. One is a board game, *tavli*, which some will recognize as backgammon: it is played at a furious rate, with much slamming and argument. The other occupation involves the little strings of amber beads which so many men finger whilst they are sitting or standing about. They are the *komboloia*—the 'worry beads'—and their function seems to be simply to relieve tension. At first glance they look like rosaries. Men can get quite attached to their 'worry beads' and it is said to be a sign of a well-spent life if a man can show a string of highly polished beads in his later years.

The Volta

Walking is another feature of Cretan social life. Not tramping overland to get somewhere—but the very special walking known as the *volta*—the promenade which takes place at given hours along a defined route in towns and villages all over Crete. The basic pattern is for a considerable section of the local population to put on its finery and stroll up and down a certain stretch of the town's main street. The usual time is in the early evening. It is quite a complex social ritual for those involved—who wears what and who is seen with whom and who looked at whom.

Time and Punctuality

If you get to know individual Cretans well enough to make appointments with them it is as well to remember that on Crete 'morning' extends until 12 noon. 'Noon' is from 12 to 3 p.m.; 'afternoon' is from 3 to 7 p.m. If a Cretan says he will meet you 'at noon', he may mean 2 p.m.; 'this afternoon' for him may be 6 p.m.

Roadside Sights

Cretan life takes place largely out of doors. It is particularly fascinating to be present during the summer grain harvest, when the farmers may be seen using tools and techniques that have remained unchanged for thousands of years. Of if you are lucky you may see flocks being moved to or from the summer pastures by shepherds straight out of Kazantzakis. In the fields women often stand guard spinning wool on the distaff—straight off an ancient vase.

If you should want to photograph such scenes you must be careful not to attract attention, for as soon as it is realized that you are going to take their picture your subjects will become stiff and formal. They may even want to go off and put on their Sunday best!

One final word about discovering Crete: on the one hand Crete seems to yield easily to the curiosity of the foreigner; the people seem open and spontaneous and their hospitality encourages one to feel that the surface has been quickly broken through. But Crete has hidden depths. It is not a tourist paradise and there are many things about it which provoke strong reactions. Life on Crete is still hard for many and can appear unrefined, to say the least. But it is a rich, unique, intense way of life, and the longer one stays the more this can be appreciated. For the discerning, a visit to Crete cannot fail to be an exciting and rewarding adventure.

Facilities on Crete

Shops and Services

Villages and the smaller towns can provide little beyond the basic amenities, but several of the larger cities offer a full range of shops and services—including laundry and dry cleaning, films and photographic supplies, pharmacies and jewellers, clothing and hardware. Prices are usually marked—and fixed. (See 'Haggling', p. 61.) Many of the better shops now have some English-speaking personnel, and people around will always help you with any difficult purchase.

The only large stock of foreign periodicals and books—English, American, French, and German—is at Alexiou's Bookstore near the Morosini fountain, a few doors from the Caprice Restaurant, in Iraklion: special orders may also be placed there.

With regard to souvenirs and handicrafts, Crete's specialities include: knives, hand-woven materials, bags, carpets, lace, embroidery, shawls, hand-made gold and silver beads, baskets and ceramics. The larger cities have a wide selection in the shops; if you are lucky you may be able to pick up some things in the villages.

In general, shops are open every day except Sunday, although certain ones manage to open even then—little meat shops, for instance, or village shops that are practically homes and which seem to be open around the clock. But in the cities some shops (including foodshops, barbers, etc.) close on Wednesdays at noon, while others close on Saturdays at noon. In general, shops open at 8 a.m., close for the long siesta at 1 p.m., open again around 4 p.m., and close for the night at 8 p.m.

Hotels, larger restaurants, souvenir shops and some selected shops in the main cities will usually cash travellers' cheques.

Kiosks are open at almost any time of day or night: here you can get cigarettes, toilet articles and cosmetics, pencils and postcards, sweets, etc., and sometimes postage stamps.

Water

There is good, safe drinking water in plentiful supply over the entire island and throughout the entire year. All the main cities and larger villages have chemically treated supplies, while fresh springs are abundant elsewhere, In the larger cities, bottled mineral water (*metalliko nero*) is available; and even in the most obscure and isolated villages there always seems to be some sort of bottled lemonade.

Electricity

All the larger towns and most big villages have electricity. The voltage is variously 110 or 220, and the current is either AC or DC. (Anyone planning a very long stay on Crete with elaborate electrical equipment would need to bring transformers to convert the voltage and current.)

Getting to Crete

The most recent means of getting to Greece—the ferry from Brindisi —promises to revolutionize tourism in Greece. What is not generally known is that Crete itself may be reached directly from foreign shores. At present there are scheduled air connections only with the mainland and Rhodes, via Olympic Airways, but ships from many ports frequently put into one of Crete's main harbours—usually Iraklion.

Ships to Crete from Foreign Ports

Most of these are freighters, coming from various Mediterranean ports, and stop only if they have cargo to load or discharge. The average traveller, therefore, will have little opportunity of reaching Crete by this means. Inquiries could however be made with an appropriate shipping line, taking particular care to verify that the ship will definitely stop at Crete. Such lines include the Swedish S.O.L., the Deutsche Orient-Linie, the Argo Nah-Ost Linie, the Atlas-Levante Linie, Hellenic Lines and the K.N.S.M. Company.

In addition to these international freighters, there are more regularly scheduled sailings of the Adriatica Steamship Lines and the Yugoslavia Steamship Lines, both of which usually put into Crete about twice a month. The following cities along the Italian and Dalmatian coasts are among their regular ports of call: Livorno, Genoa, Naples, Ancona, Venice, Trieste, Split, Kotor, Dubrovnik and Bar. Two passenger ships leave Brindisi, Italy, weekly for Crete via Piraeus.

And, throughout the year, special cruise and tour ships depart from foreign ports, and some include Crete in their itineraries. Such ships, however, usually make a very limited stay at Crete and will take on only those who intend to remain with the ship for the complete cruise.

Anyone planning to come to Crete with unusual quantities of luggage, and unable to get it there by normal means, should apply to one of the big international freight agents. A company such as

American Express or Schenker & Co. can save an individual immense amounts of trouble in such matters.

Ships to Crete from the Mainland

There are regular and frequent connections between the mainland and the three ports along the north coast—Iraklion, Khania and Rethymnon. The ships leave the mainland at Piraeus (the port of Athens) at least once a day, except Sunday, throughout the year, with a similar return schedule. The direct run to Iraklion takes 14 hours; direct run to Khania is 12 hours; if Rethymnon is to be your port of entry, you must first call at one of the other ports, which will add about four hours to your trip.

As the various ships are owned by different companies, it is advisable to buy your tickets at one of the travel agents, either in Athens or Piraeus. There will be no extra fee for this. In Piraeus, the ticket agents are in the vicinity of Karaiskakis Square; in Athens, they are in the centre of the town. In an emergency you can buy your tickets on the ship itself.

Schedule of Fares

The fares are the same for all three ports. We give below the single rates—for the round trip, simply double these. Meals and service tips are extra, and it is possible to buy passable meals and light refreshments on board.

Class	Fare
1st (2 per cabin)	Drs. 279
2nd (3 per cabin)	Drs. 190
3rd, or Tourist (4-6 per cabin)	Drs. 143
Deck	Drs. 93

(Deck Class means that you will pass the night either stretched out alone on a wooden bench or else packed in with a large and varied crowd. It is not recommended, except for the most intrepid travellers.)

In addition to the scheduled public sailings, it is possible to get to Crete on one of the cruise ships that sail from Piraeus. During the high season, five or six may call each week—usually only at Iraklion and usually only for one day. This allows a quick tour of Knossos, a walk through the Archaeological Museum, a tour of Iraklion—and sometimes a dash down to Phaestos. Failing all else, it is one way to get a glimpse of Crete—but you must sign up for the entire cruise. Arrangements can be made through any travel agency.

Planes to Crete from the Mainland

Internal air traffic in Greece is a monopoly of Olympic Airways, which has an excellent safety record. Transport to the airports is provided by the airline. For flights within Greece, travellers are limited to 30 pounds of luggage free of charge. Flights from the Athens Airport connect with one of two cities—Iraklion or Khania.

Athens-Iraklion-Athens:
2 to 3 flights daily, in each direction. Flight-time, 55 to 70 minutes, depending on whether it is a 2- or 4-engine plane.
Fare: Drs. 380 single; Drs. 684 return.

Athens-Khania-Athens:
1 to 2 flights daily, in each direction. Flight-time, 65 minutes.
Fare: Drs. 322 single; Drs. 580 return.

Ships to Crete from Rhodes

There is one ship each week, in each direction, connecting Crete to Rhodes. The ports of call on Crete are Ayios Nikolaos and Sitia; the ship does *not* call at Iraklion. An overnight stay at either of these two ports is therefore necessary.

The ship leaves Ayios Nikolaos every Wednesday at 4 a.m., calls at Sitia, leaving again at about 5.30 a.m., and then goes on to Rhodes, arriving about 11.30 that night.

It leaves Rhodes every Thursday, about 2.30 a.m., arrives at Sitia late on Thursday morning, and at Ayios Nikolaos on Thursday afternoon.

The ship is the *Arcadia*, operated by the Diamantis Line, which has an office in Iraklion. Arrangements can therefore be made there. Single fares are as follows:

	Rhodes-Sitia	*Rhodes-Ayios Nikolaos*
1st Class	Drs. 273	Drs. 296
2nd Class	Drs. 181	Drs. 195
Tourist Class	Drs. 136	Drs. 145
Deck	Drs. 97	Drs. 103

By Air to Crete from Rhodes

From April to October only, Olympic Airways provides 2 to 4 flights weekly, in each direction, between Rhodes and Iraklion. Flight time about one hour. Single Fare is Drs. 385; return Drs. 693.

Connections with Crete from other Greek Islands

There are no scheduled connections, either by sea or air, between Crete and the other Greek islands. In general, it is necessary to return to Piraeus, where there are many ships that ply between there and the other islands. However, the adventurous traveller with a little time to spare could eventually find one of the smaller freight or fishing vessels to take him to one or another of these islands. These are the boats widely known as caiques. It is safe to assume that the boat will not set out unless it is going to have a comparatively smooth crossing and a good chance of arriving; no one has more respect for the winds and seas of this part of the Mediterranean than the native.

Fares are somewhat elastic. If it is left entirely to you to decide what the trip is worth, much will depend on how you encountered the crew and your relations with the men on the trip. It may be that you can only pay your debt in wine.

Documents and Regulations

Passport and Visa

Since Crete is part of the Greek State, there are no special arrangements required for entering Crete, other than those required for Greece. A valid passport, in fact, is enough. If you come over to Crete from the mainland, there is not even any question of producing this. (The exception arises if you come to Crete with a vehicle or with an unusual amount of luggage or gear; while checking to make sure that these have already passed through customs, the officials are likely to check your passport. For the special regulations governing the entry of vehicles, see p. 48.) For travellers coming to Crete direct from a foreign country there will be the usual passport control and customs formalities.

If your stay in Greece and/or Crete is to be of any duration you must apply for a renewal or extension of your passport privilege at the Department for Foreigners of the Ministry of Internal Affairs (head office at 9 Chalkokondeli Street in Athens; central office on Crete at 25th August Street, down by the harbour of Iraklion).

Foreigners whose stay in Greece has been exactly one year or more must obtain a tax-clearance certificate from the Finance Ministry before they will be allowed to leave. For further information consult the Tourist Organization or Police on Crete. Indeed, anyone who stays for long in Greece soon learns to save all papers, documents, receipts, forms, seals and scraps of paper picked up along the way. It is astonishing how often these can be required.

Customs Regulations

The usual Greek customs regulations apply on Crete. While the foreigner may of course take in any sum in travellers' cheques the basic restriction is that you are only allowed to bring in Drs. 2,000. Only 200 cigarettes (or 30 cigars or 200 grams of tobacco) are admitted free. Cameras, typewriters, field-glasses and similar equipment must be entered on your passport, and shown on leaving.

As for export restrictions, technically only Drs. 2,000 may be taken out of Greece. There is also a limit on how much olive oil an individual is allowed to take out duty free. Finally, taking out ancient works of art (these are defined as anything dated before 1830) is prohibited, but this is a regulation more honoured in the breach . . .

Those planning to stay for some time, and who intend bringing in a lot of special gear, should check with their nearest Greek Consulate.

Preliminaries

Information

Information of every kind may be obtained from the National Tourist Organization of Greece. Its Main Office is at 4 Stadiou Street, Athens; its chief Information Office is 8 Venizelou Avenue, Athens. Other offices in the world's principal cities include:

London: 195-7 Regent Street, London W1
New York: 69 East 79th Street, New York 21
Ottawa: 215 Metcalfe Street
Paris: 31 Avenue de l'Opéra
Rome: Via Bissolati 78-80
Frankfurt/Main: Baselerstrasse 35-37

Greek Consulates and Embassies in all cities will of course assist the prospective visitor. There are also the private travel and tourist agencies. On Crete itself there are many sources of information (see p. 44). The main one in Iraklion is the National Tourist Organization, 25th August Street.

Reductions and Discounts

Certain discounts are available to special classes of visitors to Greece —particularly students, teachers, artists and journalists. Almost all of these, however, apply only to costs of getting to and from Greece and foreign ports; none apply to transport on Crete itself. Anyone who thinks he might qualify for a discount should enquire at a travel agent, Greek Consulate, or the National Tourist Organization. If your plans include making a direct connection with Crete by freight-steamship line (see p. 38) it is possible you will find something applicable.

There is one pass available to the above-mentioned groups of tourists which is valid on Crete: it is the one that entitles the holder to free access to the various archaeological sites and museums of Greece. Knossos, Phaestos, Mallia, and Iraklion's Archaeological Museum all charge Drs. 10. Ayia Triadha, Gournia, Tylissos, Iraklion's Historical Museum, and the Archaeological Museums of Khania, Rethymnon, and Ayios Nikolaos all charge Drs. 5. For those who are also travelling on the mainland, the pass is even more worthwhile.

The pass may be obtained upon personal application at the Greek Ministry of Education, 2 Evangelistrias Street, Athens. Identification of some sort must be presented: e.g. your status must be entered on your passport. (You will also need two extra passport photos.)

Seasons and Hours

Statistics show that most tourists arrive during July, August and September—with another slight rise in April owing to Easter festivities. But it must be said that as yet Crete is never overrun with tourists: Iraklion alone, on certain days, may give the impression that organized tourism has taken over, but these are only cruises ashore for the day. Apart from this, and an occasional traffic jam at Knossos, any visitor can pretty much feel as though he has the island to himself.

All the principal archaeological sites are accessible throughout the year, though some of the caves, mountain peaks, isolated villages and chapels might be cut off by winter storms.

The island's bus lines operate throughout the year, with the possible withdrawal of an occasional bus to some isolated area. Winter and summer schedules are slightly different. The summer season is from April 15 to October 15, but very few routes and villages are seriously affected by winter changes.

Shops are open throughout the year and banks are open Monday to Saturday from 9 a.m. to 1 p.m.

Climate

Crete has one of the most favourable climates of the Mediterranean, with mild to hot weather prevailing throughout most of the year. Tomatoes and swallows flourish the year round in a few places. In general, you can count on almost 300 days of sunny, clear skies each year, with moderate temperatures. For those who have the whole year to choose from, May or September is recommended as the ideal time to travel on Crete.

Spring moves in during April, and the rains usually stop by the end of the month: quite literally, barely a drop of rain falls during May, June, July, August and September. During the peak summer season, the visitor is advised to avoid ambitious expeditions during the middle of the day, when the temperature on the plains ranges from 80° to 100° F., but that still leaves many hours for sight-seeing. Evenings, too, are generally mild, cooling to 60° to 75°, even during the hottest spell. Fortunately, too, cool breezes play along the coasts and through the mountains, thus breaking the dead heat. Autumn is mild. Winter can occasionally be severe—especially the end of January and early February. Freezing temperatures are rare, though, in any locale where the traveller is likely to be. Mountain winters can be rough, and snow covers certain slopes and trails, making travel impossible. Snow is all but unknown along the coastal regions.

There are two minor diversions from this climate-pattern; neither need deter the prospective visitor. One is the hot, dry sirocco that occasionally sweeps up from Africa and which can be a minor nuisance. The other consists of earthquakes, but these occur so infrequently and so slightly as to count for nothing in the traveller's plans.

Travel on Crete

Once on Crete, it is possible to get help and advice from several sources. Iraklion, Khania and Ayios Nikolaos have branch offices of the National Tourist Organization of Greece:

Iraklion:	25th August Street (Phone: 80-96)
	Open weekdays and Sundays
Khania:	Megaron Nomarkhias (Phone: 4-76)
	Open weekdays only, 8-2.30.
Ayios Nikolaos:	Near the harbour by the 'Bottomless Pool' (Phone: 121)

If you want to know where there is to be some village festival, or clear up a point about an obscure Byzantine chapel, or make contact with the local authority on cheeses, antiquities, or caves, go to one of these offices.

They can also put you in touch with private tourist agencies, with shipping lines, and with private guides. These guides—usually young, and fluent in your own language—will accompany you on anything from a two-hour visit to the Museum to a six-day tour of the island.

Another official institution which you will find yourself relying on throughout your stay on the island is the Tourist Police. This is simply one of the main branches of the Greek National Police Force and is to be found all over Greece. Its members wear a greenish uniform, and are identified by the words 'Tourist Police' on their sleeve. In addition, those who speak a foreign language wear the flag of that nation on their jacket. (English-speaking ones wear the American flag!) Tourist Police are to be met all over the island and will do anything possible to help the traveller. They can help you find a room in a villager's house, can arrange a ride over the mountain with some local lorry-driver, or can find a boy to guide you to an isolated chapel. Main offices of the Tourist Police:

Iraklion:	25th August Street (Phone: 91-90)
Khania:	Nea Demotiki Agora (Phone: 84-41)

Incidentally, any complaints you may have, about prices or anything else, should be directed to the Tourist Police.

Buses

Most people will depend on the buses to get around the island. And in spite of the rickety appearance of some of them, they always get to their destinations.

Bus fares average about 50 lepta per kilometre.

There are scheduled connections with practically every village and site on the island, usually departing from one of the four capitals of the Nomes: Iraklion, Khania, Rethymnon, and Ayios Nikolaos.

A few of the private travel agencies operate small buses for organized tours; large parties may hire buses from the transport companies.

Taxis

In certain situations hiring a taxi is the best way to get to some place. It is not as extravagant as it may sound; nor will it mark you as a 'rich tourist'. Greeks use taxis at the drop of a hat, and think nothing of it when three or four people decide to share one and avoid the crowded buses. In the large cities it is easy to hire a cab and even smaller villages support at least one cab. Foreigners sometimes cannot understand how an isolated village can support some mammoth American vehicle, but in places where no private individual owns a car it is a necessity to have some means of transport.

Some excursions take longer than one would wish, owing to the fact that bus schedules are arranged for the villagers and not for tourists. Thus an excursion which might take three days to make by depending on buses could be done in one day if you had a taxi at your disposal. When three or four people share expenses the cost can be quite reasonable. In addition there are valuable 'fringe benefits'—such as the taxi driver knowing many people and cafés and sites en route.

Official rates are given here, but to avoid misunderstanding, the trip should be discussed with the particular driver before setting out. (This is where the Tourist Information office or the Tourist Police make their usefulness felt.)

If you make a return trip by taxi, the charge is Drs. 3.20 per running km. The charge for the driver's waiting time is Drs. 12 per hour, starting from 15 minutes after arrival at a site. If you take a taxi in one direction only, and then dismiss the driver, the cost is Drs. 5.40 per running km. (These rates are for taxis taking from five to seven passengers; there should be no extra charge for reasonable amounts of baggage, nor does the rate fluctuate with the number of people.)

Guided Tours

The private agencies which operate various kinds of tours, using buses or other vehicles, have varying fees and schedules. English-speaking guides are included, and such tours have certain advantages. Ask the National Tourist office to recommend you one.

Car Hire

In Iraklion and Khania it is possible to hire a car to drive yourself. This should be arranged through the Tourist Office or Police. Most of the cars available are recent European models.

Car hire rates fluctuate, but are usually worked on a basis of about Drs. 300 per day. Sometimes a limit may be fixed with an extra charge for additional kms. Petrol is *not* included, and some sort of refundable deposit is usually required—perhaps as much as Drs. 1,500.

An International Driving Permit is technically required for driving in Greece, but if your national or State licence is clearly in good order you would be allowed to hire.

Mules

For the really determined traveller, there is still the mule or donkey. (One school of travellers claims that the only legitimate way to arrive in Mediterranean villages is over the trails with a donkey.) Quite seriously, if one wants to do much travelling among the mountains, it is a most practical means of getting about. The Tourist Police would help with arrangements for this in almost any village: if it were only the donkey you wanted to hire, you might get one for Drs. 50 a day, and if you wanted a man to come along as well it would cost about twice as much. It is even possible to buy a donkey fairly cheaply— Drs. 600 to 1,000, depending on the staying power of the beast and your own powers of bargaining. With any luck you might sell the animal back for just about what you had paid for it, which would mean you had had free transport—of a sort.

The word for donkey is *zóon*, which means 'animal', and to Cretans the donkey is *the* animal.

Caiques

A caique is the type of boat used in the local coastal and island traffic. It may vary in size from yacht-style boats to plain little fishing boats. All have motors. They may vary in comforts and conveniences, but all are perfectly reliable for what they try to do.

There are two ways of hiring caiques. One is to make arrangements through the travel agents on the mainland or on Crete itself. Naturally, the caiques they deal with tend to be more elegant than the ones you might pick up for yourself in some little fishing cove.

The second way arises when you find yourself on the coast— whether in a city like Iraklion or in some nameless village-harbour —and you want to get somewhere farther along; you approach the men on the caique and ask when they will be moving on; if it is at a convenient time for you, you can perhaps come to terms. In most cases there is no fixed rate, but by consulting the map you may get an idea of what you might have to pay.

Much would depend on whether the men were going to make the

trip anyway as part of their work. If you have to hire them to make the trip specially for you, you would naturally have to pay more. If you fall into company with a fisherman in some café and he says: 'Come on—let's go!', you can expect to get to your destination for a bottle of wine or two. Most of these excursions, though, cost about Drs. 300 a round trip, which can be taken as some sort of base.

In the harbour at Ayios Nikolaos you can also make arrangements for a boat to take you to Elounda and Spinalonga (p. 150). A cruise round the Gulf of Merabello is most enjoyable and you may be able to arrange matters with a local caique-owner. A full day would allow you to visit the islands of Psira and Mokhlos (p. 155).

Yachting

Yachting can be a good way of getting around Crete. There are small but safe harbours all around the island, and in certain places, such as Iraklion, Khania, Sitia, Rethymnon and Ayios Nikolaos, there are adequate facilities for emergencies and repairs. By putting into various harbours you would have access to every site on the island: no place would be much more than twenty miles from the sea.

It is possible to rent motor yachts and sailing yachts, with or without crews, in Piraeus, and here again arrangements can be made through the travel agencies. There is considerable range in accommodation, but when the cost has been divided among a party of six to twelve adults it is less heavy than one might expect. With a cook aboard, doing one's own food-buying, and with no hotel bills, it might even become a fairly cheap way for a group of friends to get about.

For further information, write to the Yachting Department of the National Tourist Organization, 4 Stadiou Street, Athens.

Your own car

We have saved for last the one means of transport that most people will probably be surprised to see listed at all as a possibility—your own car. Each year, though, more and more visitors from the Continent are discovering the pleasure that can be had from touring Crete with their own vehicles. It is expensive, of course, to bring a car over to Crete, but in the end it may repay you. If you have only three to five days, it probably won't be worth it. But anyone planning to spend a week or more, with a family or party of friends, may discover that it is a most reasonable proposition. Certainly your own car will allow you to see places and things that with other forms of transport cannot be managed in limited time. As this is a fairly new approach to Crete, we shall attempt to give as complete a picture as possible of the situation facing the potential driver-on-Crete.

We start at the Greek border, assuming that you have got as far as that. To enter Greece with a foreign-licensed vehicle, the following documents are required:

(1) A Carnet de Passages en Douanes, also known as a Tryptique: this rather formidable document is really a passport for your vehicle.
(2) An International Driving Permit: this is your driving licence, printed in several languages. (One passport photograph required.)
(3) The log book (or registration) of your car.
(4) The international insurance card issued by your own insurance company.

These documents are valid for one year. They may be obtained through the national automobile associations. If you arrive at the border without these documents, the Customs Authorities will issue you a special Certificate of Free Use, *valid only for four months*. (It might be extended upon application to the Finance Ministry at Athens.) Your local automobile association issues the Carnet. It is wise to check with them to make sure you have all the instructions for taking your own car abroad.

The same regulations governing entry of vehicles into Greece extend to Crete, so that once you are in the country you can bring your car over to Crete. At most you will be asked to produce your papers and passport as you disembark in Crete, just to make sure that all is in order. If you have come direct from some foreign country to Crete, then you must go through all these formalities at the Cretan port of entry.

Mainland to Crete

We are assuming that almost all people planning to bring their vehicles to Crete will be approaching from the Greek mainland. (Anyone who is obliged to bring his vehicle from some foreign port could make the necessary arrangements there.)

Starting in Athens, you should first visit one of the travel agencies. They will probably direct you to the office of the actual shipping line in Piraeus where you can get your own ticket as well as the car's —or the agents could make the arrangements for you. The ship you take will depend on the day you want to sail and it may also have some effect on the price you pay for your vehicle. For one thing, if you had to take your car over on one of the small ships it might have to go lashed to the deck—which is cheaper than the hold passage.

The fare from Piraeus to one of the three Cretan ports, *one way*, may be anything from Drs. 600 to 1,000 depending on the weight of your vehicle. (This does not include your own passenger fares.) This rate will usually include only the loading fees and fare from the port of embarkation; when you arrive at Iraklion—or, upon returning, at Piraeus—you must be prepared to pay the particular fees and unloading charges of the port. This will run into another Drs. 90 to 150.

These various port charges and unloading fees may seem to be calculated on the whim of the particular individual assigned to you, so there is a wide range reported. In fact the men have their charts and schedules of rates: language difficulties usually cause any trouble there may be. At the same time there does seem to be a lack of system. If you have reason to feel that there has been a serious injustice, then take your papers and receipts and go to the Tourist Police. You may find, though, that the reason your unloading fee is more than that of another tourist in your hotel is that you landed on Sunday—and he came on Saturday.

Once ashore and the formalities over, you are on your own. Driving is on the right of the road. There is no speed limit on the open roads, but in towns and built-up areas there is a legal speed limit of 18 mph.

Petrol and oil are available all over the island—including several of the better grade American and European brands. There are plenty of filling stations, and distances are short, but it is as well to keep as full a tank as possible.

In the smaller villages filling stations offer little except petrol and oil, but there are plenty of repair shops in the larger villages and cities. You will not get the *most* expert service and repair work in the world, but the men are certainly experienced with American and foreign cars. Here and there you will even come across an 'authorized' dealer or repair station; and in a serious emergency there is always an appeal to Athens.

Roads: Crete has its share of bad roads—but also its share of good roads. From Khania along the coast to Ayios Nikolaos in the east, the main coast road is entirely asphalt; there is a new asphalt road from Iraklion halfway to Phaestos; and there are several other stretches of asphalt around the island—some of them in the most unexpected places. (An isolated stretch of asphalt usually means that the nearby village was prosperous enough to afford it—or else that the government put it down for some strategic purpose.) After these 'first-class' roads come the good 'secondary' hard-packed dirt roads: they can get a bit dusty during the dry season and a bit slippery in the rainy season, but by and large they are good solid roads. Here and there is a washboard stretch, now and again a patch under repair—but you make progress. And finally there are one or two stretches to sites indicated in this book which, frankly, are very bad roads. Yet with a little patience and a car you can get there. The heavy low-slung American car is apt to be at a disadvantage on these stretches, but most of the taxis on Crete are just such vehicles and their drivers are able to penetrate into the most isolated spots. The author of this book, moreover, can speak from experience: in the course of four months' excursions to some very isolated sites, he never ran into a road that couldn't be taken. It is largely a matter of being willing to crawl. Considering Crete's situation—geographically, historically, economically—the island has better roads than one has a right to expect.

Driving Conditions: Roads are not as well marked as an American or European would like them to be. Curves, bad gradients, soft shoulders, hazardous conditions—you cannot count on signs for any of these. Nor will crucial turn-offs always be marked: you will have been directed to go straight ahead to the site you want, and two seconds later there will be a forked road—one as good as the other, and with no sign to indicate which leads to your destination.

As for asking directions—care is needed. The average villager can only estimate distances or times—and usually his estimate is based on the way he knows best: a donkey trail, overland. Your destination is always 'straight ahead': it is assumed that you know about those forked roads and turn-offs. Roads are either 'very good' or 'very bad'—and the native's criteria may not be yours.

Finally, Greeks seldom use light or hand signals. They often ignore through-traffic, and will turn on to the main road from some little driveway just when you are convinced that you have the right of way. (The right of way in Greece, in fact, goes to the fastest and first—except for pedestrians. Pedestrians still have the right of way in Greece, and no matter how frivolous their actions you must make it your business to avoid them if you are behind a wheel.) At night, on-coming vehicles will blink their lights on and off. During the day, the driver of the car in front of you will suddenly halt to chat with a friend at the roadside. Driving through a city's main street is like taking part in an old Keystone comedy—but, somehow, everyone survives.

Accommodation on Crete

Taking the island as a whole, travellers on Crete have a wide choice of accommodation. Outside the principal cities, however, there is little or no choice. On the other hand, all accommodation is regulated and inspected by the National Tourist Organization and Tourist Police (as it is throughout Greece) and standards are fixed in respect of prices and facilities.

Overnight accommodation can often be arranged at monasteries.

Hotels

There are five main classes of hotels; in addition, there are the 'boarding-houses' and 'tourist cottages' or 'inns'. Clean linen and safe water are provided for every class, but other conveniences may vary. Categories are assigned on the basis of such things as whether there is a reception hall, telephones, hot running water, etc.

Prices are set by the National Tourist Organization. They will be listed both in the office and in each individual room. In the following chart we have tried to give the latest minimum rates for the several classes of hotels. This cannot, of course, be regarded as absolute; it is simply to give a fair idea of the relative costs.

(a) All prices are given in Drachmas.

(b) These rates are for a stay of *more* than two days; for a stay of only two days or less you must pay 10 per cent extra.

(c) All service charges (up to 15 per cent in the better hotels) and Municipal Taxes are included in these prices.

(d) Tourists taking rooms without private baths or showers can usually make arrangements for these: the usual rates are Drs. 12 for a bath and Drs. 7 for a shower.

(e) Heating is not included in the prices quoted: the charge is Drs. 9 for a single room, Drs. 14 for a double room, per day.

(f) Meals are always extra. If you should send out for breakfast—usually no more than coffee and some sort of roll, with jam or honey—this will usually cost between 10 and 12 drachmas.

(g) There are no official 'off-season' rates on Crete.

(h) Certain hotels—either because they are newly built or have made extensive alterations—may make a surcharge of a percentage beyond the usual rate for the class. The following hotels at present make an extra charge: in Iraklion—the Astir, the Candia Palace, the Cosmopolite, Knossos and Ariane; in Khania—the Cyprus, the Elyros and the Plaza; and in Neapolis—the Vassilikon.

(i) Tipping, of course, is at the discretion of the individual. See note p. 62.

Accommodation	Class	A	B	C	D	E
Suite (with bath)		250				
Single: with bath		120				
Single: with shower			75			
Single: no bath or shower		80	60	45	35	30
Double: with bath (twin beds)		190				
Double: with shower (twin beds)			100	75		
Double: no bath or shower (twin beds)			90	70	50	45
Double bed: with bath		160				
Double bed: with shower			90			
Double bed: no bath or shower			80	60	45	40
Room with 3 beds: no bath or shower				70	65	60

Boarding Houses

In Iraklion there are now several houses where you can stay for about Drs. 37 for a single, and Drs. 59 for a double, room. Meals can also be arranged for about Drs. 30 to 35, per day.

Tourist Cottages (Inns)

In some isolated villages, these modest little inns are the only accommodation and are perfectly reliable. Beds are about Drs. 15 per night.

Tourist Pavilions

There are several tourist pavilions, erected by the National Tourist Organization, on Crete, but the only one at present equipped to accommodate overnight guests throughout the year is at Phaestos. Its rates are the same as a Class D hotel, but it has showers. The Hotel Astir in Iraklion is the only real luxury hotel on Crete; Class B and Class C hotels are good; Class E, can be rather Spartan.

List of Hotels

Hotel	Class	Hotel	Class	Hotel	Class
Iraklion Nome		*Khania Nome*		*Lasithi Nome*	
Iraklion		**Khania**		**Ayios Nikolaos**	
Astir	A	Minoa	A	Lato	B
Ariadne	B	Cyprus	C	Aegeon	E
Candia Palace	B	Elyros	C	Athinai	E
Cosmopolite	B	Plaza	C	Minos Beach Bungalows	
Knossos	B	Hellas	D		
Florida	C	Hermes	D	**Elounda**	
Hellas	C	Nea Ionia	D	Nea Elounda	E
Palladion	C	Acropolis	E		
Phaestos	D	Arkadhi	E	**Ierapetra**	
Rex	D	Averoff	E	Creta	C
Venetia	D	Bristol	E	Lyvikon	D
Arkadhi	E	Crete	E	Aigli	E
Diathnes	E	Europa	E		
Egyptus	E	Kentron	E	**Neapolis**	
Emporikon	E	Kipos	E	Vassilikon	C
Ethnikon	E	Minerva	E		
Helvetia	E	Paradise	E	**Sitia**	
Idaeon Andron	E	Psiloritis	E	Krystall	C
Kentrikon	E			Mysson	D
Khania	E	**Kastelli-Kissamos**			
Moderno	E	Kissamos	E	*Rethymnon Nome*	
Olympos	E	Morfes	E	**Rethymnon**	
				Acropole	C
Arkhanai		**Mournies**		Minoa	C
Zeus	B	Koukounara	B	Emporon	D
				Hellas	D
Mallia		**Palaiokhora**		Hermes	D
Grammatikakis	—	Lyvikon	D	Nea Ionia	D
Bananies	E			Arkadhi	E
		Soudha Bay		Akhillion	E
Phaestos		Knossos	D	Paradise	E
Tourist Pavilion	D	Parthenon	D		
				Arkadhi Monastery	
				Tourist Pavilion	D
				Ayia Galini	
				Libya	Inn
				Pantheon	Inn

Village Accommodation

In isolated villages, where there are no commercial hotels or inns, you can always be sure of finding a bed for a night or two. The local Tourist Policeman will usually see to this for you. If he isn't around ask for the *proedros*—the president of the local community. And if *he* isn't available, almost anyone in the local café will be willing to help you. Once you have begun to 'seek lodging for the night', you had best resign yourself to accepting hospitality: if people seem to be giving up their own beds, if they obviously bring out the best family linen, if they insist on putting themselves out in many little ways— accept it all graciously: they do it because they want to.

What you pay—and whether you pay—for such accommodation depends largely on the circumstances under which you approached the particular village. If you have simply walked out of nowhere, sought a bed for one night, and intend to pass on the next morning, then Drs. 10 or 15 will probably be expected. If you have been spending some time in the neighbourhood, have come to know some of the villagers and are all but invited to spend a night or so, then you will probably 'feel' whether your host is going to be insulted when you try to force money on him. (One way around such situations is to indicate that it is 'for the children'—not just payment for goods received.) The more time you happen to pass with a village and its people, the more you are likely to be indebted to their hospitality in ways you can't repay with money.

Monasteries

There remains one other possibility for those seeking shelter for the night—the monasteries. In certain isolated places they may be the only convenient shelter—and certainly the most interesting. They are often quite comfortable, and in a few instances meals can be provided. There is no rule against women being received as guests.

Overnight lodging and a meal for the wayfarer are traditionally provided free by monasteries. But as the Cretan monasteries are poor and struggling, it is equally as traditional to leave some payment. As with Greek hospitality in general, much depends on the circumstances. If you arrive and simply use a bed, then you should offer to pay or at least leave some offering in the chapel. If you have received some special services from the abbot in charge or one of the monks, then offer some gratuity directly to him; if he refuses, there is nothing you can do.

Baths and Lavatories

If your hotel room has a private bath or shower, this is no problem. If you are staying at an hotel where there are bath or shower facilities, it is easy here, too: speak to your maid or the desk clerk, and you will be able to take a bath for about Drs. 12, a shower for about Drs. 7. If the place you are staying at has no bathing facilities, you can usually make arrangements with some hotel to use theirs.

As for lavatories, while travelling through the countryside it's advisable to go native and depend on 'the great outdoors'. In the villages, lavatories are pretty crude, and usually the 'Turkish' variety —a stand-up affair. There are public lavatories in a few of the larger cities—usually in some central square. Hotels of course have proper facilities although nothing very elegant in the cheaper places.

Doctors and Hospitals

All the large cities have clinics. Iraklion has full medical facilities, including X-ray and surgery, in its public hospital and several private clinics.

Doctors are either on hand or on call in all villages: a phone call, a taxi-ride—and a doctor will be there. Many of the doctors will have studied in England, America, France or Germany and language will not be a problem.

Camping

As yet there are no official camp sites on Crete, let alone anything approaching the elaborate camping network which is now to be found across much of Europe. It will probably be some time, too, before anything in the way of organized camping is provided. Still, it is possible to camp on Crete, and many people are doing it every year.

The first thing to do upon arriving is to go to the nearest office of the Tourist Police or the Tourist Organization, describe what you have in mind, and get information about possible locations and restrictions. (This is best done in person, on Crete itself: if you write in advance you may get a letter full of misleading information owing to their having a totally different conception of your needs.) You will find, in general, that you will be given complete co-operation by the local authorities and inhabitants. The former may forbid you to set up your tent in the middle of some historic site, and the latter may not want you camping in the middle of their olive groves, but you will certainly find a location. There is an almost limitless choice of scenic spots—whether on the coasts, in the mountains, or along the roadside. The basic problem is to avoid intruding on someone's private property.

Water could become a problem, but springs are never very far away. Check with the local people: failing anything else, you can make arrangements with one of the village boys to haul you a couple of buckets per day—in fact they will probably insist on this. Fruit and vegetables in season will be easily come by, and other provisions can be obtained in nearby villages. The larger cities and villages will have equipment such as lanterns and cooking-stoves and rope.

Foods and Eating

Restaurants and Cafés

If there is one thing that Greece and Crete have an abundance of it is eating and refreshment places and most of them are open 7 days a week. The quality and atmosphere may vary, but no one need ever go hungry or thirsty: even the meanest village will have a café or two where some sort of meal can be scraped together. (Incidentally, 'café' is literally *kapheneion*, but in the villages it may be called *magazi*—'the shop').

In the larger cities, restaurants are classed 'A', 'B', 'C', etc., depending on the extent of the menu, the facilities, the atmosphere, etc. In listing the individual places here, however, we shall indicate the class only when it seems worth making some distinction. Taking the best and the worst, there is a wide gap, but the general run are similar. Some may have white tablecloths; some will have bare wooden boards; some offer a large choice of foods; some can offer only what they have on the stove at the moment. The foreigner will be well-received in all and should try as wide a range as possible. It is customary in Greek restaurants to go into the kitchen—or over to the cooking area—to see what is on the stove. Besides ensuring that you get what you want, it saves a struggle with the menu. Simply point to what interests you, try to find out what it is, and indicate whether or not you want it. And if you don't like what is brought to your place, don't hesitate to express your disapproval: Greeks send food back for all sorts of reasons.

In addition to the restaurants, there is a class of eating place known as *tavernas*. Although these cannot offer a choice of menu comparable with real restaurants, they can produce all kinds of interesting meals —cooked to your personal taste. Almost every little café, too, can offer something to eat—hardboiled eggs, bits of meat, cheese, olives, bread, vegetables and fruits in season. Even when drinking, it is customary to munch something—a bit of cheese, fresh artichoke leaves, tomato slices: these are known as *mezes*, a sort of Greek hors d'oeuvres.

Prices vary, but not greatly. It is quite usual to spend less than Drs. 30 per person (drink included) in even the better places. Service is usually included in the bill—10 per cent, or 15 per cent in some of the more stylish places. (For tipping, see p. 62.)

The Menu

In Greece, as with most national cuisines, many foods that might not appeal to you if taken separately turn out to be most satisfying when blended with a total meal. The notorious resinated wine— *retsina*—is a case in point: by itself, it leaves most foreigners aghast but when drunk with Greek foods, it combines with the other textures and flavours to make a real Greek 'bouquet'.

Some foods are specialities of Crete; a few are even confined to limited areas on Crete. Menus also reflect the season—when something is in season you will see it everywhere; then quite suddenly it will disappear and you switch to another food.

Bread

In the villages people still bake their own bread, so there is variety from house to house. But even in the bakeries of the cities there is a choice. Most of the varieties have names—*dakos*, *kafkala*, etc. Bread itself is *psomi*. On saints' days and special occasions there is a slightly sweet bread, *artos*, which is blessed and then broken to be passed around. And in some villages they make a stone-hard bread—*paximadia* ('toast'): this must be soaked in water before you can get your teeth into it—and then it goes surprisingly well with the other foods.

Cheese

There is a variety of goats' cheeses. But the best-known and best-liked are *anthotiro*, *myzithra* and *manouri*.

Meat

The staple meat is some form of lamb-sheep-mutton—and usually very tasty. Diced, and placed on a little spit, it is called *souvlakia*. Charcoal-grilled chops are known as *brizoles*. And what we would call offal is wrapped around a large spit to make up what is known as *kokoretsi*—and despite the sound of it, it is delicious. Veal and beef are obtainable in the cities—even some pork. But lamb is the thing to eat if you are living off the land.

Fish and Fowl

Fish are more of a rarity than one would expect on an island. But they will be very fresh when you do have an opportunity to try some. The *barbounia*, a red mullet, is especially good. Try shrimp or shellfish, if you are lucky; try octopus or squid, if you are brave. Chickens are pretty rare; eggs, though, are plentiful.

Vegetables

There are plenty of tomatoes, cucumbers, and little green squashes. Egg-plants, too, are widely eaten, and a variety of green bean. A novelty for most foreigners is to see Cretans eating raw artichoke leaves in the spring.

Fruit

The prices fall rapidly from day to day as the various fruits come into full season. Oranges, peaches, water-melons, grapes and bananas are the most common; there are also quinces, pears, apples, mulberries, cherries. Try the less familiar ones—fresh figs, fresh apricots, pomegranates.

Prepared Dishes

A great favourite is a casserole made of layers of egg-plant, chopped meat, macaroni, and egg (*mousaka*). Or there are *dolmas*: vine leaves stuffed with ground meat or rice.

Olive Oil

Greeks like olive oil, but with a little persistence you can persuade them to reduce it for you.

Desserts

Most of the typical Greek sweets are some variety of *baklava*—a flaky layered pastry with fine-chopped nuts, soaked in honey: most foreigners find it excessively sweet. There is *halva*—a mildly sweet, crisp paste made of honey and sesame seeds; and there are *loukumades* —doughnut-like lumps, covered with honey.

Drinks

Oddly enough, water is the 'national drink' of Crete. Cretans like it cold and they like to savour its taste. They like compliments about it, too.

Wine

Cretan wines have not the quality of French wines, of course, but they go with the local food. *Retsina* is not nearly so popular on Crete as it is in Athens. Ask for *aretsinoto*, unresinated wine. Two of the better Cretan red wines are *brousko* and *kissamos*. Often a good white wine called *Minos* is obtainable, another is *Gortys*—and local vermouths and Greek brandy should be tried.

Beer

Beer is popular: it seems to be quite 'fashionable' in the restaurants. The only brands of beer available are of Greek origin: these are Alpha, Fix, and Mamos. They stand up surprisingly well to the better known brands.

Ouzo and Raki

Ouzo is the Greek schnapps: it is made by distilling the crushed mash after the wine-juice has been pressed from the grapes, with anisette added to give a slight flavour. On Crete the men are distinguished from the boys by drinking *raki* (also known as *tzikoudia*)—a still stronger distillation, with no flavouring.

Coffee

In spite of the claim just made for water, coffee-drinking will strike the visitor as the national pastime, and most foreigners come to enjoy the ritual, the locales—and sometimes the coffee. For Greek coffee is served Turkish style: in a small cup with the muddy lees in the bottom, and usually very sweet. You soon learn how to make the little cup last an hour. (As for the dregs, plan to stop about two-thirds down!) As a rule, the sugar is boiled together with the coffee. If you don't want any, ask for *sketos*; if you require just a little, say *Me olighi*; medium, *metrios*; sweet and well-boiled, *glyki vrastos*; and very sweet, *polli glykos*. These are only some of the gradations. The waiter will bring you sweet coffee unless you indicate otherwise. In the better restaurants or cafés you may be able to order a cup of 'American' or 'French' coffee, but in many cases this will turn out to be Nescafé. If you send out for breakfast, be prepared to get Turkish coffee unless you have made yourself very clear on the point.

Regional Food Specialities

Iraklion Nome:

Stiffado (meat with onions and spices)
Dolmas (grape leaves stuffed with rice)
Giouvarlakia (meat-balls with rice and sauce)
Fresh cheese pies
Fresh grapes: *rosaki* and *sultania*
Oranges from Fodhele

Khania Nome:

Honey from Akrotiri and from Sfakia
Wines and chestnuts from Kissamos
Olive oil of Apokorona
Snails with potatoes
Boiled *radikia* (herbs) as salad
Oranges and tangerines
Kalitsounia: mint-flavoured cream-cheese pastries (traditional Easter food)

Rethymnon Nome:

Pork with *maratha* (herbs)
Snails with potatoes
Mizithra (white soft cheese) with honey
Graviera (cheese) from Mount Idha

Lasithi Nome:

Grilled fish
Local cheeses
Wine from Mouliana

Drinking and Eating Traditions

Besides knowing the names of some of the foods and drinks, it is useful to know about some of the customs and rituals that often accompany a meal.

When you enter a private home, for instance, no matter how humble, you will, as a guest, be offered a little glass of *ouzo*: men take it in one gulp—women usually just wet their lips with it. This is followed by a sweet—either a piece of hard candy, or a little dish of preserves or candied fruit (very sweet!). A glass of refreshing water is then brought. Don't feel embarrassed if you alone are treated to this round of good things, while your host and other natives sit by: traditions of hospitality demand this ritual.

If you stay to eat a meal, you may notice several other unfamiliar ways. In the large cities, among more sophisticated people, and in the restaurants, manners are much the same as everywhere. But if you should become involved with village life or with rural families or festivals, it is as well to be forewarned about several things. There is, for example, considerable eating from common dishes. Plates and bowls are set on the table, you are handed a fork and knife—and it's every man for himself. At a high festive occasion, such eating can become quite intense. Then, a sort of 'duel' with forks may ensue: a man will thrust his fork into a piece of meat and plunge forward, offering it to some table companion—perhaps you! You are expected to eat it straight off the fork, then swallow a chaser of wine. (As a guest, indeed, you will find yourself getting far more than your share of such attentions.) You are not expected to return the service at once, but if you are with the spirit of things you will eventually pass your fork around. A banquet like this can become almost aggressive, to put it mildly.

Drinking, as in every land, is surrounded with a great deal of ritual. One is the snack—the *mezes*—taken with drinks. Then, too, almost every gulp is accompanied by a toast: glasses are knocked against each other or on the table, a toast is shouted, another is returned, and the drink is swallowed in a gulp. These are toasts that might prove useful:

Stin yassou! 'To your health!'
Stin ihya! 'To your health!'
Panta khara! 'May you always be happy!'
Epissis! 'Same to you!' (Used in reply to any toast.)

And as do most Europeans, Greeks wish each other 'bon appetit', which sounds like *Kali orexi!*

Outdoor Sports

Swimming

Crete is ringed by beaches—some like Pacific lagoons, others of a harsher grandeur, but all attractive in their various ways. The main towns have fine public beaches; in the less frequented parts the usual precautions are advised.

Hiking and Climbing

For those who would like to see something of Crete 'on foot', there are outing and climbing clubs in Iraklion and Khania, which arrange frequent excursions—some involving only a few hours of walking, others quite ambitious climbs. Foreigners would always be most welcome and contacts can be made through the Tourist Organization. For those who prefer to go alone and would like some hints from men who have actually walked over much of Crete, the following books are best: Pendlebury's *The Archaeology of Crete*, Grantham's *Minotaur and Crete*, Brewster's *Island of Zeus*, and Trevor-Battye's *Camping in Crete*. There are several quite challenging climbs to be made on Cretan peaks, but most people go to the mountains to enjoy their beauties rather than for spectacular ascents. Snow stays on some peaks through much of the year and these can be cold and windy. Proper preparations should be made before setting out.

Hunting

There is a fair amount of small game on Crete, including rabbits and hares, as well as partridges, woodcock, ducks, thrush, etc. It is forbidden to shoot the wild goat of Crete—the *agrimi* (p. 66). Seasons are observed, and a licence—probably costing the foreigner Drs. 300 —is required. The Tourist Police in Iraklion or Khania will give you information.

Fishing

Although the coastal waters in this part of the Mediterranean are no longer as productive as might be expected, there is still some fairly good fishing for the amateur. No licence is required, but anyone intending to use fishing guns or spears should consult the Tourist Police or Harbourmaster about restrictions.

Skin-diving

The latest international sport has its adherents even on Crete. In addition to the glories of underwater flora and fauna, there are one or two ancient sites to be explored—at Elounda (p. 150) and Rethymnon (p. 157). Masks and harpoons can be obtained in Iraklion and Khania; anything more ambitious would have to be brought from the mainland.

Haggling and Tipping

Many tourists believe that haggling is a required constituent of all transactions in Mediterranean regions and are more or less nervous of it according to their individual aptitude for this pastime. It may not be entirely avoided, but it need not be so unnerving: we give here a list of goods and services and show how the custom applies.

Hotel Rooms: These charges are fixed by law and are exhibited as a matter of course. Extra fees are for extra services, such as heating.

Restaurants: Prices are clearly marked on menus. Where there are no menus you may find yourself paying a few drachmas more than a native—but only a few.

Coffee: This varies in price all over the island, according to the locale, manner of serving, etc.

Beer and other beverages: As with coffee, prices will vary considerably.

Bus and taxi fares: These are officially fixed.

Groceries, fruit, etc.: Prices in shops and markets are usually clearly marked. It is as well to memorize standard prices of a few basic commodities and allow for small differences according to locality.

Souvenirs: Prices will usually be marked. This is a competitive business and shop-owners must keep a constant watch on prices. If a shop-owner knocks 10—or even 30—drachmas from an article he has been asking Drs. 120 for it may be that he has seen you waver—and he may need the sale more than you realize. Haggle if you feel like it, and see what happens.

Postcards: There is probably a fixed price for certain qualities of card. If you see the same view at a higher price, inspection will probably reveal a better card.

Sunglasses: In a shop, you will probably have to pay the marked price. But if you see a pair at an outdoor stand or kiosk, then take your stand for haggling.

Camping gear, etc.: You need a lantern or a stove, so you go to a hardware shop. You are quoted a price that is Drs. 30 more than your Greek friend told you it would be. It may be that your Greek friend doesn't know the real price. But if he did, and if the dealer is in fact trying to get 30 drachmas more from you than he would from a native Cretan, you must just decide how much it is worth to you and play the game on that basis. Nor should you feel you might have been cheated when the price is reduced. That is why you are haggling. And for all you know the shopman may need your money so badly that he is prepared to cut down on his fair profit.

If you should really feel that you have been cheated, you should quietly ask for a receipt—completely itemized—before handing over your money. Then take the receipt to the Tourist Police at the first opportunity, and you will have their assistance.

Notes on Tipping

Tipping is always a problem for visitors. On Crete many people will be helpful to you and there will be occasions when you just do not know whether to tip or not. Cigarettes, and particularly American or English cigarettes, are always welcome. Take with you a stock of cigarettes in packets of 5 and 10, and you will easily be able to get over this difficulty. It is also possible to give a tip and indicate that it is for the children.

Hotels: There is a 10 per cent, and in some cases, a 15 per cent service charge on the bill, but it is customary to give a few drachmas to anyone who has been particularly helpful—the man who carries your bags, and the chambermaid, for instance.

Restaurants: After a meal it is customary to tip over and above the service charge included in the bill. Give your waiter, personally, a few drachmas extra when he returns your change, or leave the tip on the plate with the bill. It is important to know that drachmas left on the table are considered to be the property of the water-boy. (It is usual to leave two for him as well if the party consists of two or three people). In little tavernas or cafés where it is obviously the proprietor himself who is serving you, tipping is not customary.

Your car: When you bring your own car to Crete how much you tip depends upon how helpful the men have been. A recommended way of tipping is to single out whoever seems to be the leader of the stevedores and, when your car is safely aboard or ashore, walk over to him and tip him fairly in full sight of the whole group, indicating that the money is meant for them all.

Taxi drivers: You are not expected, in Crete, to give taxi drivers any sort of percentage of the fare, but it is usual to give them a few drachmas.

Ladies' Hairdressers: For a shampoo and set the correct tip is 5 drachmas to the hairdresser in charge, and 2 to the assistant.

Shoeshine boys get a 50 lepta tip. The shine itself costs about Drs. 2.

Geography of Crete

General Situation and Features

Crete lies in the Mediterranean, almost equidistant from Greece,
Asia Minor and Africa—a fact which should be kept in mind whenever
the point is being made that Crete is the first recognizably *European*
civilization. After Sicily, Sardinia, and Cyprus, Crete is the largest
island in the Mediterranean. It is approximately 160 miles long, and
varies in width from about 7½ to 38 miles; its area is about 3,200
square miles. Altogether Crete has some 650 miles of coastline. The
northern coast is irregular, with five major bays; the chief of which
is Soudha Bay, considered to be one of the finest harbours in the Mediterranean (p. 163). The southern coast is less irregular, but possesses
no natural harbours of any great extent. Crete is distinguished by
several physical peculiarities: its many deep narrow ravines (*pharangi*);
its upland plains—some quite large, flat and fertile; numerous caves;
one fresh-water lake and three brackish waterholes (*almyros*); and
many unique species and endemic varieties of flora. The predominant
aspect of the island is its rocky, scrubby, mountainous terrain.

Geological Background

Crete's dominant formation is the limestone deposited during the
Cretaceous period. In this dim geological past, Crete was part of a
great arc of mountains connecting it to the mainland masses of
Europe and Asia Minor. For the layman, perhaps the most dramatic
evidence for this is the fossil remains of the dwarf hippopotamus
that have been found on Crete—proof, also, that the island was
still connected even in the comparatively recent Pliocene times. All
this was millions of years before the coming of man. In the last six
thousand years Crete has been racked by innumerable earthquakes,
but the most catastrophic event in historical times seems to have
occurred in the sixth century AD, when some massive submarine
movement tilted the entire island on its axis. The western end was
raised about 26 feet out of the water, while the eastern end subsided
accordingly. Striking evidence for this may be seen at the site of
Phalasarna (p. 185), where the old port facilities are now 150 yards
inland, and at Elounda (p. 150), where its harbour installations are
submerged. It has been surmised, too, that Mokhlos Island (p. 155)
was joined to the mainland before this event.

The Mountains

If one feature of Crete's geography had to be singled out as having
played the starring role, it would be the mountains. They are not
exactly spectacular in height, but they do express the Cretan character.
(As on the mainland they have probably influenced the island's history

by isolating the various settlements.) There are four principal mountain ranges and one is never very far away from them: they are the backbone of Crete.

(1) In the west are the White Mountains (*Levka Ori*: literally, 'white landmarks'). The highest point is at Pakhnes—8,045 feet.

(2) In the centre is the Idha Range, now generally known as the Psiloritis. Its peak, the highest point on Crete, is at Stavros—8,058 feet.

(3) Just east of the Idha Range are the Dhikti Mountains, the highest point of which is Mount Dhikti—7,047 feet.

(4) At the extreme east are the Thrifti Mountains, whose highest point is at 4,843 feet.

In addition to these principal ranges are the Asterousia Mountains (also known as the Kofinos range), which separate the Messara Plain from the southern coast in central Crete. The summit here is 4,039 feet.

Snow may remain on the highest peaks throughout most of the year.

Flat Land and Plateaux

The largest flat land is the Messara Plain, which is about 25 miles long, and averages 5 miles in width. It runs roughly on an east-west axis in the south-central region of Crete. Rich in history (p. 116), it is also one of the richest agricultural areas of the island. The other intensively cultivated flat lands are found chiefly on the narrow coastal plains bordering the gulfs along the northern coast.

Crete also has three major upland plains—basin-like plateaux formed of irregular mountain masses with flat bottoms that furnish excellent pasture and farm-land. The one of most interest to the visitor is the Lasithi Plain, below Mt Dhikti, at an elevation of about 3,000 feet. The Omalos (at about 3,780 feet) and the Nidha (about 4,560 feet) are the other two plains. All tend to draw rain and water from the adjacent slopes through potholes and the limestone rock strata, the water subsequently running down to the sea.

Water Sources

There are only a few rivers of any consequence on Crete—the Platanos, the Anopodharis, the Mylopotamos, Yeropotamos—and their water-shed basins cover one-fifth of the island and contain the major grain and fruit areas. Although travellers until and even throughout the 19th century spoke of an abundance of water on Crete, there has been a drastic decline and most rivers and streams there today are small, short and seasonal. The one fresh-water lake—Lake Kournas—which is about 25 miles west of Rethymnon (p. 163), has an area of only some 160 acres. There are several large springs, many smaller ones, and conditions are good for well-sinking. The highly seasonal character of the rains and the scarcity of permanent rivers, together with the cavernous limestone rock formations throughout the island, make

storage dams impractical—at least on any grand scale. Water remains
the principal challenge to Crete's development.

Climate

Crete's climate is principally characterized by the dryness that prevails
throughout most of the year—the rain occurring largely from October
to March. Even then, the rainfall varies considerably over the island
as a whole, with the mountain and upland regions getting more than
their share, and this wide variation in locale and season plays a dominant role in the type of crops as well as irrigation needs. The prevailing
winds blow across the Aegean from the north, often with such force
as to keep down tree growth in many exposed places along the coast.
At the same time, these winds furnish power for irrigation in many
areas—by propelling windmills. Once again, the focus is on Crete's
need for water.

Trees and Forest

Now we come to perhaps the reason for the water shortage: there
are no really extensive forests left on Crete. Yet the island is reputed
to have been covered with dense cypress forests in ancient times, the
export of the timber being one of the chief sources of Minoan prosperity.
Cedars grew, too, and the island was famed for its trees well into
classical times. Centuries of subsequent neglect, deforestation, grazing
and warfare left Crete denuded. Today small forests of pine, cypress
and oak, scattered over the island, cover only about two per cent of
the land. The ilex tree is predominant in the eastern half, the cypress
in the western half and upland regions; there are chestnut trees in
the Province of Selinou; particularly noteworthy are the fine old plane
trees that flourish near springs and water sources and grow to astound-
ing sizes. There are the olive trees and the carob trees which are
discussed in some detail on page 68.

Flora

Crete provides unusually interesting territory for the botanist, for
it has a great variety of flowers, plants, trees, herbs, etc.: there are
said to be over 1,500 species or varieties, at least 100 of which are
indigenous. (Quince, for instance, is said to be an indigenous Cretan
fruit.) Some are more familiar Mediterranean species, modified by
the environment: the mountain heights, with their sharp climatic
changes, have been the chief influence here. Flowers will be with you
wherever you go on Crete. And there are many thorny bushes and
spiky plants—hence the high boots worn by the mountain men. Herbs
are among Crete's most distinctive growths and if one species of all
Crete's flora had to be singled out it should be the endemic herb,
dittany. (*Origanum dictamnus*: from Mt Dhikti, where it flourished.
A plant of the mint family, it is of the same genus as wild marjoram.)

It is given several names by the natives—*Erondas, Stamatohorton,* or —as it is most widely known—*Dictamon.* Cretan dittany is mentioned in many classical texts, and it is still prized for its pharmaceutical qualities: it is believed to be of special comfort to women in childbirth. It may be found growing throughout the island, particularly in the mountainous reaches, and even in the gorges and caves. You will find yourself eating it as a flavouring with many of the Cretan foods; it is also popular in an herb-tea.

Fauna

Crete also offers a variety of wild life. The following mammals have been reported by reputable observers in recent decades: the shrew, hedgehog, bat, badger, marten, weasel, wild cat, rabbit, hare, mouse and rat. There are no poisonous snakes: tradition credits St Titus with expelling them from Crete (as St Patrick did from Ireland). The fish population is scanty, but there are many butterflies. There are some surprising native and migrant birds. The one really notable and unique animal on Crete is the wild goat—*Capra aegagrus.* Zoologists deny it the rank of a species, but it is not to be confused with the ibex and bouquetin of the European Alps; it is related to the wild goat found in the Caucasus and Mt Taurus. The Cretans refer to it as the *agrimi*—a generic word for wild animals. It has been known to weigh up to 100 pounds and have horns up to 31 inches in spread, but it is chiefly noted for its nimbleness at racing and jumping across the rocky cliffs of the Gorge of Samaria (p. 177)—its last natural habitat. It is so adept that it would seem almost impossible to catch or kill, but over the years so many *agrimi* were taken for their flesh or hides that they almost became extinct. Some years ago, however, the government and local organizations instructed the inhabitants of the region in the need to protect these goats; hunting was prohibited and strict penalties for poaching imposed. And sanctuaries were established on several off-shore islands; the future of the species on Crete, therefore, now seems secure.

The Land

Two-thirds of Crete's land area is taken up by largely barren mountains, leaving only one-third for crop production, although nomadic grazing, fuel wood, oils, honey and some other produce are also furnished by the mountain areas. More crucial is the fact that the best soils for cultivation comprise less than seven per cent of the total area of the island—and more than two-thirds of these better soils are located in the Messara Plain, where lack of water poses a serious problem. A large percentage of the soil lacks nitrogen and phosphorus, and full advantage is not yet being taken of modern fertilizers and soil conservation techniques. The land problem has been further complicated by the custom of dividing land among children upon the death of the owner or as dowries for the girls. This has reduced the size of the farms and scattered the land in each holding, until the farms have become impossibly small and inefficient.

Animal Husbandry

In the sheep and the goat we see the paradox confronting Crete: they are the mainstays of a way of life—yet they devastate the land. Their meat, of course, provides the staple flesh-diet; the wool has a multitude of uses; they provide cheeses and milk—you will see very few cows on Crete. (For that matter, you will not see many sheep and goats, considering how many there must be, unless you chance across flocks as they are passing to or from spring and winter pastures.) Chickens are fairly plentiful; pigs and rabbits less so.

Agriculture

Throughout history—and despite this history—Crete has managed to feed its population. In the 16th and 17th centuries AD, under the Venetians, Crete was a virtual garden, famed for its fruit, olives, wines, grain and cheeses, which were exported—together with products such as silk and leather—all over Europe. Today the most remarkable aspect of Cretan agriculture is the extent to which the primitive methods prevail: in many respects, little has changed since Minoan times. Many of the implements used are classic—although tractors and some other farm machinery are appearing on the scene. If you are fortunate enough to observe a grain harvest, you will see that the grain is cut by hand, gathered and carried to the threshing floor, where cattle tread it—or perhaps a sleigh is dragged over it. The winnowing is still done by tossing it to the wind until the chaff is blown away. At any time of year, you may observe the extremes farmers must resort to for water; a few lucky individuals have small petrol pumps for their well; some make do with windmills; others use donkeys to turn the crank; but many men are forced to haul water by hand, hour after hour, in the heat of the summer, pouring bucket after bucket into little irrigation ditches. Much of the cultivation, moreover, is on far from desirable terrain—burnt-out soil or mountain-sides.

The wonder of it all, then, is that yields are as high as they are. Crete cannot grow enough grain for self-support, but fresh fruit and vegetables make up a large part of the island's diet. Nuts—almonds, chestnuts, peanuts—provide a supplement. Almost any edible growth is made use of somehow. In the end, Crete is able to export considerable quantities of its vegetables and fruit, largely to Athens.

We have left until last three of Crete's crops of which two are the most important products of the island; the other is unfamiliar.

The Olive

The number of olive trees on Crete is 13 million. If you keep to the main routes you may find this hard to believe; it is only when you wander in the hinterland and among the foothills that you begin to realize how many olive trees there are. They thrive in the most unlikely places—not, as is commonly supposed, because they don't require water, but because their roots strike deep to underground sources. The olives are picked all during the winter months and although the oil is widely used on the island there is still plenty left for export. In addition, after the oil has been extracted, the crushed seeds and pulp are dried and pressed and subsequently burnt as a cheap—if foul-smelling—fuel. And last but not least, the aged gnarled trees have traditionally provided hiding places from the oppressors and occupiers of the island.

The Grape

In terms of export and economic value, it is the dried grape—alias the raisin—that has the greatest importance. But thanks to its mild climate and fertile soil, Crete's wines have been noted from earliest times: Dionysus and the grape are motifs of early Cretan coinage, and classical authors often extolled the fine quality of Cretan wines. By the 14th century, wine was a principal export; vine cuttings from Crete were so highly regarded that Prince Henry of Portugal is said to have sent for plants to stock the island of Madeira. By the 16th century the English were foremost among the Europeans who sang the praises of Crete's malmsey. The first English consul on Crete, indeed, was a merchant appointed by Henry VII in 1522 to supervise the wine exports. But by the 18th century, Cretan wines had lost their international popularity and were forced out of the market. Today their quality varies considerably: some claim that only the monasteries have first-rate wines—thanks to the care they lavish. Nevertheless it is still possible to be served with an excellent wine in some isolated taverna or home.

Carob Tree

The carob is a small evergreen tree found throughout the Mediterranean; on Crete it grows most extensively in the eastern part of the island. It has long pods looking like overgrown green beans which are rich in sugar and proteins and have been used since ancient times for cattle fodder, human food and fermented beverages. They are still much in demand as cattle fodder. In addition, a gum is made from the pods which is used in papermaking and tobacco curing, as a stabilizer in food products, and as a celluloid in photographic supplies. Sometimes the actual pods are exported for these purposes, but usually it is only the gum which has been extracted. The gum has many names—including St John's bread, because it was the carob that St John the Baptist ate when he wandered in the wilderness. This is an interesting example of a crop all but unknown to most of us in the West providing an income for a whole people. But, in fact, we have all come in contact with the carob: the carat—the standard unit for precious stones and gold alloys—is derived from the Greek *keraton* —'little horn': the carob bean that once served as a standard measure.

Mineral Resources

It is alleged that both copper and iron have been mined on Crete, but it seems probable that the Minoans imported the bulk of their raw ores. Stone quarries and gypsum mines, in any case, are all that operate today. Some surveys have turned up lead, talc, manganese, lignite, sulphur and zinc, as well as iron and copper. But at the moment the income being derived from Crete's mineral assets is negligible.

Occupations

By far the majority of Cretans are engaged in agricultural occupations: most are self-employed, eking a living out of scattered plots of land. Outside the few larger cities the visitor will hardly be aware of any other occupations. There are some, though. In addition to the hundreds of olive crushers and grape pressers and distillers that require operators at harvest season, there are a number of small factories and plants: most employ only a few people and utilize little power or equipment, but they process foods, produce soap and make building materials. There are harbour installations to be manned, as well as numerous garages and repair shops in the cities. And a stroll through the side-streets of cities like Iraklion will reveal many other crafts and trades being practised in little holes-in-walls. Crete has always been famous for its metalwork—especially its knives. (Once, too, the silkworm was cultivated on Crete, and Crete could boast of a domestic silk industry!) What the foreigner seldom gets a chance to see are the many people working at small home 'industries': spinning, weaving, knitting, embroidering, basket-making and turning out various other handicrafts and tourist articles. And as Crete advances into the twentieth century, more and more Cretans find employment in transport, trade, government and office work.

Human Resources

As with any organic society, the real potential finally lies in the people. Crete's population today numbers only about 482,000 in comparison to the million inhabitants that some scholars say were there during the peak of the Minoan civilization. Because of the climate, soil and harbour facilities, the majority live in clusters along the northern coastline. Less than one-fourth—including over 50,000 inhabitants of the rich Messara Plain—live on the southern half of the island, where Ierapetra is the only large town. Many mountain dwellers traditionally descend to the lower villages and coastal towns for the winter, of course. The capital resources of Crete are largely in Iraklion,

Khania and Rethymnon, which results in a concentration of the educated and skilled in these cities. Athens, too, has come to represent an irresistible magnet for the young and ambitious.

Population Figures (1960 Census)

Nomes		Principal Cities	
Iraklion:	207,437	Iraklion:	64,492
Khania:	130,898	Khania:	38,268
Rethymnon:	69,843	Rethymnon:	13,513
Lasithi:	73,843	Ayios Nikolaos:	3,665
		Ierapetra:	6,581
Total:	482,021	Sitia:	5,521

Caves of Crete

The caves of Crete are among its most remarkable attractions. It has caves of every conceivable size and location. Some are simple grottoes —mere holes in the ground or on the sides of mountains. Others are many-chambered, with complicated passages, with stalactites and stalagmites, or pools of water. Some have been thoroughly explored and have yielded rich archaeological treasures; others have barely been looked into. As recently as 1961, for instance, a large cave was discovered on the Omalos Plain and the first investigators, spending a whole day there, estimated its length at 20 km and its depth at 1,000 metres; they also reported an internal river or lake.

The first settlers on Crete probably used the caves as dwellings. Gradually they came to use them increasingly as religious shrines and burial sites. Finds from some of the caves have been most valuable in piecing together Crete's history—from fossil remains of prehistoric animal life to human skulls and bones, and later to votive offerings of pottery and bronze. The caves attracted pilgrims and petitioners long after the Minoan Era, also—and even now some of them are still approached with veneration. In addition they have provided a refuge for the islanders in times of trouble—as for instance the Cave of Melidhoni (p. 162).

But, cave-exploring aside, it is the mythical associations of the caves that generate the most controversy. Take the matter of Zeus's birthplace. There are many caves throughout Greece (throughout the Aegean and the Near East, for that matter) which claim to be the site. Obviously, in such a matter, everything depends on the classical source you accept. Hesiod in his *Theogony* seems to link Zeus with the cave at Psykhro. But many students in this field (Robert Graves, for one) dispute this cave's right to the honour. And technically—i.e. on the basis of geographical allusions—the Cave of Zeus should be farther east, perhaps near Praisos or Palaikastro.

And even after reaching agreement as to where Zeus was born, a second question arises as to whether he was brought up in the same cave. In the end neither 'true believers' nor classical scholars can decide and the Tourist Organization has the last word. For them Zeus was born at Psykhro's Dhiktian Cave and was brought up, under the protection of the Curetes, in the Cave of Idha. Another strong candidate, the Cave at Arkalokhorio, seems to have lost ground in modern times, although it was frequented and famous during the first millennia of Crete's history.

There are many other myths involving the caves of Crete. Minos was said to have returned every nine years to the birth-cave of Zeus where he was re-consecrated by Zeus and given a 'refresher course' in law. Elsewhere it is mentioned that the 6th century Cretan mystic, Epimenides, slept 57 years in the Cave of Idha. Here, too, it was alleged, the mysteries of Zagreus took place. And finally, the cave on Mt Iouktas is claimed as the burial site of Zeus—although not by the mainland Greeks of classical times, for whom Olympian Zeus could never have died.

Those who have had no experience of cave-exploring are advised not to go unattended. Some of the caves are soon explored, but others are true labyrinths. Candles and strong flashlights are minimum requirements; rolled newspapers, ignited, provide a clear view for a short time. A good length of string is a necessity for ambitious expeditions; rubber-soled shoes, and a light stock of food and water are also advised.

History of Crete

With every year that passes, our knowledge of the Minoan era is having to be reassessed, for modern archaeology and scholarship do more than reveal the history of such a place as Crete: they force a continual reappraisal of this history. The earlier concept of a unique indigenous Minoan civilization has been revised, and the history of the whole Eastern Mediterranean world has now to be viewed as a dynamic process and not as though it were a set of building blocks.

It is not surprising, therefore, that many of the theories and conclusions of Sir Arthur Evans have had to be modified. With the decipherment of Linear B, for instance, and the re-examination of the relationship between Crete and Greece, scholars are coming to recognize that there was a complicated network of contacts and influences between Mycenae and Knossos. Indeed, it now seems evident that the later phases of Minoan civilization owe a good deal more to mainland Mycenaeans than had ever been suspected.

'Minoan' is the name given by Sir Arthur Evans to the specifically Cretan culture that would otherwise be classified as Copper and

Bronze Age. Evans decided—not altogether arbitrarily—that there had been three definite periods: Early, Middle and Late Minoan, each of these being subdivided into three phases. Archaeology's findings since Evans' pioneering days, however, have necessitated many adjustments in his strict chronology, together with some reappraisal of the evidence. There is still no universally-agreed chronology for the history of Crete until 1000 BC. One of the more widely-accepted schemes, however, which is based upon internal evidence from the principal sites, uses the terms Pre-, Proto-, Neo-, and Post-Palatial. This is the framework adopted for this book.

Not all of Crete, of course, participated in this recorded culture from the outset. In the early centuries it seems to have been confined mainly to eastern and central settlements; only gradually was there a spread to the west. Moreover, even where several sites are contemporary, they are not necessarily at the same stage of development.

Stone Age: ? to 2500 BC

I. *Pre-Neolithic*: On the shores of the eastern Mediterranean and even on some of the other Greek islands there have been finds indicating palaeolithic settlements, but nothing has been found on Crete that allows scholars to date man's arrival there before 6000 BC.

II. *Neolithic: 5500 BC to 2500 BC*. In general, archaeologists postulate that the first people to 'settle' in Crete were semi-nomadic groups from Asia Minor and/or North Africa, who came over between 6000 and 5000 BC. Their way of life must have been most primitive at first: hunting and fishing, using stone and bone tools, making simple clay pottery, dwelling in or near caves. Relatively soon, though, they turned to elementary agriculture, to decorating their pottery, and to constructing simple dwellings of clay bricks on stone foundations. As for religion, we can assume from the finds of the small steatopygous idols familiar from many primitive cultures that they worshipped some aspect of the maternal-fertility goddess. But the most important fact for our purposes is that some of the earliest settlements were at sites such as Knossos and Phaestos, as well as at Katsamba, the Cave of Eileithyia, and the eastern plain near Sitia.

Copper and Bronze Age: The Minoan Era: 2500 BC to 1150 BC

I. *Prepalatial*: *2500 BC to 2000 BC*. The development of Crete's culture proceeded fairly steadily until around 2500 BC, when there seems to have been a new wave of settlers, from Asia Minor, the Cyclades—perhaps even Egypt. They brought their own culture, but the new environment stimulated a more rapid and individual development. Whatever social organization there was must have been of the basic pattern of tribes or clans, whose settlements were separated and independent. The indigenous neolithic population seems to have been gradually overwhelmed by the newcomers. (The Minoans, by the way, were short: their average height was about 5 feet, according to the evidence.) The Mother Goddess was still worshipped, accompanied by such of her symbols as the double axe, pillar, horns, dove, snakes and flowers.

The circular and vaulted tombs found on the Messara have not only yielded many of the treasured possessions buried with the dead— jewels, tools, sealstones, votive offerings—but their construction suggests that they were antecedents of the later 'beehive' tombs of Mycenae. Copper was worked and later bronze. How much trade there was is not certain, but obsidian knives from the earliest times have been found—and obsidian had to be imported from the island of Milo. A new artistry appeared in the treatment of pottery—the Pyrgos style and the Vasiliki 'flameware'. Metals and stone revealed an advance in craftsmanship, and the handling of ivory, rock-crystal, precious and semi-precious stones in the sealstones indicates a remarkable sensitivity.

During this period the principal centres of life and culture—at least as revealed by modern archaeology—were on the Messara Plain and at the eastern end of the island (sites such as Mokhlos Island, Vasiliki, Zakros, and Palaikastro). Knossos, Phaestos, and Mallia remained settled.

II. *Protopalatial*: *2000 BC to 1700 BC*. The construction of the first palaces at Knossos, Phaestos and Mallia accompanied what would appear to have been a rather sudden concentration of power in the ruling families at these settlements. (Today's visitor sees little of these early structures, but enough has been excavated to show that they contained the core of the later and greater palaces.) A more systematic and hierarchic society came into being over the island as a whole. Increased trade with Egypt, Asia Minor, Africa, the Aegean islands and the Mediterranean world in general laid the foundations for the Minoan thalassocracy as well as providing immediate cultural and commercial gains. Situated in the centre of the maritime routes, Crete became a distributor, an importer and exporter: she imported tin and copper, processed them to make bronze, and then sent her products at least as far as the Troad and Italy in ships made of cypress and cedarwood. The Keftiu who appear in Egyptian tomb frescoes and in the Bible are claimed as Cretans by some experts.

A form of hieroglyphics was in use, at least for special state and religious functions, from the year 2000 BC. There were many developments in arts and crafts—most notably, the Kamares 'egg-shell' pottery. Stone carving, goldwork, jewellery of all sorts, metalwork, sculpture, pottery, architecture—all are harbingers of the 'golden age' to come.

Then, about 1700 BC, the main palace centres seem to have undergone some transformation. Perhaps it was an earthquake, perhaps an invasion. There is no drastic break, however, in the continuity of Minoan culture. What does appear, though, is Linear A, a script used to record commercial and administrative transactions. Although scholars have not agreed as to what tongue is recorded in Linear A, it seems certain that some language from Asia Minor is involved. And if this is so, then it also seems certain that a new wave of settlers came to dominate Crete about this time.

III. *Neopalatial*: *1700 BC to 1400 BC*. Whoever or whatever was responsible, the palaces at Knossos, Phaestos and Mallia, whose remains we see today, were reconstructed on an even grander scale: several storeys, majestic stairways, great courts, murals, corridors, columns, workshops, ritual chambers, plus all the technical achievements that would mark them as advanced in many parts of the world even today. There seems to have been a concentration of power at Knossos, but the numerous towns and megarons constructed throughout the island indicate the extent of the total wealth and energies of this period. Cretan society became stratified, with the Priest-King of Knossos (the legendary Minos) at the pinnacle, and a vast body of workers supporting its manifold activities. ('Minos' was, in fact, a generic title, like Pharaoh, and not applicable to one ruler only.)

Advanced technical and engineering accomplishments—roads, aqueducts and irrigation systems—are also evident: the most famous are the palace sanitation systems. It should be remembered, however, that such refinements were confined to the palaces: there are no grounds for thinking that the mass of Cretans enjoyed any of this style or comfort.

The epitome of aristocratic refinement is to be seen in the role that women appear to have enjoyed in the life at court. This is the sophisticated Minoan social life that can be deduced from frescoes and other remains. Crete was not a matriarchal society, however, even if some women at the palaces may have had a fair amount of independence and influence.

Crete may not have been a woman's world, but the Snake Goddess seems to have reigned supreme. She was, in fact, only one of various manifestations of Mother Nature, the object of religious devotion all over the Mediterranean and Near East of this time. The Minoans adopted some rituals and symbols, and developed others on their own: the bull-fighting, for instance, seems to have been involved with some religious ceremony.

By now, Crete was one of the chief maritime powers in the Mediterranean. Its influence can be detected in the names of colonies and in finds of artifacts all over the Mediterranean. There is a theory, too, based on resemblances of grave and tomb types, and some few artifacts, that Cretan merchant ships went through the Straits of Gibraltar and up the coast of Europe as far as Iceland and Scandinavia. For some time, now, it has been surmised that the Minoans traded with the British Isles: the discovery of stone markings very similar to the Minoans' double axe at Stonehenge has suggested a Cretan architect. And even if the Minoans did not go as far as this, they certainly imported amber from Jutland, which came down across Europe on the 'amber route'.

Crete's far-ranging ships not only enriched the island's economy, but they protected the island to the extent that the great palaces needed virtually no special fortifications, though undoubtedly they had a defensive warning system. Minoan society, indeed, is characterized more as a vast commercial complex than as a militaristic power. All the arts and crafts were practised. Vase-making particularly flourished, with decoration becoming more naturalistic in its use of marine and floral motifs.

Between 1500 and 1400 BC, the written script of Linear A was adapted to record a new language. Until 1953 this was known only as Linear B, but, primarily owing to the efforts of Michael Ventris, it is now revealed as a proto-Greek tongue. The extant records are largely inventories and such mundane accounts, but the implications of this discovery cannot be dismissed: if a Greek tongue was being heard, there must have been mainland Greeks on Crete—and in positions of some influence. If so, they were most likely the Mycenaeans who had hitherto been thought of as more dependent on Crete. It follows that the Mycenaeans played a more active role in Minoan culture—and from an earlier time—than had been supposed.

What is more, around the year 1400 BC Knossos and some of the other centres of Minoan society seem to have been simultaneously overwhelmed. Some scholars believe that the calamity was the result of earthquakes; others think that invaders descended and burnt the palaces; still others have suggested that a natural disaster merely exposed the island to new influences. Sir Arthur Evans and his followers believed that, whatever the calamity, it marked the effective end of Minoan society and culture: in his view, 'squatters' took over the abandoned palaces, merely biding their time until the coming of the Dorians some centuries later.

IV: *Postpalatial: 1400 BC to 1150 BC*. More recent scholarship—based on philological and archaeological evidence from the mainland as well as from Crete—indicates that Crete continued to exercise considerable influence, albeit as a link in the Achaean-Mycenaean chain of power. And whether or not the Mycenaeans were responsible for the collapse of the distinctive Minoan culture, they were certainly on the scene during these centuries. At least some of the palaces and sites—including Knossos, Tylissos, Ayia Triadha, and Palaikastro—were restored and reoccupied.

Although some of the peculiarly Minoan social, religious and artistic patterns seem to have been broken up, the arts and crafts did not completely disappear. And what the Mycenaeans may have lacked in grace and refinement, they made up for in a certain rugged strength.

With the balance of power shifted to the mainland, and with some of the Mediterranean routes usurped by the Phoenicians, the commercial dominance of Crete disappeared. She continued to export, however, and even to exert some influence over mainland styles. And when the Mycenaean Greeks undertook the expedition against Troy, Crete joined in the struggle.

Around the year 1150 BC, the major sites of the Cretan-Mycenaean world were simultaneously destroyed. Among the chief witnesses to this are the tablets inscribed in Linear B, baked by the flames in the final hours of the palaces. Dates and specifics may be in dispute, but it is generally agreed that the Dorians were responsible for the destruction.

Iron Age: The Greeks: 1150 BC to 67 BC

I. *Geometric—Orientalizing—Archaic Periods: 1150 BC to 480 BC.* A wave of new invader-settlers—accepted as Dorians by most historians —moved into the vacuum created by the collapse of the Mycenaean empire. For Crete, this meant the end of the specific Minoan civilization; the Dorians brought a more rugged spirit and disciplined social organization.

Iron began to be used and swords grew longer. Proto-geometric designs developed into the full-fledged geometric style of pottery decoration. Increased contacts with eastern Mediterranean lands brought oriental influences into art: metalwork, goldwork, pottery and sculpture. Cretan art once again blossomed, the older Minoan-Mycenaean spirit now blending with the Dorian and oriental modes. Architecture and sculpture passed through a brief renaissance— especially with the 'Daedalic' style in sculpture. Crete appears to have acted as a transition between the static Asiatic forms and the first stirrings of the classical mainland spirit.

Cretan cities were revived, several autonomous cities issuing laws. If we accept Gortyne, with its Code of about 500 BC, as the climax, we see Crete's position at the edge of the final Greek triumph.

II. *Classic—Hellenistic Periods: 480 BC to 67 BC.* Here and there, remains indicate that Crete existed at the fringe of the Attic culture. Left on the sidelines, there was no great challenge and therefore no great response. Crete had had its day. (Perhaps Crete's failure lay in the inability of the settlements to pool their resources; but the mainland city-states remained basically divided, too.) Crete continued to be honoured, however, as allusions in classical texts and myths reveal, but it produced nothing of its own at that time. Trade brought a certain prosperity and there was also some building. Cities issued their own coinage. Knossos, Gortyne and Kydonia exercised some rule over lesser settlements. Around the year 300 BC certain cities in the west—Elyros, Lissos, Hyrtakina, Tarrha, Syia, Poikilassos—formed the Confederation of Oreioi with Gortyne and King Magas of Cyrenaica.

Throughout the next 250 years Cretan cities and settlements made and broke alliances with various Aegean and Mediterranean powers—Sparta, Macedonia, Egypt, Rhodes. There were continual feuds, skirmishes and wars, and the island came to be known as the haunt of lawless pirates, mercenaries—and liars! In actual fact, there was a fair amount of building during the twilight years of the Hellenistic period, but Crete as a whole declined. By the first century BC the Romans were interfering more and more in the island's quarrels. Rome was perturbed, moreover, by the alliances with such foreign powers as Mithridates the Great from Pontus.

Roman—Byzantine—Medieval Era: 67 BC to AD 1669

I. *Roman Occupation: 67 BC to AD 395.* The Romans came to settle the island's feuds: they stayed to conquer. After sporadic campaigning for three years—with Quintus Caecilius Metellus gaining the final triumphs—they acquired another province. Gortyne became the capital of Crete and Cyrenaica (part of North Africa). The Romans had ambitious plans for Crete, and after initial repressions prosperity of a sort was established. There was extensive building at Gortyne and elsewhere on the island—including an impressive settlement near Knossos. The Romans left their familiar landmarks all over the island, in villas, mosaics and temples, sculptures, aqueducts, roads and brickwork. The Apostle Paul made his first landing on European soil circa AD 47 at Kaloi Limenes ('Fair Havens') while en route to Rome as a prisoner. Tradition has it that he appointed Titus as Bishop of Gortyne, and it was Titus who spread the Christian faith on Crete.

II. *First Byzantine Period: AD 395 to AD 828.* With the division of the Roman Empire into the western and eastern sections, Crete fell under the sway of Byzantium. Christianity prospered, with considerable building of basilicas: the most notable was Ayios Titos at Gortyne, around the 6th century. In the political-economic sphere, Crete was virtually an abandoned outpost. Trade routes shifted, and the Arabs slowly absorbed the Mediterranean territories.

III. *Arabic Occupation: AD 828 to AD 961.* Abou Hafs Omar—having been driven out of both Spain and Alexandria—came to Crete with his band of brigands, attacked and destroyed Gortyne, and overran the island, establishing a fort at Rabd-el-Kandek—alias Iraklion. During the next century or so Crete was used by the Arabs as a pirates' base; all attempts to regain the island for Byzantium failed. There was no colonizing on any scale, but there were some inter-marriages and conversions.

IV. *Second Byzantine Period: AD 961 to AD 1204*. Eventually the Byzantine general, Nikephoros Phocas, liberated Crete. (It is said that he catapulted the chopped-off heads of his Moslem prisoners against the garrison.) Aristocratic families from the Greek mainland, Christians from eastern territories and European merchants were 'imported' to effect a revival of Crete. A variety of feudalism developed—the former Moslems being retained as slaves. (Phocas, meanwhile, had moved on to become (963) one of the great Byzantine Emperors—and patron of one of the monasteries on Mt Athos.) Crete once more had a place on the perimeter of affairs.

V. *Venetian Occupation: AD 1204 to AD 1669*. Byzantium fell to the Fourth Crusade, and Crete was 'given' to Boniface of Monferato, who in turn sold it to the Venetians for 10,000 silver marks. In the meantime the Genoese had set themselves up, and together with the native Cretans they resisted the Venetians. But in 1210 Jacob Tiepolo was appointed first Governor and the Venetians began their long occupation. They named the island and its capital city 'Candia' and set to work to organize, fortify and adorn their new territory. (Many of the fortifications and castles remain to this day.) The island was divided up on feudal principles: six sections, corresponding to the six quarters of Venice, were thrown open to Venetian colonizers and entrepreneurs. But the native Cretans were never quiet for very long and there were several bloody revolts. The Venetians had hoped to impose their own way of life, but actually many of the Italian colonists joined the Cretans in revolting against the unjust taxes and privileges of the Mother City, Venice.

With the decline of the Byzantine Empire and the fall of its capital in 1453, Crete became a refuge for artists and scholars from the mainland. Orthodox monasteries, schools, literature and painting flourished, borrowing details from the Venetians but essentially preserving the Greek traditions. Now and again the Cretans pressed their attacks on the Venetian overlords. In certain parts they practi-cally had self-rule; but also many Cretans had accepted positions and privileges from the Venetians: the barriers were falling down. In the meantime, during the 16th century, pirates under the Turkish 'Bar-barossa', Khair Eddin, were ravaging the Cretan coastal towns. The Venetians set about restoring and enlarging the various walls and forts. The Turks had come to see Crete as one of the last barriers to the West and in 1645 they mounted a fleet and took Khania; Rethymnon fell the next year, and in 1648 there began the epic siege of 'Candia' (Iraklion).

For the next 22 years all Europe waited and watched what was probably the longest siege of its kind in history. It was the last outpost of Christianity against the Ottoman Empire in that part of the world, and when its downfall seemed imminent Pope Clement IX appealed for aid. Louis XIV sent a French force under the Duc de Beaufort, but it was wiped out. In the final two years Candia's defence was undertaken by Francesco Morosini, but he was finally forced to surrender. The Turks let the defenders leave with honour, and most of the Cretans deserted the city. (Some Cretans went to settle in Mani, the southern tip of the Peloponnesos—as they had done earlier, when the Venetians took over: from the Mani, some moved on to Corsica, where a variation of the Cretan dialect may still be heard to this day!) It was alleged that the Venetians lost 31,000 men in the defence of Candia, while the Turks lost 118,000.

Turkish Occupation: 1669 to 1898

I. *Years of Suppression: 1669 to 1821.* The island was once again divided among foreign conquerors and administrators—this time the Pashas. There were, however, no great numbers of Turkish colonists.

At first the Cretans willingly traded Turks for Venetians. But relations soon deteriorated. The Turks took over the cities, the Cretans clung to their mountains and the Janissaries roamed at will. Under the non-administration of the Turks, agriculture and commerce declined, roads fell into disrepair, walls and forts crumbled and building largely ceased—even the mosques were converted churches. Taxes and tariffs took so much that the Cretans lost all incentive; the population declined, and earthquakes and insurrections defeated construction.

In spite of this sad history, however, it is estimated that by the mid-18th century there were 60,000 Christians and 200,000 Moslems on Crete—but almost all the last were converted Cretans! This may not be one of the proudest statistics of Crete's history but for most people it was a simple question of survival. Moreover many of them were Moslem in name only: the Orthodox faith was practised and sustained. Nor were the Cretans entirely passive during these years. There were several uprisings—the best known being the one led by Daskaloyiannis in 1770. Unfortunately, though, mountaineers like the Sfakians, who raided and then retired, brought persecution and bloodshed onto the exposed villages.

II. *Years of Revolution: 1821 to 1898.* With the uprising against the Turks on the mainland in 1821, Greece set off on the road to independence. Crete joined in, but was unable to keep up the pace. When the new Greek state was proclaimed in 1832, the Allied Powers ceded Crete to the Egyptians—who had actually been called in by the Turks to put down the revolution in 1824. But by 1840 the Turks were back in possession.

The 19th century on Crete is one of the most shameful episodes in Great Power politics. Decisive action by England, France, Italy and Russia—acting in consort or in any combination—could have resulted in the final handing over of Crete to Greece. Instead there were compromises, intrigues, rivalry—and inaction. But on Crete there was insurrection and bloodshed. The major uprisings were in '24, '30, '58, '66-'69, '78, '96-'98, but these fail to tell the full story of suffering and slaughter. The rallying cry during these decades was 'Freedom or Death': for most Cretans, there was only the latter.

Finally, in 1898, after a relatively minor incident—which happened to involve loss of life among some of the British soldiers stationed on Crete—the Allied Powers stepped in, forced the Turks to leave, and granted the island autonomous status under a High Commissioner, Prince George, younger son of the Greek King.

20th-Century Crete: 1898 to Present

I. *Towards Union: 1898 to 1913.* Prince George was warmly welcomed in December 1898; in the next year a Cretan assembly met to draw up a constitution and a new spirit of order and co-operation prevailed. Many Cretans refused to settle for half, however; they wanted union with Greece—or no outside interference. Turmoil set in once more; Venizelos actually led an abortive revolution in 1905; Prince George —despite his good works and intentions—was forced to resign. The next few years were merely a biding of time until Crete could openly be taken into the Greek nation. Finally—and not until the whole Balkan region had been embroiled in a war—Crete was officially recognized as united to Greece.

II. *Settlement—and Occupation: 1913 to 1944.* Crete quietened down and went unscathed during World War I; but in 1922 it was exposed to another severe strain by the exchanges of population between Greece and Turkey: the Turkish population left, and thousands of Greek refugees from Asia Minor came in their place. So once more Crete settled back, to build and prosper. Agriculture and commerce were increasing; archaeology and tourism gave promise of a new future. Then, in 1941, the British—driven from the Greek mainland—crossed over to Crete. A decision was made to stand, but the troops were no longer equipped to meet a full-scale assault such as the Germans now launched: the notorious paratroops descended on Crete on May 20, and by June 1 the battle of Crete was over.

Many British Commonwealth troops managed to get across the mountains to the coast of Sfakia; thousands more failed. The Cretan citizenry also had made a valiant stand. But once the Germans held the airport at Maleme, reinforcements poured in. (After the war it came out that the German High Command regarded the Cretan airborne operation as a failure, owing to the high mortality rate.)

For the next three and a half years Crete was an occupied land. At times it was a bitter one, with forced labour, insufficient food, deprivations of all kinds and punitive retaliations against many villages. The Cretans continued the struggle as guerillas and partisans—helped by special British agents—against the German and Italian troops. (The latter occupied the eastern end of Crete.) The most famous incident of this period was the kidnapping of the German Commandant, who was then taken off to Egypt by an English submarine. With the end of the occupation in October 1944—after the Germans had made a last-ditch stand at Khania—Crete surveyed the damage. Iraklion had been particularly hard hit, and so had several other coastal towns; many villages lay in ruins; transport, roads and commerce were idle; food was a pressing problem.

III. *Post-War Years: 1944 to Present*. UNRRA moved in to save Crete during the first months, but the islanders soon recovered their equilibrium. In the next few years, although there were still some lingering conflicts between the several resistance groups, Crete even had an advantage over mainland Greece in avoiding civil war. With its commerce and agriculture restored, Crete in fact attained new levels of prosperity and construction increased. Further excavations, with publicity for the archaeological sites, has brought increasing numbers of tourists to the island: the future of Crete may well lie in its past.

Crete's Contribution to Art and Letters

Considering its smallness, its isolation, its uneven history, Crete has made some truly remarkable contributions to both Greek and Western European culture. The art and artifacts of the Minoan civilization are widely known—vases and ceramics in a dazzling variety of forms, techniques and motifs; sealstones and jewellery with an unusual delicacy of style and observation; statuettes and carvings created with a perception and freedom transcending their times; frescoes almost bewildering in the range and reality of their subjects. These have all been pictured and publicized, although one should still make the pilgrimage to Iraklion's Archaeological Museum to see them in their actual glory. (Oxford's Ashmolean Museum has the second finest collection of Cretan art and antiquities, thanks to Sir Arthur Evans' bequests.) Even when adapting or transmitting the art of others, Crete gave its inimitable imprint.

In one medium above all Minoan Crete attained unique dimensions. That was architecture. Its palaces were Crete's distinctive achievement. Nor is there any possibility of confusing Minoan architecture with that of classical Greece: to put it briefly, in place of symmetry there is improvisation. Small rooms and various structures cluster around a central court; additions seem to be accidental; the sites themselves are irregular; the total complex seems to 'grow' at random levels. Yet the more one examines the different palaces, the more one appreciates the design of the whole. It is dynamic, organic—an architecture that anticipates the modern style of a Frank Lloyd Wright.

As regards literature, the Minoans left none that we are aware of. (The Phaestos Disc—if 'literature'—is in any case an imported object.) But when all the evidence is considered who knows how influential—even crucial, Crete was in transmitting the alphabet to the western world? One thing seems certain: the Minoans must have had a rich stock of folklore if they were anything like their descendants. Songs, tales, ballads, proverbs, popular lore of every kind, were surely passed on orally from generation to generation. And of far more importance than a barren legacy of fragments and minor texts, Crete left a vital corpus to the classic world—and to our own—in mythology.

The traveller to Crete who wishes to recognize its oldest traditions should prepare himself by reviewing these myths. 'Review', because it is surprising how many of the familiar personages and episodes of classical mythology concern Crete. In a book such as *The Greek Myths* by Robert Graves, almost every page contains at least a passing allusion to Crete. It must, however, be admitted that most of these myths were transplanted to Crete long after the decline of the indigenous culture. The Minoans, it is true, remained faithful to the Great Mother Goddess in all her manifestations; on the other hand, Crete must have offered a fertile soil for the proliferation of such myths.

There is the birth of Zeus himself, involving Cronus and Rhea, as well as several episodes in his youth: these are associated with specific Cretan caves, although the scholars haven't agreed as to which is which (p. 70). Later, Zeus returns to Crete, this time in the guise of a bull, carrying Europa on his back: the associations here run through 3,000 years of European art. Europa bears Zeus three sons—Sarpedon, Rhadamanthys, and Minos. It is the last-named who became the dominating force in Crete's myth-history: the repercussions have never really stopped. There is a certain ambiguity in the figure of Minos: on the one hand, he is the harsh tyrant whose ships scour the seas while he sacrifices to the Minotaur; on the other hand, he is the just and benevolent law-giver who attains immortality as a judge in the after-life. But that is only part of Minos' drama. He had a wife, Pasiphae, who had a god-willed lust for a bull; their union produced the Minotaur. This was the occasion for the Labyrinth, constructed by the legendary craftsman Daedalus to hide the Minotaur. Then comes Theseus—who would seem to embody some semi-historical figure or event—the slaying of the Minotaur, the flight with Ariadne. Later, Theseus marries Phaedra, another of Crete's ill-starred daughters, and there follows the classic tale of her passion for Hippolytus. It is an endless thread, indeed. Meantime, Heracles had accomplished the seventh of his Twelve Labours on Crete. There is also Daedalus, back in the Labyrinth: his escape with his son Icarus has never ceased to engage man's wonder. In addition there are all the secondary figures— Britomartis, Miletus, Talos the Bronze Monster. Crete may not have given birth to all these gods and heroes, but they have all wanted to claim Cretan ancestry.

At the time of the Homeric Age the balance of power had shifted, but in some versions of the Trojan War the Cretan Idomeneus was accepted as an equal of Agamemnon. *The Iliad* and *The Odyssey* are matchless sources for this period in Crete's history, although the island appears only indirectly in the narrative. Judging from the behaviour of Idomeneus in *The Iliad*, the Cretans had a reputation as rather rugged fighters. This same Idomeneus appears some 3,000 years later in a considerably less boisterous setting—Mozart's *Idomeneo*, which deals with his return to Crete after the Trojan War.

With the coming of the Dorians, Crete entered into the mainstream of the cultural world as it was developing in that part of the Mediterranean. There was a minor resurgence of the Cretan genius in ceramics, and although it cannot be claimed that Crete originated the forms it certainly contributed its share to the emerging art of the geometric and oriental styles. By the end of the 7th century BC still another force was at work—this time in the archaic sculpture of the Greek world. Crete has generally been credited with taking the lead in the movement, which was away from rigid formalism and towards more lifelike representations, and has even given a name to its characteristic features. The 'Daedalic' style was so called after the mythical craftsman who achieved his greatest feats on Crete. Other historical Cretan sculptors such as Dipoinos and Skyllis carried the lessons of the master to the Peloponnesos, thus helping to liberate the mainland from the restricting conventions of the day. (In addition to the Daedalic sculptures on view in Iraklion, there is the 'Lady of Auxerre' in the Louvre, a bronze statuette at Delphi, and figures in New York and other museums.)

With the triumph of the Attic-Athenian culture, Crete was completely overshadowed. It can, however, be fairly claimed that Crete was the cradle of many of the manifestations of the classical civilization. Some students have traced a Cretan influence in much of its art and architecture; certainly it can be said that Crete played a dominant role in its mythology and religion—there was even a legend that the first priests at Delphi were Cretans from Knossos. Then, too, there is a fragment of a lost tragedy by Euripides, *The Cretans*, that appears to deal with a religious cult. Beneath the classical veneer, a Cretan influence seems always to be present. There is even a theory that Plato's 'Atlantis' is really Crete. Or take, for instance, one of the most famous Cretans of this period—Epimenides. Said to have flourished around the turn of the 6th century, he came to Sparta and Athens about the time of Solon and is credited with shaping the legislation of the times. Numerous works are attributed to him, including the constitution of Crete and mythical-mystical texts. In due time, many myths accrued to him, such as that he was a son of Zeus, slept in a Cretan cave for 57 years, had prophetic revelations and was reincarnated. Obviously something of an apocryphal figure, his most famous line, alas, is his claim, 'All Cretans are liars!'

It was in the domain of law, however, that Cretans were particularly honoured. Both Minos and Rhadamanthys were installed as judges in the underworld. Lycurgus was said to have studied on Crete. Solon was said to have been inspired and influenced by Cretan law: once he counselled Athens to bring a wise man from Crete to help purify the city. Plato and Aristotle paid frequent tribute to Crete. And if more tangible evidence is required, we have only to consider the Code of Gortyne, still standing as irrefutable testimony to Crete's achievement.

Gortyne itself stands as a symbol of the Romans' ambitions on Crete: they came, conquered and built, but the Empire declined before Crete could contribute to the greater glory of Rome. And Rome did little for Crete. Instead, the winds blew from the East. Paul of Tarsus passed through. Paul's immediate heir on Crete was Titus; his testament is in *Acts* XXVII and the *Epistle to Titus*. With the absorption of Crete by the Eastern Empire at the end of the 4th century AD, the island was left pretty much to its own devices; church buildings and mosaics seem to have been the sole expressions of any aspirations. The Arabs came and went, from 828 to 961; then mainland Greeks asserted themselves on Crete under the banner of Nikephoros Phocas—later to be one of the most prominent Byzantine Emperors. In the 13th century, all Greece became prey to the plundering Crusaders and warring commercial states of Europe: Crete fell to the Venetians.

For the next four-and-a-half centuries Crete was a Venetian colony. During the first half of this occupation there were frequent and bloody uprisings, but the Venetians imposed their *castelli* and order, and a cosmopolitanism gradually took over in the main port cities. Yet, somehow, Cretans survived as such, in their language, their religion, their folklore, their dances, their art and their traditions: the people kept their identity. All this time the Venetians were effecting a relative prosperity: in fact, it became clear that they were there to convert only one thing—produce into gold. So that, with the fall of Byzantium in 1453, Crete was one of the last outposts of Orthodox Greek culture; scholars and artists, fleeing from the mainland, often landed on Crete. Thus, the three traditions met: the indigenous vigour, the links with the West via Venice, and the cultivated forms of Byzantium. The result was Crete's version of the Renaissance.

The literary products of this period are not generally known outside

Greece, which is a pity. There is the poetry of Saklikis, who recounts his escapades in a Rabelaisian manner. There is a pastoral poem—*The Fair Shepherdess*—perhaps somewhat incongruous on the island. The most noted work is the long epic poem *Erotokritos* by Vincenzo Cornaros: it strikes those who read it today as a marathon of conventions, but it exercised considerable influence on modern Greek literature —and even now can still be heard in the villages of Crete. It was the drama, however, that experienced the most solid revival. Six plays have been preserved from the period 1550 to 1670, and if none is a masterpiece—and all are highly derivative—they represent a significant achievement. The finest is *The Sacrifice of Abraham*, attributed to Cornaros: it is in the familiar vein of the medieval mysteries, but there are individual touches and its insight makes it truly Cretan. There is a pastoral comedy, *Gyparis*, of some distinction. Another play, *Erophile*, was revived for the Athens Festival in 1961; even mainland Greeks pay their respects to Crete's contributions to the language.

But it is in another medium that medieval-renaissance Crete has held the attention of the world: in painting—both of frescoes and icons. Scholars have not yet separated all the strands in the tapestry of Cretan-Byzantine painting: besides indigenous art there is an imported influence. The Byzantine schools of Macedonia and Mistra evidently made some impact; later there was the influence of Italy. Yet it is agreed that there is a recognizable 'Cretan school' of Byzantine art, even though this may be more a style and technique than the work of a circle of friends. In either case, the Cretan spirit speaks with an intense masculine energy: figures are often exaggerated in length, realistic detail is brought forth, a chiaroscuro effect is achieved by the use of bold colours over dark backgrounds.

When used in a restrictive sense, the term 'Cretan school' refers to the iconography that developed towards the end of the 15th century, but the earlier frescoes reveal the same spirit. Among the 600 or more chapels and churches on Crete, there are many that still have their wall-paintings intact—albeit restored. The most notable examples are at Kritsa, Valsamonero, Potamies, in the chapels around Kastelli-Pedhiadha and in the provinces of Amari and Kydonias. In more accessible places, many of these would attract thousands of viewers. In the 16th century, several Cretan painters worked on the mainland: Theophanes, Anthony, and Tzortzis are the best known and their works—perhaps the master works of the 'Cretan school'—are to be seen in the monasteries of Mt Athos and Meteora.

At the beginning of the 16th century the Cretan spirit tended to express itself rather in icons than in large-scale frescoes. The tradition, of course, had been long established: recognizably *Cretan* icons can be found from the 14th century. Here again mainland influences came into play; by the later 16th century, Italy—particularly Venice

—exercised her spell; and eventually, in the 17th century, a Creto-Venetian school flourished in the Ionian islands. Michael Damaskinos, one of the true Cretan masters, absorbed much from his years in Italy; when he returned to Crete to paint his major works—largely from 1570 to 1591—he blended the Italian-Renaissance style with his own Byzantine manner. Finally there came the man who made a bridge between the Byzantine and Western forms, the medieval and modern worlds, the orthodox and the catholic—the man from 'Candia' who moved on to other lands but who could never quite forget his homeland —its landscape, its patterns, its eyes: Domenico Theotocopoli, 'El Greco'. He was born in 1541 and died in 1614. None of his work is to be seen on Crete, but Crete is to be seen in much of his painting. Not all Westerners find the Byzantine iconography congenial, but even for such El Greco vindicates the tradition.

To round out the picture of Crete's peculiar vitality during this period, three other Cretans who left their mark on the world must be mentioned. In 1340, a certain Peter Philargis was born outside Neapolis; he went to study in European universities, advanced in the Roman Catholic hierarchy, and crowned his career by being elected as Pope in 1409. As Alexander V he served for only ten months; it is suspected that he was poisoned—a suitable end for a Cretan and Pope of that day. Then there was Kyrillos Loukaris, another Cretan who wandered forth to get a European education some two centuries later. A man of true culture and learning, he became Patriarch of Constantinople and took the lead in educating Greeks in their traditions, even to the extent of sponsoring a translation of the Bible into a less archaic, more colloquial Greek. But such activities were too advanced for the times and he only succeeded in offending Orthodox, Moslem and Catholic (he had studied at Geneva) and he paid with his life. Finally, there was yet another Cretan scholar, whose achievement would seem to have gained him the blessings—or curses—of all faiths. Nathaniel Kanopios was at Balliol College, Oxford, for ten years—until Cromwell expelled him in 1648. In the course of his time there he is credited with having introduced coffee drinking into England.

By the end of the 17th century and with the final conquests of the Turks, Crete once more passed out of the mainstream of European history. Again, though, popular traditions—songs, poetry, music, dancing, folklore of all varieties—kept the Cretan character alive, renewing the life and language of the island. Every event provided its hero, and subsequent songs and epics. The most admired of these poems is *The Song of Daskaloyiannis*, based on the uprising of the Sfakians in 1770. But in the 19th century, when the rest of Greece had gained independence and was sharing the artistic harvest of the new spirit, Crete was still occupied territory. Its energies went into the continual struggles and uprisings against the Turks.

Yet when Crete re-entered the Western community in the 20th

century, a man came out of Crete who was destined to become the only modern Greek statesman who can be classed in the grand European tradition. His ancestors, it is true, had come from the mainland, but Eleftherios Venizelos, born in 1864 at Mournies (p. 171), was forged in and out of the Cretan struggles. A staunch republican and politician, he first raised his banner by forming a party pledged to seek union with Greece; in 1905, he convened a revolutionary assembly at Theriso, in violation of the government of Prince George and the Allied Powers; when he resorted to arms he was beaten down, but he forced the retirement of Prince George and gave notice that Venizelos and Crete would be heard of someday soon in the parliament of Greece. Eventually he had his way; he was Premier of Greece during several tempestuous administrations; he was listened to at the Treaty of Versailles; he lost a great deal, for himself and for Greece, but the net gain was the modern Greek nation.

Curiously enough, the only other modern Greek who has gained an international reputation is also a Cretan: Nikos Kazantzakis. He left Crete as a young man, but he could never get it out of his system: *Zorba the Greek* and *Freedom and Death* are literally set there; *Christ Recrucified* is animated by a Cretan energy; and even his Odysseus becomes deeply involved with Crete. Philosopher, poet, dramatist, novelist—a genuine man of letters—the translations and the publicity of his last years gave Kazantzakis a somewhat distorted status in relation to the total Greek literature of this century. But no one can deny his power, his intensity, and the provocative nature of his work.

Nor was he the only Cretan writer of this century. Several others have made significant contributions to Greek literature—Kondylakis, Prevelakis, Dimakis, Chatzidakis. In addition, the leading Greek actor of our time, Alexis Minotis, is also from Crete. What is the secret? Why should so many of Crete's sons and daughters achieve a place in the pantheon of the immortals? It could be that if there is one theme peculiar to the Cretan spirit, one thread that links Minoan pottery, Cretan frescoes and the novels of Kazantzakis, it is an affirmation of life in all its diversity, a spontaneous—yet intense—celebration of man's joys and mysteries.

Excavating Crete

One of the most frustrating sensations while exploring some ancient site is to know nothing about the circumstances of the excavations themselves: When were the remains discovered? Who excavated them? For how many years have visitors been able to view them as we know them today? Such questions often rush to mind—and usually must remain unanswered. Here, though, we offer a brief survey of the exploration and excavation of Crete in order to put the whole field into some perspective. For it is one of the most common fallacies in the entire realm of archaeology that until Sir Arthur Evans excavated the great palace at Knossos no one had ever suspected the greatness of Crete's past. According to this version, Evans was the first to stumble onto Crete, the first to dig, the first to reveal the existence of a Cretan culture: before Evans there was nothing but vague mythology and a few classical allusions.

The plain fact is that Crete's sites had never been completely lost to men's eyes or minds. Indeed, the list of those who had come to Crete before Evans is a long and honourable one, which includes the Homeric heroes as well as Schliemann. In *The Iliad* and *The Odyssey*, Crete appears only indirectly, but it is cited as the home of populous cities—either 90 or 100, many of which are named—and as a land of great wealth. (In Hesiod, on the other hand, Crete is a land of the gods: it is he who sets the tone of mythology that is later associated with Crete.) The disguised Odysseus pretends to have come from there—he even mentions the Cave of Eileithyia—and part of Menelaus' fleet is blown ashore south of Phaestos—but in general Crete is a distant prospect.

By the time of the classical mainland civilization the Cretan cities and their glories were all but legendary—although one, Gortyne, was yet to enjoy its heyday. Numerous classical sources refer to Crete: historians, commentators, geographers, travellers. To men such as Thucydides, Aristotle, Apollodorus, Diodorus Siculus, Pliny, Strabo, Appian, Ptolemy, as well as many others, Crete was a very real place, even if all their facts weren't quite correct. But Strabo, in the first century BC, gives quite accurate distances between Cretan sites.

After the Roman adventure in the island, Crete passed into obscurity. The *Stadiasmus*, an anonymous 'Admiralty Chart' of the 6th to 11th centuries AD, mentions many places and routes on Crete, but like much of the Mediterranean world Crete fell into disrepair. For hundreds of years its cities and sites, temples and tombs were abandoned to the ravages of time and climate, earthquakes, marauders and—perhaps most destructive of all—Cretans themselves, seeking materials for new structures.

The arrival of the Venetians in the 13th century provided both losses and gains, but at least Crete re-entered the awareness of the western world. The name of 'Candia' began to appear in dispatches and men passing through the eastern Mediterranean en route to the Levant or Asia often made a point of stopping off on Crete. The Italian Buondelmonti, in the 15th century, was among the first to record his visit; he was able to say of Gortyne that he 'counted two thousand columns and statues upturned by time. For grandeur it is the equal of our Florence'. Belon and Belli in the 16th century; Boschini and Lithgow in the 17th; Tournefort, Savary and Pococke in the 18th; Tancoigne, Olivier, Sieber and Hartley in the early decades of the 19th—these are only a few of the men who set down their impressions of Crete. In addition, scholarly works such as those of Meursius (1675), Dapper (1688), Cornelius (1755) and Hoeck (1823-9) kept the academic light burning for later archaeologists.

With the publication of Robert Pashley's *Travels in Crete* in 1837 a new era began. Pashley was one of England's indefatigable scholar-travellers: after finishing his book the reader is left feeling that there was nothing for anyone else to discover. He had in fact a remarkably high score in his identification of sites. However, when he reaches what he feels is 'undoubtedly the site of Knossos', he says: 'All the now existing vestiges of the ancient "metropolis" of Crete are some rude masses of Roman brickwork . . .' The fact is that Pashley, like his predecessors, had no idea of how much he was missing: despite all they did see and despite all they knew of Crete's past, they lacked one simple tool—the spade.

Pashley was followed by men such as Raulin and Spratt, just as knowledgeable in their own ways—so that by 1870 most of Crete had been brought into the area of the *known*. But what all these men had settled for were fragments protruding above ground, or random surface finds of artifacts; some were scholars, of course, and cited a classical allusion for every remain they saw; at most they might dig up a column or sarcophagus. Yet if none excavated, as we understand the term today, some of them certainly looked very hard and turned up things that provided material links to Crete's past. From the time of Pashley on, there could be no doubting the existence of historical Crete: it was only a question of digging it up.

Two events in the year 1878 gave the impetus to Cretan archaeology. One was when a Cretan merchant and amateur archaeologist (most fittingly named Minos Kalokairinos) was digging in an olive grove a few miles south of Iraklion, not far from the known Roman ruins. His spade struck a buried structure, and before long he was uncovering extensive walls, stones with masons' marks on them, and huge storage urns. W. J. Stillman, an American archaeologist-journalist, who had once served as Consul on Crete, went off to explore with Minos. Before they could proceed much further the Turkish authorities put a stop to the excavations, but not before Stillman had sent out various dispatches. Heinrich Schliemann read the accounts and in 1886 he arrived in Crete, determined to buy the land concerned. He was unable to come to terms with its owner, however, and abandoned his 'hope of discovering the original home of Mycenaean civilization'. What Minos Kalokairinos had excavated, by the way, were storerooms of the palace of Knossos.

In that same year a group of prominent Cretans formed an association to advance the education and culture of the islanders: within a few years they were concentrating on preserving the historical and archaeological remains, collecting antiquities and generally encouraging excavation. (From this enterprise, incidentally, developed the Archaeological Museum of Iraklion.) The guiding spirit behind all this was Joseph Hadzidakis of Iraklion. Scholar, active archaeologist, first curator of Cretan antiquities, not the least of his achievements is the aid he lent to the various foreign archaeologists during the early years of 'digging up' Crete.

In the meantime—starting in 1884—an Italian mission was travelling about the island making significant discoveries of both epigraphical materials and ancient sites. To the Italians, in fact—headed by Professor Federigo Halbherr—should go the credit for the first really sustained and professional excavations on Crete. By 1900, parts of Gortyne, the Caves of Idha, Eileithyia and Kamares, many tombs, and other sites had been revealed by the combined efforts of Greek, Italian and other foreign archaeologists.

Then came the spectacular excavations at Knossos. Sir Arthur Evans had originally come to Crete in 1894 in search of linguistic materials: he was looking for sealstones with pictographs, and in the course of his searches he actually uncovered several sites, explored caves and tombs and made finds that were later to occupy many other archaeologists. After several attempts he was finally able to buy the entire plot of land at Knossos. There, armed with his personal fortune, his knowledge and insight, and aided by a staff of technicians, archaeologists and artists, he supervised the literal unearthing of Minoan civilization. It was to take many decades, and the whole world looked over his shoulder. It is little wonder that Evans has come to stand as the Columbus of Crete. And it does not belittle his achievement to recognize all those who had gone before.

From 1900 onwards, the excavation of Crete proceeded by leaps and bounds, stimulated by the finds at Knossos. Some were the results of individual quests; others came about through patient searching by teams of archaeologists. The Greeks were active throughout the island, finding the tombs of the Messara and the megarons of Tylissos, Nirou and Amnisos. The Italians were uncovering many sites: concentrating on the Messara, they excavated Phaestos, Ayia Triadha, Gortyne. English archaeologists spread over the island and were particularly active in eastern Crete, as well as exploring caves generally. The French undertook such sites as Mallia, Lato and Dreros. Americans excavated Gournia, Mokhlos and Psira. By 1940, the major patterns of Cretan archaeology had been established.

Excavating has by no means ceased. (Even during the German occupation it went on to some extent.) The Greek government and various archaeological missions from foreign lands bear the burden of the expenses now, and some of the glamour may seem to have passed. But to dedicated archaeologists the day-to-day finds at even some of the more modest sites can be exciting. Since the war there have even been some quite dramatic finds, at both old sites and new discoveries—such as Vathypetro, Katsamba, Leben, Phaestos and Knossos. With the refinement of techniques—e.g. stratigraphic excavation: the precise recording of levels—and dating methods, some of the previous categories have had to be modified, with a resultant refinement of conclusions about Crete's history. Excavations all over the eastern Mediterranean, in fact, have revealed contacts, sources and influences—via religion, trade and art, for example—so that each find on Crete reveals the island as part of a grander pattern than Evans or any of his contemporaries could ever have realized.

Crete now stands like some great jigsaw puzzle: most of the pieces are there, but the problem of arrangement still remains. And although it is unlikely that anything as spectacular as Knossos lies buried, there is a good chance of major finds yet to come.

The Greek Language

The history of the Greek language can here be noted briefly, to the extent that it impinges on modern spoken Greek. One thing should be said at once: there *is* a definite relationship between classical Greek and modern Greek. Having been given the impression that there is little or none, most students of the classical language are amazed at how far it can take them.

After the decline of the classic Attic civilization, a common Greek tongue came into use throughout the Hellenistic-Mediterranean world: this was the *koine*, the Greek of the Bible. It is the basis of modern Greek. Over the centuries, through the rise and fall of the Byzantine Empire, a gap developed between the language of the masses and the refined language of the lettered. The clergy especially tried to maintain the archaic Greek, but the vulgar tongue was evolving on its own: foreign words were absorbed, idioms crept in, and each region developed its own dialect. When the independence of the modern Greek nation was established in the 19th century, the movement to impose a unified and purified language gained the support of many educated men: this was the *katharevusa*—the pure, correct, formal language. But for all their sincere intentions, the proponents of this somewhat artificial language were doomed from the start, because the colloquial tongue—despite its inconsistencies and faults—was an organic living language. At the end of the 19th century the struggle between the adherents of the two languages was still in full swing, affecting every aspect of national life and capable of causing academic quarrels and popular riots. To a certain degree the struggle is still going on, but the *katharevusa* is now largely confined to newspapers, the law, science, academic circles, government administration and formal use in general. The demotic or 'popular' language is Greek as it is spoken in the streets; among other victories, it has won over most modern creative writers, and it has proved itself an expressive instrument.

To understand what it means to have two languages in competition with each other, the English speaker need only imagine all those situations where he employs only the most formal and literary language (legal documents, scholarly papers, formal announcements, conversations with foreign dignitaries) and oppose them to situations where he uses the most colloquial and familiar language. In other words English —as well as every other language—is subject to the same forces. The significant difference, though, is that strict boundaries were never set up between these other pairs of languages, so there has always been some intermingling. Britain could support a Dr Johnson *and* a Robert Burns; America could support a Henry James *and* a Mark Twain. But the Greek language-psychology found them incompatible. Contemporary educated Greeks, all the same, are finding it easier to bridge the two languages in speech, literature, radio and the theatre. (When a classic Greek tragedy is performed today, for instance, it is translated into a modified *katharevusa*.) The differences—in sounds, grammar and vocabulary—still exist: everything depends on how much modern Greeks want to make of them.

Few visitors to Greece ever come to grips with the language and fewer still master it. The alphabet defeats most people in the first place: until one is in control of that there is no gratuitous gain in vocabulary—as is the case when the English-speaking traveller tries other European languages. The result is that most foreigners give up —or at best struggle along with about three words.

This is to be regretted, because the Greeks are among those people who truly enjoy having a foreigner use their language—even when it is not used well. So few do try to use it that the Greeks are pleased when anyone does make the effort. The foreigner need never feel embarrassed while he is learning, and he will never lack encouragement and praise, even though accompanied by good-natured laughter.

Anyone who wants to try to use Greek needs a phrase-book: several are available and they are all more or less the same. Most of them are to be found in the bookstores of Athens. The really ambitious may try to teach themselves Greek before setting out, and there are several courses available. Useful books include *Cortina's Modern Greek* and *Modern Greek in a Nutshell*. Record courses include Dover Publications' *Say It In Greek*, the Linguaphone Institute's course, and another by the Institute for Language Study. There is also a small, cheap record, *Pronounce It Correctly in Modern Greek*.

Between phrase-book and complete course lies the dictionary—a necessity for anyone planning to strike out on his own. There are many available—again, mostly to be found in Athens. It is important to make sure you are getting a dictionary of *modern* Greek. The most up-to-date one, designed specifically for the current visitor, is *Vocabulary of Modern Spoken Greek* by Professor Donald C. Swanson of the University of Minnesota. (Published in Athens by Minas Myrtidis, 9 Thiseos Street; price about Drs. 100.)

When travelling with a dictionary, it is of course of no use to hand it to unschooled people and expect them to pick out words for you: they are not accustomed to treating their language as an alphabetical list and are apt to be as baffled as you are by the mass of words. Moreover, just as important as learning the proper sounds of Greek pronunciation is learning the correct syllable to be accented. The accent is a crucial element in the Greek language—a mark is always written over the syllable which must receive the major stress—and when the accent is misplaced it leads either to confusion or to a complete blank. The average Greek finds it hard to disassociate the sounds from the accent. It can be most frustrating when you have taken the trouble to learn some long, difficult word and you know you have the sounds correct—and still no contact is being made. (When you finally do shift the accent to the proper syllable, your word will be greeted with immediate recognition and a 'Why didn't you say so?'!)

There is a distinct dialect spoken on Crete, and as might be expected the farther one goes into the hills the more pronounced it becomes. In the matter of vocabulary, too, there is a rich fund of local words and expressions. The main pronunciation variations are as follows: the Greek gamma—γ—thickens into a sound like 'rou*ge*' before 'i' and 'e'; the kappa—κ—behaves like the Italian 'c', being hard before 'a', 'o', and 'u' and soft (like English 'ch') before 'i' and 'e'; and the khi—χ—ordinarily a guttural 'kh', on Crete behaves like the Italian 'sc', becoming a soft 'sh' before 'i' and 'e'.

Cretans, like all Greeks, use many nicknames, diminutives, and terms of affection. Even the commonest words will frequently have affectionate diminutives, such as '-aki': thus, *nero* is 'water', while *neraki* is more like 'lovely bit of water'. (Incidentally, if you meet a Greek whose name ends in '-akis'—'son of', the probability is that he comes from Crete.)

The English Language

Many of the younger people speak a little English. Some are learning it in school or by following the bilingual lessons the BBC gives regularly several times a week; but the majority are studying at one of the many 'institutes', or private evening schools. People of all ages and all walks of life give up a considerable proportion of their time and money to acquire this new way to success. You will be doing a real service to exchange a few words with such students when opportunity presents itself.

The Greek-Americans

Almost every town and village, no matter how isolated, has its 'Greek-American', an ex-immigrant who has returned to live out his retirement in his home town. He will make your acquaintance very quickly, and although his English is not exactly polished it will probably be better than your Greek. He will be of great help, saving you a lot of time and trouble, but you may not gain in the eyes of the other inhabitants of the town or village if you let yourself be adopted by him. Preserve your independence with goodwill and still seek to make your own contacts.

Government and Administration

Crete is one of the governmental districts of the highly centralized Greek government, and it is from Athens that Crete's ministers of agriculture, education, finance, justice, public works, etc., are appointed, as are also the Nomarchs, or Prefects, at the head of each Nome. The island elects 18 representatives, or deputies, to the Greek Parliament.

Khania is the official capital of Crete. Each city elects its own mayor, as do the villages (though 'presidents of the community' might be a better translation of the title, *proedros*). But there is no common legislative body for Crete: the government of the island as a whole is carried on largely by the appointees of Athens. Most taxes are collected and disbursed by Athens. The police belong to the national force, too, although the enlisted men are usually Cretans who have been more or less permanently assigned to the island. Even teachers must go for their training to Athens before being assigned to Crete.

All this is to a certain extent only a technicality, but the fact remains that the initiative comes from Athens and local responsibility for government and social institutions is relatively small. Nevertheless, Crete's true parliament is to be found in its cafés.

Religion and the Church

Commentators on modern Crete all remark the continuity of Cretan culture: despite a history of violent disruptive forces, Crete seems to have maintained intact many fundamentals from even the earliest eras. In nothing is this more apparent than in its religious beliefs and practices. The Greek Orthodox Church exacts adherence to the Christian faith of course. But it also stresses its own continuity, taking pride in its own faithfulness to the roots and sources of earliest Christianity. For the visitor, Crete provides a fascinating glimpse of age-old sources of the religious impulse and of religious behaviour. To Cretans, who are almost all Orthodox, there is nothing contradictory or curious about worshipping in the ways of their ancestors, but it is one of the most interesting and attractive features of a stay on Crete.

The priest, or Papas, in his stove-pipe hat and flowing gown, soon becomes a familiar figure as he strides across the fields or sits in the cafés. In the Orthodox Church, if a priest wants to rise in the hierarchy or to enter a monastery, he remains celibate, but the village priests are allowed to marry and are encouraged to take part in the life of the community. It is therefore no cause for surprise to see a bearded old Papas showing off his grandchildren. The village priests will often be obliged to do some other work to support their families, despite the fact that they receive part of their salary from the government, Orthodoxy being recognized as the official state religion. The Church's hierarchy, in fact, has a status analogous to the civil service or the military: the Metropolitan of Iraklion, who is head of the Church on Crete, has the 'rank' of a General—and should even be saluted by members of the military when he passes in his official capacity.

During the centuries of occupation the Orthodox clergy always helped to keep Cretan aspirations alive, both by word and deed, and the Greeks' Independence Day, in fact, celebrates the occasion on March 25, 1821, when Bishop Germanos of Patras raised the flag of revolution against the Turks.

Of the chapels and churches on Crete (there are reputedly over 600) many are tiny, and are used only on one day of the year to commemorate a particular saint, or the name-day of the donor. Some are new and have no significance for the visitor. But some are very old indeed, and many of these have frescoes and other works of art that are worth going out of one's way to see. They are to be found everywhere—on the barren coast, perhaps, or high on a peak. They are worth looking into, deserted or not (the key is usually on the ledge over one of the doors), for they have a special atmosphere. Often candles will be burning in the most isolated chapels. The simple icons are often interesting and sometimes, flanking the picture of a saint, a heap of little metal tags is to be seen. These are *tassima*—simulacra—moulded in the image of the afflicted part of the body, or an animal, or someone the petitioner wants cured or protected.

Sites, Cities and Excursions

Crete has hundreds of villages and chapels, scores of monasteries and caves, dozens of archaeological sites and remains. It would take months to explore Crete thoroughly. On the following pages, all sites of major interest are described in detail, most secondary sites are also described, and many other places of interest are briefly mentioned. The visitor is also introduced to all available sources of information, both official and unofficial. Anyone who discovers a fragment or ruin in an out of the way place should ask its location from local people, for on returning to Iraklion or Khania he is sure to find some museum official or local antiquary who can give him information about his find.

The scheme followed in this section is that sites and excursions have been arranged according to the four Nomes (divisions for administrative purposes) of Crete, which are Iraklion, Rethymnon, Khania and Lasithi. The capital city of each Nome has been taken as the starting point for each excursion, but in cases where it is equally convenient to start from the capital of one Nome for an excursion to a site in another Nome, this also has been indicated. Within each Nome we start with a description of the capital city and its resources. A number of major excursions are then outlined, a return to the capital city after a day or two being intended. Various side-trips are also indicated for those who would have the time for them. A number of secondary excursions starting from the capital cities are also given. And in the case of Iraklion, which is likely to be the point of departure for most visitors, the routes connecting it with the other capital cities have been described in some detail.

Finally, comprehensive tours which take in the most important sites have been plotted in the Chart for people with limited time at their disposal: a four-day tour, a five-day tour, etc. These have to be planned with great care because bus time-tables in Crete are not yet arranged for the convenience of tourists. For such round trips, Iraklion has been taken as the starting-point.

The chart opposite is designed for those who have independent transport—their own vehicle or a rented one. The chart represents one day per block, so that the visitor to Crete may plan his trip for anything from one day at Knossos and Iraklion to a complete 40-day tour of the island. (W) indicates some overland hike or trip that involves walking.

	Major Sites & Excursions		Seconds		Minor Side Trips		Special Excursions	
	Brief visit	Fuller investigation						
	a	**b**	**c**	**e**	**f**	**g**	**h**	
1	**Iraklion:** Archaeological Museum **Knossos:** Palace complex *Remain in Iraklion*	**Knossos:** Palace, dependencies and environs including Roman ruins and tombs [W] **Iraklion:** City sights and landmarks, Historical Museum	**Arvi** via Knos... Ano Via...oudhia; ...a *Return t...aklion or on to ...non road 3e* ...on to 1e, 5b	**Rethymnon** *Ship to mainland via Fodhele and/or Arkadhi; Rethymnon, city and landmarks; Monastery of Preveli Amari Province: via Asomatos and Fourfouras; Ayia Galini On via Phaestos to Iraklion. Return to Rethymnon, or overnight in Preveli, or Ayia Galini*	**Mount Iouktas:** [W] **Vathypetro;** Arkhanai *Return to Iraklion*		Ascent to Mt Idha and cave of Kamares [W] *3-5 days via Kamares Village, Vrondisi and Valsamonero, or via Anoyia and Tylissos Overnight on mountain or at Kamares or Anoyia*	**1**
2	**Phaestos** Ayia Triadha Gortyne *Return to Iraklion or overnight at Phaestos*	Phaestos, Ayia Triadha and Gortyne; Ayia Dheka; The Messara (village and farm life) *Overnight at Phaestos*	Matala ... Kaloi Lines [W] ...ie *Return t... Phaestos* ...haestos		**Ayia Galini** Timbaki; Kochinos Pyrgos; *On to Rethymnon via Spili; or overnight at Ayia Galini, Phaestos, or Timbaki; or boat to Sfakia, 5c; or Ayia Roumeli, 5e*			**2**
3	**Gournia** Pakhia Ammos Ayios Nikolaos Mallia *Return to Iraklion or overnight at Mallia, Neopolis, Ayios Nikolaos or Pakhia Ammos*	Cave of Eileithyia Amnisos; megaron of Nirou; Khersonisos; Ayios Georgios of Selinaris; Kritsa; Pakhia Ammos; Neapolis) roads to Ayios) Dhiktian Nikolaos) Cave, 4a	Ayios ... *Ship to ...les* Kritsa ...f Lato [...os Eloun...stro Spinal... ...Sitia *Overn... Nikola...os Sitia, ...*	**Ierapetra** via Gournia, 3a *Return to Iraklion via Arvi, 1c; or overnight at Ierapetra; or return to Ayios Nikolaos, 3c; or Sitia, 3d*	**Eastern Crete:** Itanos; Palaikastro; Zakros; Praisos; Akhlada *Return to Sitia*		**Gulf of Merabello:** *1-2 days* Ayios Nikolaos (rent boat): Elounda and Spinalonga, 3c; **Islands of Mokhlos and Psira;** Gournia, 3a (Pakhia Ammos) *Overnight at Pakhia Ammos; return to Ayios Nikolaos, or go on to Sitia, 3d*	**3**
4	**Dhiktian Cave** [W] Lasithi Plateau (10,000 windmills) Psykhro *Return to Iraklion or overnight at Psykhro*	Cave of Eileithyia Amnisos; megaron of Nirou; Potamies and Avdou; Krasi; Lasithi Plateau *On to Neapolis, 3b, or Ayios Nikolaos, 3c*						**4**
5	**Khania** Fodhele; Rethymnon; Soudha Bay; Aptera; Khania landmarks and Hill of Elias *Back to Iraklion; ship to mainland; or overnight at Khania*	**Melidhoni Cave; Arkadhi Monastery;** Rethymnon— Venetian Fort; Lake Kournas; Khania—city and landmarks *Overnight at Arkadhi, Rethymnon, or Khania; return to Iraklion*	Sfakia...amos; Khora...f Frango... [W]; ... Ayia C...W Prevel... or wes... Roumb...back Selino... *Return ... or ove... Sfakia... Galini, Roum... Palaio...*	**Ayia Roumeli— Tarrha:** East to Sfakia [W]: 5c St Paul's; Aradin— Ayios Ioannis; Phoenix—Loutro; Anopolis **West to Palaiokhora** [W] 5f; Gorge of Samaria [W]: 5h *Overnight at Ayia Roumeli, or return to Khania*	**Province of Selinou:** Kandanos; Hyrtakina; Lissos; Elyros; Syia-Souyia; Poikilassos [W] **Palaiokhora** *Return to Khania or overnight at Palaiokhora, or walk to Ayia Roumeli, and overnight, 5e*	**The Akrotiri:** Hill of Elias; Ayia Triadha; Gouvernetou [W] Katholiko [W] Sternes—Minoa *Return to Khania*	**Gorge of Samaria** [W] *3-5 days* Meskla and Rizinia; Omalos Plateau; Ayia Roumeli— Tarrha, 5e *Overnight in Gorge or Ayia Roumeli* **Island of Gavdhos:** *1-2 days* Rent boat passage at Palaiokhora, Khora, Sfakia, or Ayia Roumeli	**5**

Iraklion

Hotels

Iraklion has a wide choice of accommodation (see pp. 52). All the hotels are more or less central. If the one you go to is full the receptionist or proprietor will help you to get placed in another. The word for hotel is *xenodokhion*.

Restaurants

There are countless restaurants and eating-places in Iraklion, not all first-class, but all offering a wide choice in menu and atmosphere. At the places listed below regular meals can be obtained at more or less regular hours. There are also numerous cafés and sweetshops where cold drinks, coffee, ice cream, cakes, yoghurt and light snacks may be bought.

    Class A: Caprice, Knossos, Peripteron Limenikon (Glass House)
        B: Ionia
        C: Nikokirakes, Karazou, Triana

    Tavernas (with more limited menu)

    Class B: Kallithea, Voyiatzis, Shik, Ariadne (summer only)
        C: Vardavas, Lakis, Kastella

    Snack-Bars (these are drinking places, but light snacks are available)

    Class B: Oasis, Ouzeri
        C: Costas, Apostolos

·In addition to trying some of the above, no one should leave Iraklion without visiting one of the little eating places lining the street known as 'Dirty Alley'. This connects Market Street with Evans Street, one block up from the main cross roads of the city. It provides a fascinating glimpse of a fast-disappearing world. Each little restaurant jostles the next, spilling out on to a narrow street filled with smells, noise and people. The food is appetising—especially the charcoal-grilled meats. To sit over a meal here is to realize that you are indeed on a unique island.

Dining and Dancing

There are a few places in and around Iraklion that offer music and dancing as well as food. When spirits get high enough there is likely to be dancing at almost any taverna, but the places listed below make a special feature of dancing (in the case of the first two, continental style with orchestras).

The Glass House:	Class A restaurant, ideally situated overlooking the harbour. Well patronized in summer time.
Taverna Ariadne:	Class A restaurant, only open during summer season. On the road near Knossos about 4 miles from Iraklion. Has a delightful garden and often provides musical entertainment as well as an orchestra for dancing.
Tzobanakis:	Class C. An outdoor taverna in Ayios Ioannis, on the perimeter of Iraklion.
Verikokes:	Class C. An outdoor taverna in Ayios Ioannis.
Tzitziphies:	Class C. On the water's edge past the Khania Gate. This is the real thing, not some quaint tourist dive. The popular 'bouzouki' is played and danced here and things have been known to get rough. ('Bouzouki' is named after the instrument, a type of long-handled mandolin.)

Cinemas

During winter film-shows are indoors; cinemas open at 4 p.m. on weekdays and 2 p.m. on Sundays. Prices from 5-10 Drachmas. In summer films are shown out of doors, beginning at 8 p.m.

Other Entertainments

On the waterfront, not far from the Glass House Restaurant, is a place where in summer shadow-puppets perform. These are the famous Karaghiozis (inherited by the Greeks from the Turks), and are well worth seeing.

There is a special organization of young girls, the Lyceon Ellinidon (Girls' Lyceum) who study and perform the authentic Cretan dances. Shows with costumes, music and dancing can be arranged through the Tourist Organization office, but are expensive and only practical for large parties.

Bus Lines

Buses for the various cities and sites leave from four points in Iraklion: Kornarou Square, Daskaloyiannis Square, Kalnouria Porta (South Gate) and outside the Khania Gate. Tickets may be bought at the time of departure but it is wise to arrive in good time.

Post Office

Address: Koronaiou Street

During the summer stamps can be obtained here between 7.30 a.m. and 8.30 p.m. During winter the hours are from 8 a.m. to 8 p.m. (all other services close between 1-3 p.m. throughout the year). Stamps may also be purchased from some of the street-corner kiosks. See p. 190 for postal services and rates.

Telephone and Telegraph

Address: Kantanoleon Street

Open 24 hours a day throughout the year. International calls can be made. For rates see p. 190.

Shops

These provide every kind of product and service. Many of the manufactured items will bear familiar names, since Greece is forced to import a great deal. Pharmacies are indicated in the street by a red cross. Dry cleaners are surprisingly cheap, laundries surprisingly expensive.

At Alexiou's Bookstore, a few doors from the Caprice Restaurant and near the Morosini Fountain, you can get books and daily papers in English as well as in other languages.

Souvenirs and Handicrafts

Many shops stock these. Some are cheap tourist items, some are examples of authentic native crafts, some are genuine antiques. The Cretan knives are of particular interest. Some of the imitations of Minoan artwork are fairly attractive. Among the best buys are textiles —wool, linen, silk, cotton, embroideries, knitwear, lace—made into handbags, rugs, and various articles of clothing. Much of it has been produced in the villages, on the old looms and with the old patterns.

Churches

In addition to the many Greek Orthodox Churches and chapels there is a Roman Catholic Church.

Sports Facilities

There is a private tennis club on Beaufort Avenue with two courts. An introduction would be required.

The Greek Touring Club arranges excursions on the island. So, too, does the Greek Climbing Club, particularly climbs. Further information about both clubs may be obtained from the National Tourist Organization.

The local boys swim in the harbour, but there is a wide choice of beaches. The nearest are those at Poros and Karteros—better known as Florida beach; buses leave for them frequently from the town centre. Both have cabins and refreshments, and small fees. The beaches of Stomnion and Stalis are farther away but have underwater fishing.

Social Contacts

There is a Chamber of Commerce which would welcome contacts with visiting businessmen, socially or otherwise. There are various language institutes, which welcome opportunities to speak English and to hear it spoken.

Iraklion

1 The Great Fort (Venetian castle)
2 Historical Museum of Crete
3 Bank of Greece
4 Astir Hotel
5 Post Office
6 National Tourist Office
7 Church of St Titus
8 Tourist Police
9 Morosini fountain (Venizelos Square)
10 Buses for Rethymnon—Khania
11 Archæological Museum
12 Taxi rank
13 Great Church and Small Church of St Menas
14 Buses for Lasithi (Daskaloyiannis Square)
15 Buses for Knossos (Kornarou Square)
16 Kazantzakis grave

Canea Gate

To Phaestos

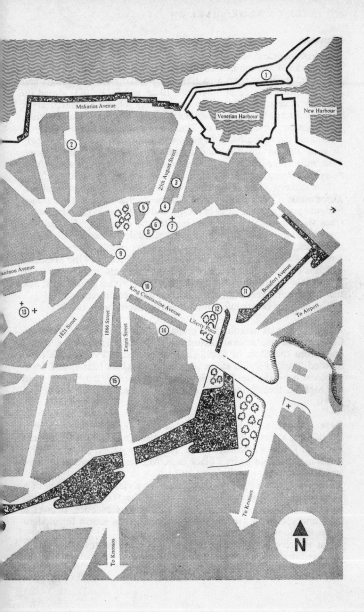

Museums

The Archaeological Museum

This is housed in a modern building, and the summer schedule (April 1 to September 30) is from 8 to 1 and 3 to 6, daily except Sundays and holidays when it is open only from 10 to 1. NOTE: It is closed on Monday afternoon. The winter schedule (October 1 to March 31) is the same except that it opens an hour later and closes an hour earlier.

Admission: Drs. 10. Free on Thursdays and Sundays.

You are strongly advised to go to the Archaeological Museum early in your stay in Iraklion, and again after seeing the various sites. You will certainly appreciate and understand these wonderful finds more fully if you can relate them to the different places they came from.

This is the world's unrivalled collection of Minoan art and culture. To examine it thoroughly would require several days: but the major finds are arranged in a series of rooms, and the general visitor can easily trace the chronology and sites, reading the clear English labels, so that those who must keep to a limited schedule can see the highlights in a quick tour. To view the collection more carefully, the visitor can buy the official Guide by Dr Nicholas Platon, Director of the Museum, which is on sale in the entrance hall. Arrangements can also be made through the Tourist Organization's office for a private guided tour, and there are several rooms which specialists may see on request.

The items of outstanding interest are described below:

Room A includes neolithic and prepalatial finds, largely from Eastern Crete. There are several distinctive styles of vases: the neolithic ones from the Cave of Eileithyia; the bucchero 'Pyrgos style'; the mottled 'Vasiliki style'; stone vases from Mokhlos Island; and some of oldest painted vases from Europe. There are also many finds from the Messara tombs, including sealstones, idols, weapons, tools, and jewels.

Room B contains finds dating from about 2000-1700 BC. There is a bewildering variety of vases from Kamares Cave, Phaestos, and the Palace of Knossos: most are in the 'Kamares style'—highly decorative forms in many colours on a black base. Also here are some of the thin 'eggshell ware'.

There are votive figurines here, including a clay representation of a Minoan religious sanctuary. Here, too, is the 'Town Mosaic' from Knossos: made up of several small earthenware plaques, it gives a fair impression of a Minoan town and has been a source for modern reconstructions.

But the chief attraction of this room is the Phaestos Disc: this is discussed in detail under Phaestos (p. 122).

Room Γ contains some of the most fascinating finds from the high point of Minoan civilization (1700-1400 BC). There is a great variety of stone vases, the most impressive of which is the bull's head rhyton from Knossos. Carved from black steatite (the horns are restored), it was used as a libation vase, with the liquid poured in the top and running out of the mouth.

There are two of the famous Snake Goddesses here, both from Knossos. (Boston's Museum has the most famous Snake Goddess, incidentally, only because some workman smuggled it out of the Knossos excavations.)

There is the ivory acrobat from Knossos: he is represented as leaping over the bull. The dynamic style makes it one of the most remarkable specimens of Minoan art.

There is the gameboard found at Knossos: made from semi-precious stones and gold and silver foil, it seems to have been used for a form of draughts (checkers) played with dice.

For those who are interested in the problems of Linear A and Linear B, this room has examples of inscribed tablets and vases. (For a discussion of these scripts, see p. 74 and p. 75.)

Room Δ has finds from the neopalatial graves and cemeteries: vases, tripods, toilet accessories, weapons, and jewellery. (See especially the gold ring from the Tomb of Isopata.)

Room E includes the rich treasures from the Villa of Ayia Triadha. The most notable are the three black steatite vases—the Chieftain's Cup, the conical rhyton depicting athletic games, and the Harvester Vase.

Here, too, are many double axes—a sacred symbol for the Minoans —found in caves and sanctuaries all over the island.

This room also has many votive offerings in bronze representing people, animals, and weapons; some of these are from the Cave of Dhikti, the birthplace of Zeus (p. 131).

Especially fascinating are the carbonized foods, found in palace storerooms.

Room Z includes finds from sites in Eastern Crete: vases, idols, and kitchen utensils from Palaikastro; bronze tools from Gournia; a bronze cup from Mokhlos Island.

The room has the masterpieces of Minoan jewellery, including the famous golden bee pendant from Mallia.

Of particular value and charm are the numerous sealstones on display in this room. (For a description of sealstones, see p. 126.)

Room H has finds from the postpalatial period, many of them revealing the Mycenaean influence.

Room θ has remains from the Geometric and Orientalizing Periods (1150-650 BC).

Room K is upstairs, but it is a necessary ascent to see the famous frescoes from Knossos. The original fragments are clearly distinguished from the restored parts.

Also here is the sarcophagus from Ayia Triadha. (Described on p. 124.)

Room N Back on the ground floor, you will find the famous works of Archaic sculpture from such sites as Dreros, Gortyne, Elevtherna, Palaikastro, and Prinias.

Giamalakis Collection
Dr Giamalakis, an Iraklion physician, was one of the few individuals allowed to purchase Minoan art and over the years he amassed an important collection. It has now been acquired by the Archaeological Museum and is displayed in separate cases. The showpiece of the collection is the 8th century BC bronze statuette of a man carrying a lamb on his shoulder.

Historical Museum of Crete
Taking up where the Archaeological Museum leaves off, this is a collection of art and handicrafts dating from the first years of the Christian era. The continuity of Cretan popular culture can be traced through the Medieval and Renaissance periods as well as during the Turkish occupation. Among its most appealing exhibits is an exact reconstruction of the room of the novelist Kazantzakis, with his books and belongings just as he left them.

Admission: 5 drachmas

April 1 to October 31:
Weekdays from 8.30 a.m. to 1 p.m. and 3 p.m. to 6.30 p.m.
Sundays 9 a.m. to 1 p.m.

November 1 to March 31:
Monday, Wednesday, Friday: 8.30 a.m. to 1 p.m. and 3 p.m. to 5.30 p.m.
Tuesday, Thursday, Saturday and Sunday: 9 a.m. to 1 p.m.

City of Iraklion

Iraklion is the largest and best-known city of Crete, its commercial capital, and the focal point for most visitors to the island. It is the gateway to Knossos—the foremost Minoan site—and houses the world's supreme collection of Minoan art.

History

Iraklion's history is best traced through the changes in its name. In Minoan times it was only a minor port for Knossos: it came to be known as Herarchtium, or Heraklaea—where Heracles landed to perform his Seventh Labour. Later, the Greeks knew it as Polimation, but it was still not much of a city. When the Arabs conquered the island in AD 828, they chose to make a fort in its harbour, calling it Rabd-el-Kandak; Phocas liberated it in 961 and the Arab name was corrupted into Khandax; this, in turn, turned into something like Chantash under the influence of the local dialect; and when the Venetians took over early in the 13th century, they named it—and the entire island—Candia. (Shakespeare knew it as Candy.) Candia-Iraklion became one of the great Venetian strongholds; but in spite of its fortifications, it fell to the Turks in 1669, after a 22-year-siege that occupied Europe's attention. During the next two centuries the city must have been known by many names, but by the 19th century the islanders seem to have been calling it Megalo Kastro ('Great Castle'): it is either by this name, or by Candia, that it is referred to in travellers' accounts. Finally, when Crete gained its union with Greece, the city was officially named Iraklion—although there are still islanders who prefer to call it Candia or Kastro.

In the last few decades it has become the island's centre of transport and communications as well as the market for central and eastern Crete. Each year sees it grow more modern, but it still retains something of a Near Eastern-bazaar atmosphere. And, although most travellers tend to treat Iraklion strictly as a gateway to Minoan culture, we hope to show that it has historical landmarks of its own to interest the thoughtful visitor, as well as modern diversions.

Sightseeing in Iraklion

Since Iraklion is usually approached by sea, we begin with the view as you enter the bay. The right arm rises steeply, with the remains of a Venetian fort, the Palaiokastro, to be seen; above this is the village of Roudhia. Inland and to the west is the prominent cone of Mt Stromboulas; more central are the peaks of the Idha range and the Zeus-profile of Mt Iouktas. In the bay, to the left, is the barren island of Dia, named after the nymph (one of the extra-marital amours of Zeus) cast there by Hera. The English-speaking community call it Dragon Island because of its shape. The city itself is most dense around the harbour, but overflows onto the inclined plain that is backed by Crete's mountain spine.

Ships tie up in the New Harbour, which has been dredged and enlarged over the years and is still developing its facilities. The entrance to the inner and older Venetian harbour—now used for yachts and smaller ships—is guarded by the impressive Venetian Castle. The Arabs may have been the first to build on an islet here—now joined by a mole to the mainland; then came the Genoese with a simple fort; and finally, the Venetians worked on the ambitious fort we see today from the 14th to the 17th centuries, constructing the major part between 1523 and 1540. It has 26 chambers and its battlements are worth a visit: the Lion of St Mark recalls the old glory. It is in a good state of preservation and is used as a gymnasium and recreation hall by local youths. Visitors may inspect the whole castle. The Venetians expended a great deal to improve this harbour: little remains except one of their 16th century *arsenali*—great vaulted chambers with arcades, now a warehouse.

The dominating structure of Iraklion is the Venetian Wall. First erected in the 14th century, these ramparts were greatly enlarged and improved in the 16th and 17th centuries: Michale Sammicheli of Verona, one of the leading 16th-century military engineers, came in 1538 to supervise. These walls were considered the strongest of their day in the Mediterranean world; in spite of the long siege by the Turks, they are well preserved and enclose the main part of the city. They have a perimeter of about 5 km, several fine bastions, and the deep moat is visible: dwellings and plant growth have spread onto the ramparts and down into sections of the moat. There are three main gates:

(1) The Gate of the Pantocrator, or Panigra Gate—now best known as Khania Porta—serves as gateway to the west. Carvings date it at about 1570.

(2) The Gate of Gesu (Jesus), or Kainourgia Porta, with ornate stonework and decorations. Dated from 1567 to 1587.

(3) The St George Gate, or Porto del Lazzareto (lepers once crowded outside this gate). Dated at 1565, it has two old fountains intact. It offers a view of the Fortress of St Demetri and the east walls.

One of the bastions, the Martinengo (west of the city) holds the grave of Nikos Kazantzakis (1883-1957), the celebrated Cretan-Greek author. Because of his somewhat unorthodox beliefs and writings the Greek Church refused to bury him with its full rites. Now he lies under massive but simple rough native stone. On it an inscription from his own works reads: 'I hope for nothing. I fear nothing. I am free.'

It is possible to visit the 'birthplace' of Kazantzakis in the street now named after him, but it seems unlikely that any of the original structure is contained in the house now standing there. The reconstruction of his last study in the Historical Museum is more stimulating.

Proceeding from the harbour, you climb 25th August Street to the centre of town. (This is the street on which are the shipping lines' offices, tourist agencies, banks, and the offices of the National Tourist Organization and the Tourist Police.) About halfway up, you reach the large new Hotel Astir, on the left. It stands on the Square of Ayios Titos (St Titus), named for the Patron Saint of the island, whose church dominates the square. An early Greek Byzantine church on the spot was enlarged by the Venetians; earthquakes, fires, and restorations followed, until the Turks made a major reconstruction as a mosque in 1862, thus accounting for its unusual shape. (Its two most famous treasures—the icon of Messopanditissa and the head of St Titus—were taken to Venice when Iraklion fell to the Turks.)

Off this square is the Venetian Armoury, now the City Hall. The Armoury backed onto the once renowned Loggia. Constructed early in the 17th century, in a 'mixed Renaissance' style, it was badly damaged by earthquakes; the last war finished it off for the most part. In the north wall of the Armoury is the small fountain of Sagredo.

Higher up 25th August Street is Venizelos Square—commonly known as 'Fountain Square' after the delightful fountain erected in 1626 under the Venetians. (A Francesco Morosini is credited with supervising its construction, as well as that of the Loggia, the Armoury, an aqueduct from Mt Iouktas to Iraklion, and several other fountains. This Morosini, a Venetian governor-general, should not be confused with the famous *Proveditore Generale* who surrendered Iraklion to the Turks in 1669.) The four lions date from the 14th century, probably brought from another Venetian fountain. There was once a statue of Neptune on the top. The eight lobes or basins have bas-reliefs, not especially fine workmanship but worth a close look: nymphs, tritons, dolphins, bulls and mythical marine animals, some playing musical instruments.

Across from the fountain, on the left of 25th August Street, is the Venetian church of St Mark: built in 1239, reconstructed after an earthquake in 1303 as the Church of the Duke, with a campanile (since destroyed), it was then transformed into a mosque. It has been restored in the original Venetian style, with Byzantine-Cretan frescoes, and is used as an auditorium for lectures and concerts.

Off Fountain Square—to the north-west—is a modern public garden with a bust of El Greco. (There are public toilet facilities beneath this park.)

Continuing on 25th August Street, you arrive at the crossroads —officially Nikephoros Phocas Square, but commonly identified as 'where the traffic policeman stands'. Straight ahead, and bearing to the right, you enter 1821 Street. On the corner, right, are the remains of the Church of the Madonnina, or Virgin of the Forum, built by Nikephoros Phocas after his liberation of Crete in 961. Little remains except parts of the roof, covering the shoe repair shops and cafés.

Back at the crossroads, the street that bears more to the left is officially 1866 Street, but no one can fail to recognize it as the Market. A stroll down its length must be made. At the far end is Kornarou Square, where the Bembo Fountain (1588) stands: the headless statuette built into it is Roman, brought from Ierapetra. The Bembo Fountain stands hidden by a café; beside it is another café, this one formerly a Turkish fountain. At the far side of the square is the former Church of San Salvatore: once part of the Augustinian monastery, it became the Mosque Validé, and is now a school.

Back again to the 'crossroads of the policeman', and still with your back to the harbour, turn left and go along King Constantine Avenue, where the better shops are found on the left and administrative buildings on the right. At the entrance to one of these latter—the Court House—is a Venetian portal from the destroyed monastery church of St Francis. The old Turkish barracks once stood along the right hand side; these were replaced by the present structures, which house the government offices. On the left hand side, incidentally, were found some of the few Byzantine remains in Iraklion. Continuing down King Constantine Avenue, you come out onto Liberty Square, with its several cinemas and many cafés. On Sunday and holiday evenings, their patrons spill out over the streets, and here is where you sit to watch the *volta*, or promenade. At the far left of the square, where the road swings down through the St George Gate to the east, is the Archaeological Museum. In its garden is a monument, in French, to the Duc de Beaufort and the French troops who lost their lives in 1668 while trying to lift the siege of Candia.

Returning to the crossroads, and this time turning right (with your back to the harbour), you proceed down a street lined with shops—with most of the goods hanging outside. (This road leads to the Khania Porta.) About five blocks to the left, after leaving the crossroads, you turn in and emerge into the square where stands the Cathedral of Iraklion, Ayios Menas. Erected between 1862 and 1895, it is remarkable largely for its six icons by Michael Damaskinos. A contemporary of El Greco, he too was known in Italy where he went to study and paint. These six icons, dating from about 1580, are his masterpieces and were brought here from the church at Valsamonero. The icons are named: *The Burning Bush, The Last Supper, The First Oecumenical Synod, Noli me tangere, The Adoration of the Magi,* and *The Sacred Mass.*

To one side of the Cathedral is the little 18th-century church of Ayios Menas; it contains some notable wood carvings as well as icons by the Gastrophylakes brothers. (If it is not open, you may get the key from the staff at the Cathedral.)

Off this same square, in a lower court, is the Church of St Katherine. It dates from 1555, and is of a plain, relatively pure style except for the elegant 17th century doorway. During the 16th and 17th centuries, this was the site of the Mt Sinai Monastery School, a centre of the Cretan 'renaissance', where painting, theology, and humanistic studies were taught (and where, it has been claimed, El Greco, Damaskinos, and Cornaros studied.)

These are the principal landmarks of Iraklion, but there are still other, if minor, sights. There are several charming little fountains—the Fountain of Priuli, for instance, in the Bodhosaki Square, dating from 1666. There are remains of other churches—one is Santa Maria dei Crociferi, in Halbherr Street (the southwest area of the town), dating from the early 14th century. And everywhere, in addition, are the pleasures and surprises of contemporary Iraklion.

Knossos

Knossos is, of course, the goal of all visitors to Crete, and it lives up to its reputation. There will always be some who feel that Sir Arthur Evans carried his reconstruction rather too far, but no one ever leaves without being impressed by the majesty of the site. While its breadth and complexity are apparent even to those who merely stroll through, a guided tour is the only way to grasp the details of the site. Private guides may be hired through the National Tourist Organization: the fee for taking a small group through a normal tour—of 2 to 3 hours —100 Drachmas. The minimum time required to tour the main palace complex is about 2 hours; the same time is needed to make a thorough inspection of the surrounding structures. A possible alternative would be to go through with Pendlebury's *Handbook to the Palace of Minos: Knossos with its Dependencies*—which guides you through the site in a clear manner, satisfying both to the scholar and the curious tourist.

Knossos is open to visitors from 8 a.m. to sunset, throughout the year, seven days a week (entrance fee: 10 Drachmas). Buses leave from Kornarou Square in Iraklion every twenty minutes.

History of Site

It had long been known that there must once have been a place called Knossos; by the last half of the nineteenth century there were frequent reports of finds in the area, but they were usually remains of the later, Roman, structures. After the revelations of an amateur Cretan archaeologist, Schliemann tried to acquire the site, but it remained for Evans to begin the real excavations in 1900. Week after week produced some amazing find; year after year continued to reveal the immensity of the site. Evans soon realized that if the various levels and the general complexity of the structures were to be presented there would have to be a certain amount of reconstruction. Working carefully with all the

fragments and evidence available—c.f. the Town Mosaic in the Museum
—Evans supervised the restoration of considerable parts of the palace:
columns, window casements, stairways, walls. All these were rendered
in reinforced concrete, and whenever possible actual remains were
incorporated in the restoration. Over the decades, Evans was assisted
by a staff of archaeologists, architects and artists. In 1960 there was a
scholars' dispute that might have appeared to cast doubt on the whole
site of Knossos. In point of fact it concerned such matters as chronology, the script, and the relationship between Minoan-Cretans and
Mycenaean-Greeks. Whatever the final adjustments, the achievement of
Evans can in no way be diminished. Excavations continue—under
the British School of Archaeology—and still turn up valuable finds
both at the palace and in the surrounding fields.

Visiting Knossos

As Knossos is only about 5 kms from Iraklion, everyone might
consider walking at least one way. In any case, you leave Iraklion via
the south-eastern section of the ramparts. At about 1 km. from the
city an old paved road descends into a ravine at the left and leads off
eastward to the plateau of St Nicholas, from which there is a fine
view of the town and bay. Not far from here were the remains of the
Tomb of Isopata, a remarkable domed tomb from the middle Minoan
period. What little survived when Evans excavated it was destroyed—
accidentally or otherwise—under the German occupation: now you
must see it through the restoration drawn by Piet de Jong, one of
Evans' assistants, in Iraklion's Museum.

From this point you could walk across the fields to Knossos,
inspecting the remains of other tombs in the region. But it would take
a knowledgeable guide to locate them—and all their valuable yields are
in the Museum.

Returning to the main road, this goes up and down hill through
several villages: this Knossos Road is in fact becoming an extended
suburb of Iraklion. About 4 kms from the city, on a curve to the left,
is a Sanatorium (built by the donations of Greek-Americans) that
commands a fine view across the valley of Kairatos, where Knossos
lies. Many tombs were discovered when the Sanatorium was being
built after World War II.

Continuing, up on the right is the Villa Ariadne, built by Sir Arthur
Evans for his private residence. During the war it became the Headquarters of the German Commandant, but now belongs to the Greek
Archaeological Service. Also on the right, below the Villa and just
as the road descends the last hundred metres to Knossos, is a little
passage leading through a wall to the Roman remains. A colony of
Roman veterans settled here after their conquest of the island, and
though they could not revive the glory of Knossos, the *Colonia Julia
Nobilis* was quite an ambitious settlement with a fair number of

buildings. Well-preserved mosaics of the Villa Dionysus are to be seen, as well as remains of the basilica and theatre across the road.

Finally you come to the stretch of little coffee houses that proclaim your arrival at Knossos. Right off the main road, to the left, are remains of an old Minoan road, but there is no access to the site at this point; you must go on to the white pavilion, where you enter the grounds. (There is a souvenir shop here, with a handsome choice of handicrafts.)

It must be emphasized that what the visitor sees at Knossos today are largely the ruins of the great palace that arose during the Neopalatial Period (Evans' MM III and LM I)—approximately 1700 to 1400 BC. At the same time, remains from both earlier and later periods are everywhere, the Cretans having continually built upon and absorbed previous structures. (At its peak, by the way, it is estimated that Knossos—as both palace and city—numbered 100,000 inhabitants, spread over 25 acres.) We see a great sprawling palace complex, amazingly modern in its treatment of space and terrain. This is not Greece of the classic proportions, but Knossos never was that; the amalgam of periods and structures we view is a legitimate effect.

Knossos is the archetype of all the Minoan palaces: the heart is always the great central courtyard—and the ones at Phaestos and Mallia are even more impressive than that at Knossos—used for everything from religious rituals to moonlight strolling. There were subsidiary courtyards also, and in fact you enter by the West Court: the altars, the raised processional causeway, and the drainage system are all typical of what lies within.

The palace site is best considered as being divided into three sections.

In the West Section are the following rooms:

> The long narrow storerooms (commonly called 'magazines')
> The Propylaeum (at the south end)
> The Temple Repositories
> The Pillar Crypts
> The Tricolumnar and Tripartite Sanctuaries
> The Throne room (with the original stone throne of the Priest-King)

In the East Section, across the Central Courtyard, are:

> The Royal Apartments
> The Hall of the Double Axes
> The Hall of the Columns
> The Queen's Chambers
> The workshops of various craftsmen
> The water-pipe system
> The East Bastion (with its ingenious drainage system)

To the north lie:

> The Main Entrance Gate
> The Guard House and Customs Control
> The Theatral Area

Knossos

1 Theatral area
2 North-west treasure house
3 Initiatory area
4 Throne room
5 Court of the stone spout
6 Hall of the Columns
7 Hall of the Double Axes
8 The Queen's Chambers
9 South house

West Court

Magazines

Gr
Stair

Palace area

South Corridor

Actual or certain masonry

Conjectural masonry

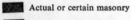

0 10 20 30 40 50
Metres

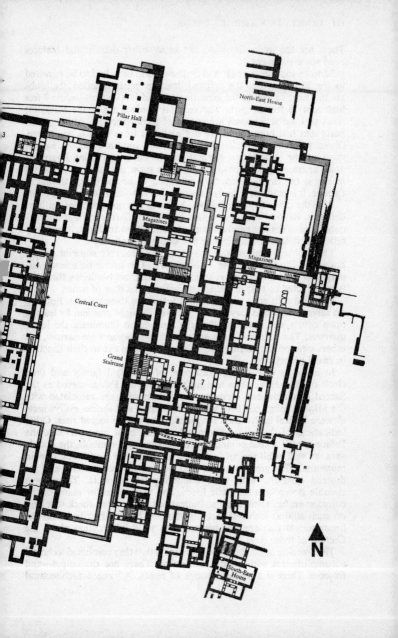

These are the main divisions, but many other details and features need some comment.

Most of the works of art and craftsmanship have had to be removed to the Museum. But the original drainage pipes function; bathtubs are in place; as well as the gigantic urns and jars (*pithoi*)—some 7 feet high and 15 feet in girth. The original frescoes are in the Museum; what you see at Knossos are copies of reconstructions, although the parts that had been found are distinguished from what is conjecture. (Swiss painters, the Gilliérons—father and son—are responsible for most of the imaginative restorations, based on surviving fragments and archaeologists' hints.) Perhaps the most dramatic original still *in situ* is the throne—generally conceded to be the oldest throne in Europe. It is made of gypsum, is well preserved—and you may sit on it!

Like the other Minoan palaces, Knossos has no particular walls or defences. Its location, on a mound in a valley, hardly made it impregnable; but as the signs and remains of fortification are slight, it evidently relied for defence on sea power and coastal installations.

The drainage and sanitation system was probably superior to any known in Europe until the 19th century. The hydraulic science displayed in the East Bastion is amazing: the channel bordering the stairs is constructed so that it breaks and governs the flow of water.

The lightwells are a distinguishing feature of these palaces. Building on several storeys as they did, they solved the light problem by leaving open courts and shafts so that the light could illuminate the lower quarters. The stairways, too, are remarkable. Some were narrow, but others were on the grand plan, no doubt with an eye to their function in ritual processions.

In addition to being the residence of the royal family and their circle of attendant nobles and functionaries, the Palace served as the Sacred Precincts, and many rooms and remains are associated with the Minoan religion. There were little chapels and shrines everywhere, as were 'lustral baths' used for purification during sacred rites. Other indications of the religious atmosphere that must have pervaded the Palace are the sacred pillars, the carved signs and symbols, the double axes, as well as all the artifacts such as the Snake Goddesses, now in museums. This great complex also housed the commercial and industrial quarters, with their administrative adjuncts. There were sizeable storerooms for basic foods, and workshops for many of the common crafts. There are also indications that a close check was kept on such affairs: included here are the clay tablets inscribed with the linear scripts that are just beginning to yield information about the Cretans of those days.

The amazing thing about the Minoans is that they combined technical accomplishment with artistic refinement. There are drainpipes—and frescoes. There is a whole network of roads. Advanced architectural engineering goes with such adornments as colonnades, stairways, and benches.

Is it any wonder, then, that such a complex and awesome structure gained the reputation of being a labyrinth? Think of the effect such a place must have had on passing travellers or captured enemies. With earthquakes familiar, too, the bull-roaring earth-shaker was undoubtedly worshipped along with other manifestations of Nature. Finally, there is a pre-Hellenic word *Labrys*—'double axe'—and a pre-Hellenic place ending, *-nthos* (a survival in sites such as Tirinthos or Korinthos): Knossos was literally 'the house of the double axe'.

Palace Dependencies

The remains of several subsidiary structures lie around the main Palace. Another hour or two might well be spent in climbing about the gentle slopes where the following are to be found:

> *Small Palace:* This lies off the main road to Knossos, on the right, about 250 metres north-west of the Palace.
> *Royal Villa:* Below the main Palace, about 110 metres north-east, where the Kairatos River once ran.
> *Caravanserai:* A reception house for travellers, it is some 110 metres south of the main Palace, with the remains of a viaduct nearby.
> *South Royal Tomb:* Proceeding past Knossos by the new main road, some 500 metres beyond the site of the Caravanserai, up a steep path on the right.

Several other houses have also been excavated in the neighbourhood, along with many tombs and graves. After the decline of the great Palace culture, settlers tended to build on its fringes, but no very extensive excavations have been undertaken for such remains.

There is still one other point of interest in the area. If you stay on the main road, following as it curves for about 2 kms past Knossos, you come to the head of the valley of Spilia. Arching across the gorge is the aqueduct, dating from the 19th century (circa 1838), when the Egyptians were in control of Crete: it is credited to a Cretan architect.

Gortyne, Phaestos, Ayia Triadha

Here again is one of those excursions through history so peculiar to Crete. It can be managed in a day, but could just as profitably take three or four, depending on how many of the side-trips you make. Phaestos itself, as the second of the great Minoan palace-complexes, justifies a day's trip. Those with private transport will be able to set their own pace, but even those dependent on buses will find the schedule allows the three major sites to be included in a day's outing. And Phaestos, with its Tourist Pavilion, is ideal for an overnight stay.

You leave Iraklion by the Khania Gate, pass through the industrial litter at the edge of town, and then, after crossing the little bridge at the outskirts, turn sharply left, away from the coast. For several kilometres you drive through the fertile central basin of Crete; during the Middle Ages, the prized malvasia wine came from here, and today the celebrated rosaki grapes flourish. Then begins the long climb over the Idha Range.

After the village of Avyeniki, about 25 kms from Iraklion, you will see to the right a naturally-fortified hill, almost a vertical mass of stone that rises quite dramatically: this was the acropolis of ancient Rhizenia—the locale is now known as Prinias. There had been some settlement and structures here from Minoan times, but only in the post-Minoan period was the site fully exploited. The Italians, excavating in the first decade of this century, discovered the remains of two archaic temples (roughly, 7th century BC), including friezes depicting animals and warriors, and a statue of the Cretan 'mistress of animals', one of the protean forms of the Mother Goddess. It is such work that has gained the name 'Daedalic style'.

Continuing a few kilometres, you come to Ayia Varvara (29 kms), a sizeable village and a centre for this region. As you enter the village you pass a huge rock, on the right, topped by a chapel: the rock is called the *omphalos*—'the navel'—of Crete, for it is said to be the island's geographical balancing point. The road climbs another 2½ kms and then you go through the pass of Vourvoulitis, at an altitude of almost 2,000 feet. From here begins the long, winding descent to the Messara: with the Lasithi Range to the east, and the Libyan Sea to the west, it is quite a spectacular experience to come down onto the plain.

Stretching some 25 miles back from the sea, and from 5 to 7 miles wide, the Messara Plain is Crete's largest flatland. You might think that this fertile plain would have ensured the island's prosperity and nourishment, but it has never been allowed to develop properly or peacefully. It is productive, but it will take more than fertilizer and tractors to make it flourish: the people of the Messara would have to want to change their way of life. It remains to be seen whether or when this will come about. For now, the Messara provides a modest living for the villages scattered around it, and a rich harvest of sites and pleasures for the traveller.

Water is a problem for the farmers on the Messara as elsewhere on Crete, but there are two major rivers: to the east is the Anapodharis, while the Yeropotamos runs along the base of the Phaestos ridge, at the western end where you are entering.

As the road levels down on the plain, you arrive at the roadside village of Ayia Dheka (44 kms). Ayia Dheka has been called 'a living museum', for the present village is all but built on and out of the remains of ancient Gortyne. Its name means 'the holy ten', alias the

Ten Martyrs: in the 3rd century AD, ten of the inhabitants of this region refused to sacrifice to the gods of their Roman overlords, and so were beheaded. There is one church in the village—probably dating from early Byzantine times, but greatly restored—where is the stone on which the 10 Martyrs are said to have been decapitated. (There are also interesting icons, and a modern altar.) Farther out of the town is another church with the 'crypt of the martyrs'. And near this is 'the museum', with a few remains from Gortyne. (The best are in Iraklion's Museum.) But it is a stroll through the village itself that reveals the museum: columns, statues, fragments of all kinds, have been absorbed in constructing and patching up modern Ayia Dheka. If you handle it properly, you can usually get some of the local people to show choice pieces, built into courtyards, stairways, and houses. It is nothing very dramatic, mind you, but it is sobering to consider how a once-great imperial city like Gortyne can be swallowed up by the sleepy routine of this village.

Moving out of the village, you pass along a road lined by olive trees and parched fields; if you strike off across the fields to the left, you will come upon some of the ruins of Gortyne; continuing another few hundred metres, you will see more obvious remains of Gortyne to the right.

Gortyne

If there was any settlement at Gortyne during the Minoan era, it was completely overshadowed by Phaestos. Not until the great Minoan centres declined and the Dorians took over did Gortyne come into its own; it began to compete as a commercial power from the 8th century BC, eventually controlling the ports of Matala and Leben. By 500 BC Gortyne was mature enough to have its famous Law Code; by 300 BC it probably had control of most of the Messara. But there was never much time for peaceful exploitation; there were, instead, continual wars with the other Cretan city-states and Mediterranean powers, until Gortyne fell to the Romans along with the rest of the island about 67 BC. As part of Rome's imperial vision, Gortyne became the seat of a Praetor, the capital of Crete and the Province of Cyrenaica; the Messara was to become the breadbasket for this empire: Gortyne to be turned into a splendid provincial city. Indeed, for a while, there was a period of prosperity and ambitious construction: irrigation helped the fields to flourish, and brick-making allowed buildings to rise. When Byzantium replaced Rome, and Christianity the old idols, Gortyne managed to retain some of its prestige. But when it fell to the Moors in 828 AD, it was partially destroyed and never again regained its stature.

Gortyne was among the first Cretan sites to be excavated—by Halbherr and the Italian mission, back in the 1880s; it took many decades, though, before all the ruins we see were exposed, for they spread over a considerable area. They are fairly difficult to find, but that is what makes this such a fascinating spot: you walk through dry fields, across crumbling walls, past gnarled olive trees, discovering the sunken foundations, columns, statues, arches, and fragments —slowly piecing together the once-grand city of Gortyne.

The ruins of Gortyne may be seen as two major groupings, the first of which is in the fields to the left (after you have left Ayia Dheka's little 'museum'). Here are the Temple of Pythian Apollo, the Praetorium, the Sanctuary of Isis and Serapis, a theatre, an amphitheatre, a stadium, and a basilica. Most of these date from the 2nd century AD, but there had been earlier structures in several cases, and some were later adapted by the Byzantines.

The second and more interesting group of remains is found farther along the road to Phaestos, on the right. The first structure to catch your eye is the high apse of the Basilica of Ayios Titos—the Titus said to have been commissioned by Paul in person to convert the Cretans, and the first Bishop of Gortyne. (It is claimed that he was buried here, but there is no way to prove this.) The Basilica dates from the 6th century AD, with alterations up to the 10th century; eventually it fell to pieces, but enough remains to show the extent of the structure. One of the small side chapels is used as a shrine by the local people, and fragments of the original frescoes adhere to the walls. Outside stands an odd miscellany of remains in various architectural styles.

Proceeding back into the fields by a path that runs above the river Lethe (no—not the famous one), you arrive at the ruins of the Roman Odeon. Originally there was a Hellenistic structure here; in the 1st-2nd centuries AD the Romans built this 'chamber theatre' whose ruins survive. Enough is preserved to give a good idea of its appearance. Behind the Odeon is the prize exhibit of Gortyne: the Law Code. Carved on stone blocks, it stands upright as it stood when the Romans came and incorporated it into their Odeon; it is sheltered under a modern brick gallery. The separate blocks were found by Halbherr and his Italian mission in 1884; they were scattered and partly inundated by the mill stream, and it was many years before they were reassembled in their original position.

The Law Code as you see it is the original one. More than 17,000 characters are carved in the stone; the language is a regional archaic and most of its 18 letters are recognizably Greek. The code has been set down in what is called 'the ox plough script', according to which the eye travels from right to left and left to right continuously, as a field is ploughed. It is generally dated about 500 BC, and there are grounds for believing that the laws applied to more of Crete than Gortyne alone. They deal with both criminal and civil matters—divorce, adultery, adoption, dowries, lands and inheritance—and provide a fairly clear view of the social structure and life of the time. Seeing this, you can see why Crete was regarded by the mainland as being the fountainhead of law.

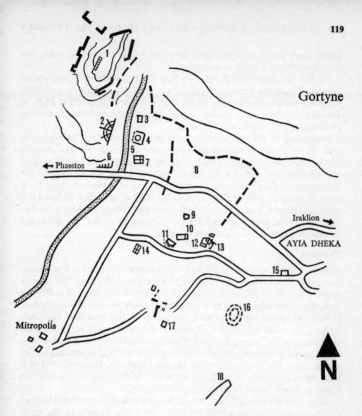

Gortyne

← Phaestos

Iraklion →

AYIA DHEKA

Mitropolis

N

1 The Acropolis
2 Hellenic Theatre
3 Venetian Watermill
4 Odeon and Law Code
5 Agora, Greco-Roman market place
6 Storage galleries
7 Basilica of Ayios Titos
8 Aqueducts
9 Sanctuary of Isis and Serapis

10 Temple of Pythian Apollo
11 Theatre
12 Praetorium
13 Nympheon
14 Byzantine Basilica
15 Museum
16 Amphitheatre
17 Main gate
18 Stadium

Behind the Law gallery is a medieval mill, used for grinding flour. If you are lucky enough to arrive when the miller is at home you may enjoy another unique experience, for he plays a primitive ancestor of the bagpipe. This is a goat's skin, turned inside out and sewn up, with small reeds inserted. The music may not be to everyone's taste, but it makes an unforgettable occasion.

On the hill to the left is the Acropolis from the earlier post-Minoan period. There are remains from Greek and Roman times, including religious shrines, an archaic altar, and a fortress. Important finds of Daedalic art have been made. Lower, towards the main road, are the remains of a Greco-Roman theatre.

Returning to the main road, and again en route for Phaestos, you pass the ruins of the storage galleries along the road—the last glimpse of Gortyne. A few kilometres farther on is the Agricultural School of the Messara, housed in a former monastery. Here, young Cretans are taught up-to-date methods of agriculture on a self-supporting farm now an integral part of the Messara farming community. A few kilometres farther (53 kms from Iraklion) is the village of Mires—a bus junction, with plenty of cafés for a refreshing pause; on Saturday mornings there is a lively market-bazaar.

Phaestos

Several kilometres on from Mires you become aware of a low mountain ridge that breasts the Messara like the prow of a ship. Here, on a spur, is the site of Phaestos, some 250 feet above the plain. It is difficult now to understand how it ever came to be covered—but this happened. It was only after several experimental digs in the area that Halbherr located the exact site, in 1900. The great palace-complex was excavated over many years, largely by the Italians and the Greeks. Cemeteries and other remains were found outside the palace proper, indicating settlements from the neolithic period through Minoan, Hellenic, and still later ages. Phaestos, indeed, has been one of the most active sites on Crete in recent years, with many revealing finds.

The turn-off to the left (61 kms) is clearly marked. A new road crosses the Yeropotamos and winds up the steep ridge, ending at the back of the site. A short walk brings you above a most spectacular combination of natural site and historic ruin. (The modern building overlooking the site is the Tourist Pavilion: see p. 122.)

Since Phaestos arouses as much enthusiasm by its location as by its ruins, it is well to get oriented. As you stand looking down the long Messara Plain to the east, Mt Dhikti and the Lasithi Range rise at the far end. To the right is the Asterousia Range, bordering the south coast. To the north, left, is the Idha Range. If you look carefully you will see a dark hole, at the extreme right of the saddle between two peaks on the Idha slopes: this is the Kamares Cave, where the famous pottery was found.

The history of Phaestos is not so well known as that of Knossos, although recent excavations are bringing much to light. Among other discoveries are extensive remains of a neolithic settlement, plus

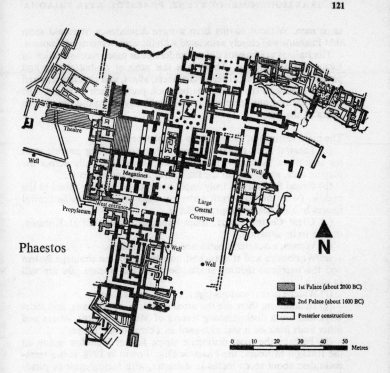

Phaestos

1st Palace (about 2000 BC)

2nd Palace (about 1600 BC)

Posterior constructions

N

0 10 20 30 40 50
Metres

various levels indicating continuous habitation of the site. It is said to have been founded by Minos, but it is traditionally associated with his brother Rhadamanthys—also a noted legislator. The weights and measures of Phaestos may have been accepted as standards throughout the Cretan 'empire'. Its people were known for their wit. Phaestos' development, both political and architectural, seems to have paralleled Knossos, although it was never so extensive in power or so intricate in structure. The materials and workmanship at the palace of Phaestos were however at least as good as at Knossos. It passed through successive series of reconstructions and additions, and it fell to some natural disaster or to invaders—or both. The rise of nearby Gortyne denied it any later glory. How closely it was linked to Knossos in its heyday is in dispute: certainly there is a similarity in the design and structure of the palaces as well as in many of the artifacts found at both sites. Some scholars place great emphasis on masons' marks on stones which, they say, show that the palaces were probably built by the same men. Without having been a mere dependency, it would seem that Phaestos was closely associated with the achievements of Knossos.

The Italians at Phaestos did not undertake as much reconstruction as Evans did at Knossos. There is a fair amount of buttressing and patching; walls, walks, cisterns, chambers, altars, and urns are repaired *in situ*; otherwise the palace has been left pretty much as found. The current excavations serve still more graphically to expose the various strata of the site.

The main features of the Phaestos complex are:

(a) Theatral area: raised steps more than 60 feet long provide seats for spectators. A narrow flagstone ramp runs diagonally across the playing area, somewhat in the manner of a Japanese theatre.

(b) Grand Stairway: a truly imperial structure, slightly raised in the middle. (Was this to permit water to drain off—or to make central figures in a procession appear taller?)

(c) Great Central Court: more impressive than that at Knossos, thanks to its situation.

(d) Women's quarters: baths and other chambers.

(e) Workshops and storerooms: note the ingenious drainage system and the overhead lighting shafts. Some of the storage jars are still in place.

(f) Water system: various pipes, drains, and cisterns.

(g) In addition, there are the usual corridors, apartments, and stairways that are a distinguishing feature of Minoan palaces. Altars and other finds indicate it was also used as a ceremonial 'temple'.

(h) Perhaps the most distinctive single find at Phaestos is now in the Iraklion Museum: the Phaestos Disc. Found in 1908, it is a terracotta disc about seven inches in diameter, with hieroglyphic or pictographic characters imprinted on both sides and spiralling into the centre. It is believed that the text has some religious significance—perhaps a hymn—because there is a rhythmical order to the signs and a 'refrain' of sorts. It was made by punching movable type into the clay, making it one of the earliest specimens of printing. It is dated about 1650 BC. Many scholars have suggested translations; the latest has declared it is related to the cuneiform Hittite language.

These are the main features of Phaestos; around the hillsides are other remains, from graves to Minoan houses. Anyone wishing to spend a night at Phaestos—and to stand beneath the stars in the Great Courtyard and gaze across the Messara is an unforgettable experience—can do so at the Tourist Pavilion. Rooms are about 50 Drachmas a bed; meals are available; campers have been allowed to sleep on the roof. The atmosphere is more like a friendly inn than an official hostelry, and it makes a congenial starting point for excursions to other sites in southern Crete.

Ayia Triadha

One side-trip can conveniently be made on foot from Phaestos, even by those who have only time between buses: to the Villa of Ayia Triadha, one of the miniature gems of the Minoan civilization.

There are two main routes. Those who have transport should go down to the main road and continue towards the coast for about 2½ kms, until a turning to the left is indicated. After following this for about 500 metres, you arrive at the river, which you can easily ford, if it isn't dried up. There is a short walk of another 100 metres —and usually someone is there to guide you.

The other route is for walkers. You pick up the trail behind the Tourist Pavilion, where the asphalt road stops; then follow the Phaestos ridge along its northern side. It is easy to find your way and it takes about 45 minutes.

The ruins of Ayia Triadha lie at the western end of the Phaestos ridge; they were excavated by the Italians early in the century, after the discovery of Phaestos. The Idha Range lies to the north; directly below, where the river meanders along the plain, is a lush, almost tropical region known as 'Paradise', where many fruit trees grow. To the west is the Bay of Messara, and it is fairly certain that the sea once came much closer to the site, making Ayia Triadha almost a

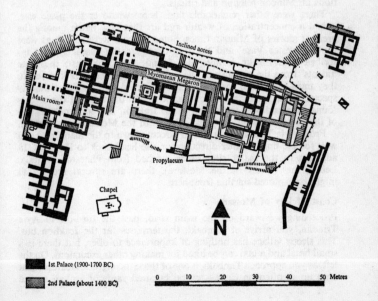

Inclined access

Mycenaean Megaron

Main room

Propylaeum

Chapel

N

■ 1st Palace (1900–1700 BC)

▨ 2nd Palace (about 1400 BC)

0   10   20   30   40   50 Metres

seaside villa. Exactly what it was is not known. Some say it was a summer palace for the Phaestos royalty; others think it was a prince's residence; some see it as the home of a wealthy vassal-chieftain; still others think it was a royal annex, used for special ceremonial occasions. Certainly it must have been dependent on, if not actually subservient to, Phaestos; the trail still taken overland must have seen its share of messengers, functionaries, and royal processions.

Whoever owned it, it was built as a sort of 'vest pocket' version of a Minoan palace. There is the little 'theatre', the courtyards, stairways, storage vaults—all the familiar forms. One of the most interesting parts is the throne room, with gypsum benches and panels, overlooking the bay. The remains are largely from the late Minoan period. A caretaker at the site will show you round.

Its name, which means 'Holy Trinity', comes from the little Byzantine chapel above the site. Beside this is another chapel, the 15th century Ayios Georgios, with frescoes and Venetian tombs.

Many tombs were excavated in the vicinity of Ayia Triadha. In one, about 100 yards to the north-east, was found one of the most significant remains of the entire Minoan culture—the sarcophagus with its surface painted to show the religious rites for the dead. It is carved from limestone, but its surface was coated with a white plaster. It dates from about 1400 BC and represents the chief source for speculations on Minoan religion and rituals.

There were other remarkable finds here: whatever the place was, it had a concentration of wealth and art that now figure among the greatest glories of Minoan times. Some frescoes were found, as were the 'Harvester Vase' and the two other steatite vases. Tablets inscribed with Linear A were also found; and, not least, the large 'talents' from the treasury of the sanctuary—weighing 29 kilos each, they must have been some official standard. Ayia Triadha, if hardly spectacular as a site, has its own appeal; and the value of the objects found here and now to be seen in the Iraklion Museum make it one of the most important pre-classical sites in the Mediterranean world.

From Ayia Triadha, you can go directly down to the main road and wait for the bus in either direction, or else head back to Phaestos. In addition to the major sites to be reached from Phaestos (Matala, Leben, the Tombs of the Messara), there are several areas that might be explored starting from here.

Coast of Bay of Messara

Proceeding westward on the main road, past the turn-off to Ayia Triadha, you arrive at Timbaki, the terminus for the Iraklion bus. This sleepy village has nothing of importance to offer, but there is a small hotel and a taxi can be hired for making other excursions. On the left, as you approach Timbaki, is one of those incongruous features that crop up so often on Crete—several hundred yards of asphalt spread over the landscape to form an airstrip. Built after World War II for strategic reasons, it is abandoned except for a small contingent of Greek military guards.

From Timbaki there is a bus to Ayia Galini, where you can take another bus to Rethymnon or a boat to Sfakia. Some 3 kms from Timbaki, along a rather primitive road, is Kochinos Pyrgos, with its tomato gardens, abandoned warehouses, unfinished shell of a church, and customs 'office'—it was once a port for the African trade. There is fair swimming here; a café serves basic drinks all year, and a small restaurant provides light meals in summer. You may also see the home of 'the mad American millionaire artist', who appeared here in 1959, rented a dilapidated house, and with remarkable energy and ingenuity —and to the amazement of the local people—converted it within a few months into a comfortable villa, complete with a hot-water shower!

Tombs of the Messara

This rather specialized excursion takes several hours and is probably of interest mainly to archaeologists. A good guide is essential and should be obtained in Iraklion. Access to the region of these tombs is by the road that turns left (southwards) just after you leave Ayia Dheka; walking the whole route would take about 6 hours, and driving to a few points would only cut off an hour or two. You should head first for the three tombs—one of which is quite well preserved—between Loukita and Koumasa. Then go on to Platanos (via Kato Anoyia) where foundations of two more tombs may be seen: one has a diameter of 13 metres, with walls nearly $2\frac{1}{2}$ metres thick, and is surrounded by 15 smaller chambers where many vases were found. Along with the tombs at Ayia Triadha, these are the most important in the area, but there are other remains at Kalathiana, Marathokephalo, Porti, Dhrakonas, Ayia Irena.

These tombs were among the earliest finds on Crete—as well as the oldest remains—some having been excavated towards the end of the 19th century by local Cretan archaeologists and the Italian mission. They were circular, probably vaulted, and although less dramatic than the great 'beehive' tombs of Mycenae (certainly not as high as the latter) were the forerunners of these later mainland tombs. They were regarded as homes for the afterworld, and it is from them and their contents that we have learned practically all we know of the people who used them for burial. It was a pre-palatial culture, based on small tribes or clans; existing well before the distinctive Minoan civilization, there were undoubtedly strong links with the Egyptian, Hittite, Mesopotamian, and Babylonian cultures, as the many finds testify. These finds—now in Iraklion's Museum—include jewellery, amulets, pottery, idols, human and animal figurines, tools, and weapons of all kinds. Some of the knives were made from obsidian, a stone found only on the island of Milo—a fact that opens up wide speculation about the trade and communications of the age.

The most revealing finds have been the sealstones—small, flat, and oval-shaped. At first these were made of soft materials like ivory and steatite; later, harder semi-precious stones were used. They were carved, intaglio fashion (often on both sides) with representations of various forms including animals and, less frequently, human figures. They seem to have been something like 'totems', expressing the personality or ideal of their owners with whom they were interred. (Some were also used for the more prosaic purpose of identifying and protecting property.) Many are truly gems of artistry, as well as revelations of the mode of life.

From the village of Platanos you can either return direct to Ayia Dheka or proceed south to one of the sites along the coast, such as Leben or Matala.

Matala

Another locale that might be visited from Phaestos is the port-village of Matala, site of ancient Matallon. There are several approaches— overland from adjacent sites or by back roads—but only one is really feasible. (Even that is hard to follow.)

Starting on the ridge of Phaestos, behind the palace site, you bear left, passing the abandoned chapel of St George, and then descend onto the plain to the south-west of Phaestos. After a few kilometres, you come to a crossroads, with a small school building to your right; bear right here, passing through the village of Ayios Ioannis. Within another few kilometres you pass a walled enclosure, within which stands one of the more unique architectural forms on Crete. It is the little early-14th century roughstone chapel of St Paul, almost sinking into the ground. Burial plots lie round it, and the charnel house is at one side; within are a few old frescoes and icons. But it is the structure that is so remarkable: it is almost as though you are witnessing the emergence of the Byzantine style out of some archaic form.

Proceeding a few more kilometres, you arrive at a crossroads, with a sizeable building (an olive press) across to the left; turn sharply right, passing through the olive groves and come out along a walled cemetery. Just beyond this is a turn-off to the right—actually a by-pass round part of the village that lies ahead on an extremely rocky road. Taking this by-pass, you reach the end of the village; continue through some fairly bleak landscape, gradually descending to the coast. On the flatland, the road passes some farmplots, and then leads right onto the sandy beach: don't drive too far onto the beach, as the sand is very soft.

This is Matala—a striking, circular cove, with fine, grey sand. The village is almost deserted during winter, but there is always someone there to serve coffee. Shacks and houses straggle along the slopes above the beach; and a new Tourist Pavilion is due to open in 1963, providing more elaborate refreshments and bathing facilities.

The really unique aspect of Matala is the great promontory that forms the right arm of the cove—a high, sheer cliff of parched yellow earth that time has packed into a sort of rock. Into this cliff, across the centuries, men have carved caves. Some are little more than pock-marks, warrens barely able to shelter a few people; others are regular rooms, complete with benches carved out of the walls; and a few are quite elaborate apartments, with steps, vestibules, framed doors and windows, and fireplaces. (The beds are reminiscent of Etruscan tombs, with their platforms for the dead, carved out of the natural stone.) The left arm of the harbour also has a few caves; some people, too, have built houses on its gentler slopes, back against the caves.

It is difficult to find an authoritative statement as to what caused this unusual terrain: one theory is that forces of water, millions of years ago, built up great sand barriers, and when a stream cut through the compressed mound the cliffs were left on both sides. In any case, men came along and scratched out the caves, and these have been inhabited off and on for a few thousand years. Neolithic settlers may have taken advantage of the site before homes were available. In Minoan times Matala was a port for Phaestos: despite the complications of getting here by road, it is only about 10 kms overland. Later, when Gortyne had assumed power, Matala's caves served as arsenal-magazines; not for the last time, either, as the Germans used them for the same purpose during their occupation. Matala has also its share of myths and legends: here Zeus, disguised as a bull, came ashore bearing Europa (perhaps signifying the arrival of some Phoenician ship with the figurehead of a bull?); here some of Menelaus' vessels were driven ashore on their return from Troy (see *The Odyssey*, Book III); here the Arabs under Abou Hafs Omar came ashore in the 9th century AD and moved on to attack Gortyne and conquer Crete.

All this time, though, it is safe to assume that local people used the caves: after all, they are at least as comfortable as many peasant dwellings—and cost nothing. Even today the caves are inhabited by people from central Crete who come for summer holidays.

There are reputed to be some underwater remains at the edge of the cliffs, as well as grottoes—an invitation to skin divers. Most people are content to enjoy the swimming, and to sit in the caves and gaze out over the cove that has seen so many illustrious strangers—yes, and pirates—come and go.

From Matala you can walk east over Cape Lithinon to Kaloi Limenes; return by the same road to Phaestos: or strike north-west to Timbaki and Ayia Galini.

Leben

Another interesting side-trip from Phaestos is to the seldom-visited site of ancient Leben—now known also as Leda, the modern village near by. You start by taking the same turn-off after Ayia Dheka as for a visit to the tombs of the Messara, then proceed through the villages of Mitropolis and Platanos, and press on across the Asterousia Mountains, lying parallel to the southern coast. There are some impressive slopes and curves, but the road is good. After several kilometres you come to the village of Miamou: in a cave (first explored by the Italians in 1894) were found remains indicating that it was inhabited in the neolithic period and later used for burials. From Miamou you descend to the southern coast: when you come to the end of the road, at a cluster of houses clinging to the coastal slopes, you are at Leben (about 30 kms from Ayia Dheka).

Leben seems to be derived from a Phoenician-Semitic word for 'lion'—referring to the promontory that juts out into the sea here, like a crouching animal. This helps to form and protect the small harbour, which must have once witnessed a fair amount of traffic. It was in the post-Minoan period that Leben came into its own—especially during the 6th and 5th centuries, when Gortyne used it as a port—and it attracted people from some distance, thanks to the curative powers of its spring. Even today, people come from as far away as the Greek mainland to drink the waters—especially recommended for ulcers. Leben is situated in such a favourable spot that tomatoes can be cultivated around the year and swallows are said to winter there. You can get little more than water, coffee and very simple meals, but the local people enjoy showing strangers around the ruins.

The remains—first excavated in the 19th century by the ubiquitous Italians, who returned to complete the work in 1910—are quite impressive for such an isolated spot. They are situated on the hillside a little to the east of the present settlement of Leda, and command a fine view across the Libyan Sea. There is the Temple of Asclepius, signifying the associations of the site with its curative waters; some remains of the portico; and the ruins of the Temple to Olympian Zeus. This last has a subterranean treasury-crypt: over this is an elegant mosaic, depicting a prancing, fanciful seahorse. Altogether it must have been a pleasant spa.

On your way back—if you have a guide—stop along the road and walk overland to the remains of some Minoan circular tombs that have recently been discovered (about 5 kms from Leda.) There was a Minoan village at the base of the promontory, and recent digging has begun to expose the extent of the site. The tombs have yielded pottery, implements, jewellery, some confirming the early trade with Egypt. Employing the most advanced methods of stratigraphic excavation, archaeologists from Iraklion's Museum are now learning still more about the Minoan era from this obscure site.

Kaloi Limenes

Another possibility while at Leben is to walk overland (about 10 kms) west to the harbour of Kaloi Limenes—the 'Fair Havens' mentioned in *Acts* XXVII. It is situated against Cape Lithinon (on the other side of which is Matala) and three rocky islets lie just off-shore. One of these is 'St Paul's Island', and there is a small chapel on shore where St Paul is said to have preached.

From Kaloi Limenes you can either walk overland to Matala or take the road north to the main road by Phaestos.

Dhiktian Cave and Lasithi Plain

This excursion—which includes the birth-cave of Zeus and a plateau known as 'The Valley of the Windmills' as its destination—requires a full day, especially if any of the sites en route are taken in. The destination actually lies in Lasithi Nome, and can be reached from either Neapolis or Ayios Nikolaos. Most people will make it as a round trip from Iraklion, however, so we describe the approach from there; those who are going on to the eastern sites might consider taking the alternative route down.

The road out of Iraklion is the one described for the excursion to Mallia (pp. 135-7). At about 23 kms, however—near Khersonisos—is a turn-off to the right: there should be a sign indicating Potamies, but you can hardly miss the turn, as it bears off gradually, a major asphalt road leading through well-kept olive groves. The asphalt gives out, and you start climbing, arriving after some 10 kms at the village of Potamies. Here stands the Byzantine Church of the Panayia Gouverniotisa, with 14th-century frescoes considered as among the most notable on Crete.

About 6 kms later—after some rather poor roads—you come to the village of Avdou. Here there are three 15th-century frescoed chapels: St George, St Constantine, and St Anthony—this last having the best frescoes. You proceed through the village of Gonies, and begin the dramatic ascent of the Lasithi range, passing after 6 kms the out-skirts of the village of Krasi. Those who can should make a halt here, and walk up to look at one of the most remarkable trees in the world: a gigantic plane tree, nourished by the endlessly gushing springs near by. You can sit beneath the tree, enjoy a glass of the wonderful water, and watch the village people come and go at the fountains.

Moving on some 4 kms, you arrive at the village of Kera. (You are now about 50 kms from Iraklion.) Just about 600 metres before the village is the Monastery of Kera: its once-famous icon of the Madonna of Perpetual Succour was taken in 1498 to the Church of St Alphonse in Rome. Finally, just when you think the road cannot go any higher or farther, you find yourself going through a pass, with old stone windmill towers banked along the steep ridges. Ahead of you, spread out like some gargantuan Olympic Stadium, is the Lasithi Plain, with Mt Dhikti at its far end, and the slopes and peaks of the Lasithi Range completely encircling it.

From 8 to 10 kms long and 4 to 6 kms wide, the plain appears almost symmetrical. After heavy spring rains or the thaw, the water may collect up to one metre's depth; this drains at the north-west entrance forming a sizeable river as the water comes down onto the north coast. The plain, thus, is virtually an alluvial plain, in that the run-off from the slopes has deposited a thick soil, making for some of the most productive land on Crete. Potatoes, apples and other fruit, and some grain are among the chief products. There are about 18 villages tucked away in the foothills—both to avoid the floods and to free the land for cultivation. Because of its peculiar situation, this total area has always been somewhat independent, yet it has never completely cut itself off from the culture of the rest of the island. Ancient sites and remains have been found all over the plain and its slopes—caves, buildings, forts, temples, tombs, with shards and artifacts of all sorts —with the British taking the lead in exploring and excavating these places. The history runs from neolithic times to the Roman period, and to describe all these sites would require a book in itself. The Venetians, determined to do away with such an enclave, removed the inhabitants and prohibited farming and pasturing on the plain, from 1362 to the end of the 15th century; but eventually its fertility could not be denied.

What makes it a spectacle today is not just the lush, flat farmland, Wherever you look there are windmills. Yes, windmills—some very slight and others quite ambitious, but when they all have their white sails unfurled, it is a unique sight, best seen in mid-morning, when the prevailing winds tend to sweep across the plateau. They are used to pump the water for irrigation. An actual count was taken some years ago, and it is reliably claimed that there must now be some 10,000 windmills on this plain. It is said that a man's wealth here is measured by the number and size of his windmills—just as the Lapps with their reindeer.

As you proceed along the north edge of the plain, you pass through the largest village there, Tzermiadha. A little to the north-east of the village is the low plateau of Trapeza, where lies a famous cave by that name. (Beware of several other caves in the area.) The Cave of Trapeza was discovered by Evans in 1896, but it was not until 1936 that the British got around to making thorough excavations. Many finds, including pottery, seals, and figurines, were taken out of the cave, but were so mixed up that it was hard to assign exact dates. It was definitely a dwelling in neolithic times; human remains indicate that it was later a burial site. In Minoan times it became a cult shrine.

Circling from the north and east, you head for the village of Psykhro. En route, you pass the Monastery of Panayia Kroustallenia, situated on its private little peak. It enjoys the singular, and rather un-monastic, luxury of its own generator, so it has electricity. You can pass the night here in quite comfortable quarters.

Finally you arrive at the village of Psykhro, the starting point for the climb to the Dhiktian Cave. The village is a popular spot for excursionists from all over Crete, with people coming to sit in the shade of the trees and enjoy the spring water. There is a modest tourist cottage, with 8 beds; light meals can be had in the village. And except for occasional weekends, there are not likely to be many going to the cave at any one time.

It is advisable to arrange with one of the local guides to take you through the cave; not that there is any risk involved, but you will be certain of seeing all the 'inner sanctums'. (The usual fee is from 20 to 30 Drachmas; this includes the candles he brings.) Within the cave there is no need to mark a trail, but it can be damp and cool: rubber-soled shoes and a sweater are advisable. The climb takes only about half an hour, and then you find yourself before a gaping split in the mountainside—the Dhiktian Cave, birthplace of Zeus.

The cave was brought to light back in the 1880s by local men; Hadzidakis and Halbherr explored the exposed parts shortly after, and Evans came there in 1894; but it was 1900 before the British undertook a thorough excavation, with the help of local people. Blasting was resorted to, and the unsuspected inner depths revealed, with local youths bringing up hundreds of votive offerings from the muddy depths. There are two great fissures, but it is the one leading down to the right that has the more spectacular interior and so has always attracted more people. There are large stalagmites and stalactites: a huge stalactite, hidden in a chamber, is known as 'the mantle of Zeus' (i.e. his swaddling clothes). There is a small underground pool. And in one tiny chamber—where there were particularly rich finds of votive offerings—it is claimed the birth occurred.

The myth, briefly, is that Cronus had a habit of devouring his offspring, so his wife Rhea fled to the Dhiktian Cave to be delivered of Zeus. It must be recalled that Zeus was no god for the Minoans; he was brought into Crete by the Greeks, and this story of the birth was evidently an attempt to relate the new god to the old mother, and to convert some Minoan deity into an acceptable Olympian figure. Hesiod is responsible for setting this down, and as noted elsewhere, it is all further complicated by the question as to just where the Dhiktian Cave should be located. In any case, this cave had a long history as a cult shrine, from the middle Minoan period on. It would seem that the upper cave was used first; then the water receded and the lower cave was attended by votaries of the Mother Goddess. By 800 BC, the cave's appeal was at its peak, and then it began to be superseded by the one on Mt Idha. But it is easy to see how such a cave would give rise to a cult and myths.

To view the cave takes about an hour. By the time you get back to the village of Psykhro, then, a good two hours will have elapsed. Depending on your mode of transport, you now have the choice of going back to Iraklion, moving down to Ayios Nikolaos, or remaining overnight in the village.

Mount Idha and Kamares Cave

Although no Alpine ascent, the climb to Mt Idha and a visit to the adjacent caves involves more than the casual traveller will be able to manage. There are alternate approaches, with various detours and diversions, but at least two or three days must be allowed. We shall describe the approach from Iraklion via the village of Kamares, not only because it offers convenient access to the summit and the caves but also because it provides an excursion with several interesting stops en route. (The other three approaches are: from the north, the village of Anoyia; from the south, the village of Voroi, near Phaestos; and from the west, the village of Fourfouras, in Amari Province.)

All except the more experienced climbers and hikers should arrange for a guide; they can be picked up in the villages, but you would do well to consult the Iraklion office of the Tourist Organization. Here you can be put in touch with guides, consult more detailed maps, or be introduced to the local Climbing and Touring Clubs who occasionally make ascents. Those who are determined to go alone will find the best available account in Robert Grantham's *Minotaur and Crete*.

Incidentally, so that no one goes to all this trouble by mistake, the Mt Idha in question is not the classically famous one of Homer and Aeschylus—that is near Troy. Crete's Mt Idha, in fact, is becoming more widely known today, at least among the natives, as Psiloritis.

You leave Iraklion by the Khania Gate, taking the Phaestos route as far as the village of Ayia Varvara. (See under Phaestos.) At Ayia Varvara (29 kms) there is a turn-off to the right that takes you west along the edge of the mountains and down into a lovely valley, on through the village of Yeryeri (with the Church of the Panayia: 15th-century frescoes), and so to Zaros (45 kms). Zaros is cleaner and more prosperous than the average Cretan village; most of the houses' doorways have carved lintels. It is also noted for its fine water, the same source that supplied ancient Gortyne (due south, behind the mountains) and that still supplies Ayia Dheka. Remains of the ancient stonework are to be seen around the spring. Above this spring is the old Church of Ayios Nikolaos, with 15th-century icons and altar panels in early renaissance style. Farther above this church, across a ravine and up the mountainside, is a chapel in a cave: it dates from the 15th century, has frescoes, and takes its name from St Efthimios who lived and died as a hermit-ascetic in the cave.

Continuing on the main road from Zaros, after three kilometres you come to a turn-off to the right, leading steeply up the hillside to the Monastery of Vrondisi. It is said to have been founded in the 16th century by pilgrims from Brindisi, Italy. It stands high on the hill, with a fine view, and there are large plane trees in the clearing before the walls. Here, too, is a 16th-century Italianate fountain, quite un-monastic in its elegance and one of the finest in the Cretan countryside: between the two pilasters are badly mutilated statues of Adam and Eve. Notable frescoes, in the Church of St Anthony, and the fine overnight accommodation (with arrangements for meals) complete the attractions of the place.

Back on the main road, and just a little farther on, you see a small, isolated chapel, across a gentle ravine to the left. This is Valsamonero, with its famous church, dedicated to St Fanourios. It has two parallel naves, and a third at right angles to these, in place of a narthex; with its gothic arches, decorated with leaves and palmettes, the exterior shows obvious Italian influence. The north nave was the original and is attributed to the 14th century; the other two, based on the inscriptions of the donors, are assigned to the early 15th century. Within, a richly sculptured iconostasis, with delicate scallops on each niche, indicates more Italian renaissance influence. The major attraction is the frescoes, considered among the most valuable on Crete. Those on the ceiling vaults portray the life of the Virgin in a naïve style and date from the 14th century; along the walls are various saints, dating from the end of the 14th or early 15th century. Konstantine Rikos is generally credited with these frescoes, although you may be told that Damaskinos and El Greco worked on them. (The six icons by Damaskinos, now in Iraklion's Cathedral of Ayios Menas, were once here at Valsamonero.)

From the church, there is a path leading directly to the next village, Voriza—also reached by the main road. After Voriza, you proceed about 3 kms to the village of Kamares. Here you can get overnight accommodation and meals, rent mules, hire guides, and generally prepare for the climb to the summit. (It is a 7 or 8 hour trip *each* way, so you must plan your day accordingly.

There are three principal destinations:

Cave of Kamares: This is about a 4-hour climb. Discovered by local men in the 1890s, it was first explored by the Italians, and finally excavated by the British in 1913. Used in neolithic times as shelter, it became a sacred cave for the Minoans; here were found some of the most eloquent witnesses to the Minoans' artistry—the thin, polychrome delicately decorated pottery that is known as 'Kamares ware'.

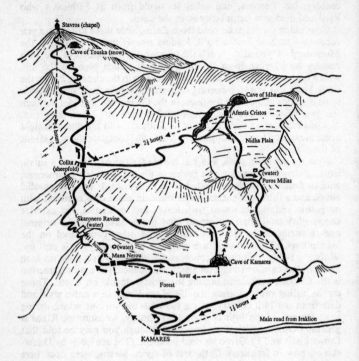

Mt Idha's Summit: This is another 5 hours from the Cave of Kamares. At 8,058 feet, it is the highest point on Crete—and there is usually snow here. A small cave lies about half an hour from the summit; those who care to spend the night here, however, should stay in the chapel of Stavros, right at the peak.

Cave of Mt Ihda: This is about 4 or 5 hours from the summit, to the north-east, on the edge of the Nidha Plain. It was discovered and explored in the 1880s and yielded many rich finds, including bronze shields dating from the 9th and 8th centuries BC and showing Assyrian influence. These finds have been taken to indicate that there was a post-Minoan cult of the Curetes, who were worshipped at this cave. (The Curetes were the warriors who danced round the cave where the baby Zeus was being nursed, covering his cries from his father Cronus by the clashing of their shields. Robert Graves claims that it was the son of Zeus, Zagreus, who was being protected at this cave.) From this cave, there is a descent of about 4 hours to the village of Voriza. It is also convenient to continue north above the Nidha Plain to the mountain village of Anoyia. During the last war, the village was completely razed, except for the church, as a reprisal against the partisans who kidnapped the German commandant, but it is now rebuilt. The people live largely on their flocks, and are noted for their handicrafts. There are several lovely chapels in the neighbourhood, one built over an ancient mosaic.

About one hour's walk to the north-west of Anoyia is the site of Axos. It lies on the summit of a spur-end from the Idha range, and its steep slopes make it practically inaccessible. First settled late in Minoan times, it became an important site in the archaic period. There are few remains except for cyclopean walls, but the view is impressive.

Heading east from Anoyia towards Iraklion, you might turn off to visit Tylissos, where three Minoan megarons were excavated by Hadzidakis after World War I. There has been a small amount of restoration, but if the remains are not too spectacular, the finds were: bits of frescoes, figurines, vases, and bronze cauldrons—testifying to the level of culture even in such isolated spots. There was also a tomb that had been used for a cremation-burial, and since this does not seem to have been the customary mode for the late Minoan period, it has been suggested that this was the tomb of some distinguished foreigner.

From Tylissos, you descend to the main road, the Rethymnon-Iraklion route, for the last 10 kms to Iraklion.

Mallia Palace

The Palace of Mallia was contemporary with the palaces of Knossos and Phaestos and together with these two sites is among the principal attractions of Crete. It is not nearly so extensive as Knossos, nor is its setting as spectacular as Phaestos, but it is certainly rewarding.

The road to Mallia provides an excursion through time. There are so many things to see on the way that this is one trip where it would be well worth while taking a taxi. Visitors intending to make a round trip from Iraklion by bus must allocate the better part of a day to it: by starting early and breaking the trip here and there it would be possible to see a few of the other sites along the way, but you would have to time it very closely to catch the buses.

Leaving Iraklion by the Gate of St George (off Liberty Square, by the Archaeological Museum), you descend sharply, round a corner, and pass a large plant (on the left); this is a distillery, and often burns compressed olive seeds as fuel—hence the foul odour pervading this stretch.

Ascending, you pass through the fairly new and bustling suburb of

Poros, which absorbs some of the overflow from Iraklion. On the shore to the left is a popular bathing beach. A little farther on, you go down to sea level again at Katsamba. This was the mouth of the Kairatos River, and was once a harbour town serving Knossos. (The river is still here, but dries up for much of the year.) Excavations continue to turn up remains of houses and tombs, some yielding rich artifacts and testifying to continuous habitation of the site from neolithic through later Minoan times.

Climbing again, you emerge on a flat plain; on the right is a Greek Army Officers' Training School. And a little farther on you pass the Municipal Airport, which is the terminal for air traffic to and from Athens and Rhodes. Swinging down a gully, you pass a small wayside chapel carved into the hillside, and then the Karteros Beach—now known as 'Florida Beach' a popular swimming spot in summer. Here the shore forms a wide arc, and on the knoll at the far (eastern) side are the remains of Amnisos, another of the ancient port settlements. Vestiges of several buildings have been discovered here, including the Minoan Villa of the Lilies and the Altar of Zeus Thanatas. It was from here that Idomeneus and his ships left for the Trojan War.

About 1 km farther on is a turning to the right, at signposts marked Episkopi and Cave of Eileithyia; turn here and go up the winding road for about $1\frac{1}{2}$ kms to where a small sign by the roadside indicates the cave. The fig tree marking the cave's entrance is a few yards below.

The fig tree—symbol of fertility—is most suitable for this 'womb of the earth', which provides a glimpse into really primitive Cretan culture. (It was first explored in the 1880s by Hadzidakis and Halbherr, although the local people had never really 'lost' it.) It is known that the cave was a shrine and habitation in the neolithic era, well before 3000 BC and the later Minoan civilization. Through Minoan times it was revered as a sacred spot, dedicated to manifestations of the Nature Goddess in general and to Eileithyia—the 'liberator', goddess of childbirth—in particular. It retained its prestige throughout Crete's history, and is mentioned in *The Odyssey* (Book XIX), when Odysseus, disguised as a beggar, lies to Penelope and claims that Odysseus put in at Amnisos, 'where the Cave of Eileithyia is'.

You can walk about 50 metres into the cave; burning rolled newspaper or brushwood is better than a flashlight. It can be slippery. There is a sacred stalagmite, or lingam, and always the possibility of finding a shard of pottery from some ancient votive offering.

Returning to the main road and continuing east you follow the shore around the flank of Kakon Oros, the mountains which descend sharply to the sea—a delightful drive. Offshore is the islet of Dia. On sea level again, you swing around a wide curve and at about 13 kms (from Iraklion) you pass a small house with a well and a tree, on the left. Opposite are the remains of the Minoan megaron of Nirou, excavated by Evans and Xanthoudides in 1919. The remains are not spectacular, but important finds were made there: great bronze double axes, oil lamps, vases, tripod altars—all to be seen now in the Iraklion Museum. They were found in such concentration that it is thought this was the dwelling of some high functionary of the Minoan state religion, who may have acted as a 'distributor' of these religious objects through the small port at this spot.

Continuing along the road, you pass first a tiny roadside chapel and then a taverna with a handsome tree: this is the 'village' of Kochini Khani. In the field to the right is a transmitter station for the American base farther down the road; and just past the taverna, on the left, is a large modern villa built by one of Iraklion's wealthy citizens. (Significantly, he made his money as men in Minoan times made theirs —through grain and bakeries.) Two kms farther on you pass the little village of Gournes, on the slopes to the right. And then, on the left, you come across one of the most unexpected sights in Crete—an American Air Force Station. It is virtually a pocket of the 20th century, and although it has acted as a great stimulus to the local economy, it is surely one of the strangest labyrinths ever erected on this island.

After about another 10 kms you find yourself looking down to the bay and plain of Mallia, spread out at the foot of the Lasithi mountains. Hundreds of windmills can be seen, which pump water for the farming carried on here. Then, to the left along the coast, at about 26.5 kms, are the remains of Khersonisos, the ancient trading port for Lyttos. The ruins are those of a Roman fountain, as well as two 6th-century Christian basilicas with mosaics. Some 4 kms farther is Stalis, another fine beach, with palm trees. (There are a few plain rooms in the vicinity where it is possible to stay, and tavernas that provide simple meals.)

Finally, you arrive at the village of Mallia—about 34 kms from Iraklion. Olives, carobs and bananas are cultivated in this area. Rooms can be rented in the village, and there are cafés and tavernas. The beach—which has the reputation of being the finest on Crete—is reached by turning out of the village to the left, then winding through fields and groves. There is an excellent little tourist hotel which provides full pension and room for about 100 Drachmas per day. With its clean white sand, and its little island and chapel, this beach makes a perfect retreat.

Having left the village, continue on the main road for another 3 kms where there is a turning to the left. (There is a signpost clearly indicating the Palace of Mallia.) Going down this road you pass, on the right, the ruins of a megaron, which although extensive are of no particular interest except to professional archaeologists. A little farther on is the small house used by the caretaker and the French Archaeological School, now responsible for the excavations. (Hadzi-dakis made the initial excavations during World War I, but the French took over the site thereafter.)

Although not as dramatic as Knossos or Phaestos, the remains of

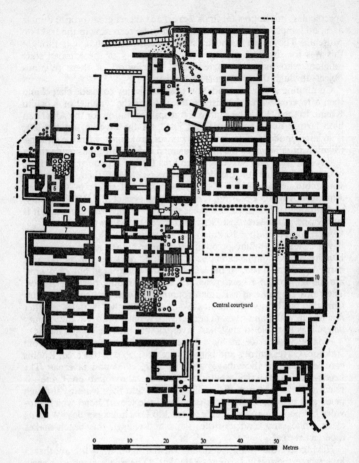

N

```
0    10    20    30    40    50
                                  Metres
```

Mallia

1 North courtyard
2 Table for offerings
3 North portico
4 Hypostyle hall
5 Corridor leading to North
  quarter

6 Bath
7 Corridor West façade
8 Loggia
9 Corridor West
10 East magazine
11 Tiled hall

the Palace of Mallia are well preserved and there has been a minimum of restoration. There is nothing more delightful than a stroll through the site on a good day, when Mallia seems to hover between mountains and sea. The history of this site is generally analogous to that of Knossos and Phaestos, as is the basic pattern of the palace: the large central court, the various corridors and chambers, the throne room, the storage magazines, the stairways. The East Magazine's walls have been rebuilt and roofed over to provide a museum for the pottery and other artifacts found on the site—signs of the domestic, commercial and ceremonial life of a Minoan palace. (Here, too, you can see the ingenious way they had of storing wines and oil.) In the middle of the central court is the sacrificial pit; the *pithoi*—giant urns—stand about the ruins. But the unique find still *in situ* is the *kernos*—the offering table, a circular stone about 2 feet in diameter, with a depression in the centre and 34 tiny concave circles carved around the rim. It is believed that each one of these was for one of the different seeds or crops produced by the land, and that the stone was an altar for offering thanks and prayers for continuing fertility. (A second such stone was found at the *Khrysolakkos* (see below); and a third, carved into an irregular stone block, stands in one of the rooms of the remains.)

Between the palace and the sea are tombs and houses that have been excavated, with remains of connecting roads. This must have been quite a prosperous palace—it is usually associated with King Sarpedon, brother of Minos and Rhadamanthys—and it was in the cemetery here that the *Khrysolakkos*—'pit of gold'—was found. Some 40 metres long and 30 metres wide, with many compartments, it evidently served as some sort of communal tomb. It was plundered long ago, and random surface finds gained it its name before it was finally excavated, giving up still more fine treasures.

From Mallia, several moves are possible: you can stay overnight in the village or at the beach; catch the bus back to Iraklion; or take a bus east, going on to Neapolis or Ayios Nikolaos.

Arvi

A visit to this unique coastal village is a full day's excursion from Iraklion; but as it is near Ierapetra, two trips might be combined.

The road past Knossos winds up through Kounavoi (15 kms) and Peza (18 kms). There is a turn-off here, to the left, to the village of Kastelli-Pedhiadha—some 17 kms east, if you detour. There are several churches in the neighbourhood of Kastelli-Pedhiadha noted for their frescoes, as well as the Church of Ayios Panteleimon of Vitzariano, from the Byzantine period but built from ancient materials including capitals that have have been stacked to make a supporting column.

Near by, situated on the slopes of the Omphalian Plain, are the remains of a once-powerful post-Minoan city, Lyttos. In the classical period it could afford to issue coins, and probably controlled the port of Khersonisos on the north coast. It once had a famous theatre, but nothing of any interest has survived.

Back on the main road to the south, you arrive at Arkalokhorio (33 kms): in a nearby grotto there were valuable finds of bronze weapons and double axes. On to Embaros (50 kms), to the right of which lies Arkades, an Hellenic site where extensive finds were in tombs from the 9th and 8th centuries BC. Then on to Ano Viannos—Upper Viannos (65 kms).

Ano Viannos is the district's focal point, boasting a school and a fine plane tree. The village is delightfully situated on the mountainside, surrounded by vineyards and olive groves. The frescoes and icons in its 14th-century Church of Pelaghia are well worth seeing; nearby are the ruins of watermills and the 15th-century Church of St George.

From here it is advisable to ask directions and drive with care. The road descends sharply out of Viannos, then crosses over the mountains before dropping to the coast. Following the shore east you pass the huge rock Keratokambos, rising nearly 2,000 feet above the sea. On its summit are ruins of the Keratonkastello ('Castle of Horn'); at its base, remains of a post-Minoan village. Proceeding along the Bay of Keraton for about 4 kms, you arrive at the tiny port-village of Arvi.

Arvi lies on a small coastal plain, backed by high hills, and an almost tropical climate prevails: bananas grow here, as well as oranges. Behind the fruit groves is the gorge that has given Arvi its name and fame: legend has it that Zeus Arbios struck the rocky cliff, creating the cleft through which the irrigating waters flow. When the wind howls through the gorge or water rushes from the 1,000-foot-high fissure, the noise is said to be like titanic thunder. When Pashley came here in the 19th century he found remains of what he decided was the Temple of Zeus Arbios ('Zeus the Thunderer'); it is claimed that the present village church is built on the platform of that ancient temple. On the hillside to the right of the cleft is the now-crumbling Monastery of St Anthony, where a few monks eke out a bare existence.

In the village itself, unexpectedly good accommodation is to be had in a one-time warehouse recently rebuilt by a returned Greek-American. It is a small inn from June to October, and there is fine swimming.

From Arvi, Ierapetra can be reached by road (largely in first gear), passing through Pevko; or you might get a fisherman to take you along the coast by boat.

Mount Iouktas

Most people will be content to enjoy this peak from a distance: from almost anywhere around Iraklion, in fact, the monstrous recumbent profile of Zeus is visible, and it is easy to believe that a god lies buried beneath those slopes. This god-who-died should not be confused with the immortal Zeus of Olympia: the name was taken over, but the concept of a dying god pre-dates the classical image.

The actual ascent of Mt Iouktas is made from the town of Arkhanai, some 15 kms from Iraklion, and easily reached. Arkhanai is quite a prosperous modern community, noted for its wines. There is a new, B class, hotel: the Dias. Nearby is the Church of Asomatos, with notable frescoes painted by Michael Patsidiotis early in the 14th century.

It is wisest to engage a man in Arkhanai to guide you to the peak, although it is only an hour's climb. On the mount you will be shown the cave where Zeus was buried: no matter what you may believe, it has been used as a shrine over the centuries. In the middle and late Minoan periods there was quite an elaborate sanctuary on the summit; some fragments remain, and votive offerings of vases and figurines have been recovered. (Evans was among the first to explore this site; the Greeks have continued the work.) The Orthodox, not to be outdone, have built a Chapel to the Lord of the Transfiguration here; and modern technology has constructed *its* shrine—a radio transmitter.

Back at Arkhanai, you might ask to be directed to another nearby site, Vathypetro, where a large Minoan megaron has been excavated since World War II by the Greeks. It is not that the ruins are so impressive but the situation—overlooking a valley rich with vines—is. One of the chief finds at the site was a Minoan wine-press.

Fodhele

People who come to Crete simply to see the home of the Minoans may be surprised at this excursion, for it is to the birthplace of Domenico Theotocopoli, known as El Greco.

That El Greco (1542-1614) came from Crete is not disputed, for he declared he was a native of Candia. But the actual place of his birth was not known until this century, when research established that references to a family named Theotocopoli living in Fodhele occurred in documents of the time; indeed, a family with a similar name still lives in the district. (The region near Gortyne has also laid claim to being his birthplace, but on very slender evidence.) In any case, Fodhele has been designated as El Greco's native village.

Little is known of El Greco until he arrived in Venice to study under Titian. It is said that he studied at the school of Mt Sinai in Iraklion, that he learned woodcarving at Vrondisi Monastery, that he painted at Valsamonero, but none of this is authenticated. He went to Italy in the 1560s and never returned to Crete. But El Greco carried the Byzantine style in his eye, and the island's landscape in his mind: he was never to free himself entirely from their grip on his technique and imagination.

There are two possible approaches to Fodhele. For both, you leave Iraklion by the Khania Gate, cross a little bridge, and then proceed straight ahead, west along the flat coastal road for about 7 kms. Then the major route, the one taken by the bus, bears left and climbs the steep winding road away from the shore. At about 20 kms the village of Marathos is reached; and about a kilometre beyond this is a sharp turn to the right, where the descent begins into the mild, lush valley where Fodhele lies, some 7 kms farther. (En route, to the left, you pass the Monastery of Ayios Panteleimon.)

Fodhele is noted today for its orange groves and mild climate. There is a modest monument to El Greco, placed there in 1934 by the University of Valladolid in Spain. For the gullible, there is a Venetian-style house that is shown as his family's home, and a chapel with his paintings. Those who insist on seeing his *real* birthplace will be taken through the village and across the fields to the ruins of an old house lying in a little gully—and imagination must do the rest.

The alternative route to Fodhele from Iraklion is harder going but can be managed by a careful driver. At the 8 km point outside Iraklion, you turn right instead of climbing into the mountains away from the coast. This is a steep road, and after a few kilometres you find yourself looking down a fairly sheer drop to the right. Below is an old mill, sited on the edge of a dark pond about 50 yards across. This is the Almyros of Malevizi—the 'salt pond', one of three such brackish pools on the north coast—and, as usual, the natives claim it is bottomless. What is left of the old mill dam may be Venetian masonry.

A few kilometres farther is the village of Roudhia, which can be seen from Iraklion as a glimmer of white in the day and a sparkle of light at night. It is worth stopping to look at the façade of a Venetian palazza near the church. The road goes through Akhlada, then deteriorates as it descends to Fodhele. On your left as you proceed is the Convent of Savathianon, where a few nuns live and work. At a distance of 20 kms (from Iraklion) there is a road to the right leading to Ayia Pelayia, an old Monastery along the coast. There are some remains of a Venetian fortress near by, as well as a Byzantine kiln that is believed to have been used to fire the rooftiles for this. The beach is especially fine, and a new Tourist Pavilion is under construction and will add considerably to the amenities for bathers. Proceeding by the 'main' road, you descend through the outskirts of Fodhele. The drive from Iraklion by this route will have taken about 1½ hours, and it makes an interesting one-way alternative to the bus route.

Iraklion to Ayios Nikolaos

To get to Ayios Nikolaos—gateway to eastern Crete—follow the coast road to Mallia (pp. 135-7). After Mallia, this road climbs away from the coast; some 4 kms later, it winds through a quite dramatic ravine. At the halfway point in this rocky pass, the road widens: here stands the monastery of Selinaris. There is a chapel dedicated to St George, and all travellers—including those in buses—stop here to say a few prayers for a safe journey. In this chapel is a rather incongruous, if typically Greek, scene: there is an impressive modern safe to hold the offerings, and alongside are the little tin simulacra (tassima) of the various parts of the human anatomy that people want cured or blessed—arms, heads, eyes, torsoes: moulded in metal, they crowd around the altar. Outside the chapel is a lovely flowering tree—in season. Fresh spring water is to be had; across the road is an inn with more elaborate refreshments. The monastery is the site of one of the largest annual festivals (April 23).

Continuing through the pass, the road climbs and winds, passing through several villages, including the mountain town of Vrakhasi. Then you descend to the town of Neapolis—54 km from Iraklion—a centre for the region. Neapolis has a leisurely, provincial air, yet just enough bustle, with buses and markets. It is the judicial capital of Lasithi Nome, so has the court traffic. The people of Neapolis pride themselves on their intellectual traditions—their schools, the library, and even a small collection of antiquities from the region, displayed in a 'museum' on the central plaza, a shaded public park. It was on the outskirts of Neapolis, too, in the village of Kares, that Peter Philargis was born in 1340—the man who became Pope Alexander V (p. 86). Neapolis has one main hotel, the Vassilikon (Class C); the Tourist Police can make other arrangements. There are several eating places: one of the local specialities is soumadha, a milky drink made from fresh almonds.

There is a fairly good road that climbs south from Neapolis to the Lasithi Plain, Psykhro, and the Dhiktian Cave.

Leaving Neapolis by the main road, about 2 kms from town you see a row of turret-like structures, banked against the hillside profile in the distance. Approaching these along the road, you discover they are old mills, placed so as to catch the winds. At the village by these mills, there is a road to the left: it is in terrible condition, but you can follow it for several kilometres to approach the site of Dreros. (You are advised to take a guide from the village, as it needs some searching—and a bit of hiking—to find the remains.) Dreros was an Archaic settlement, with an acropolis that dominated the passes and plains of the vicinity. The French, excavating in the thirties, found the remains of a small temple to Apollo

Delphinios, as well as bronze idols. The view and surroundings make the excursion worth while.

Returning to the dirt road—but not back to the village by the mills—and continuing north-east, you eventually arrive at Elounda and Spinalonga (p. 150). This is not recommended except for the most hardy vehicles and souls: the road is extremely rough and rocky, but you pass occasional villages—and wonder how anyone ekes out a living from such miserable ground—and the trip can be made. You will be rewarded by a spectacular view of the Gulf of Merabello just before you descend to Elounda.

Assuming that most travellers will be restricted to the main road, we rejoin that back at the turn-off to Dreros. This next stretch, of some 13 kms, is uneventful, except for the hairpin bends as you descend to Ayios Nikolaos. Outside and above the town, you have a fine view of the Gulf of Merabello, with the mountains of Sitia in the distance.

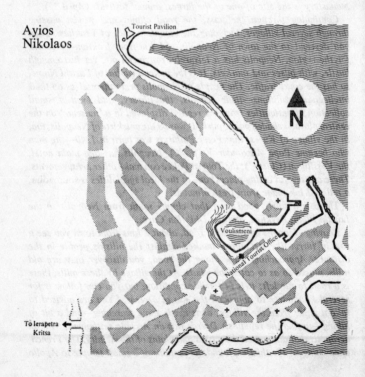

Ayios
Nikolaos

Tourist Pavilion

N

Voulismeni

National Tourist Office

To Ierapetra
Kritsa

Ayios Nikolaos

Hotels and Restaurants

See p. 52 for hotels. There is the usual choice of restaurants, tavernas, cafés; the Rififi, down by the harbour, is considered one of the best. Tourist bungalows with full pension are available at Minos Beach.

Museum

There is a small collection of antiquities from the area on the ground floor of the Town Hall.

Swimming

There are many fine beaches on the outskirts of Ayios Nikolaos. One in particular—an almost tropical lagoon west of the town—has lovely sand and excellent bathing. There is a new Tourist Pavilion, where you can get refreshments, and other eating-places with bathing facilities. (No overnight accommodation.) To get here, follow the road that leads around the harbour, to the left.

Ayios Nikolaos

Ayios Nikolaos is a quiet little port town, noted for its healthy climate and fine beaches. Although it is officially the capital of Lasithi Nome, the town and its people seem unimpressed by this. It would be a delightful place to settle in while making excursions to some of the sites in eastern Crete. It is an especially neat and clean town: shady trees, white-washed kerbs, everything well tended—down by the harbour you could almost believe you were in a Dutch or Scandinavian village. But it pays a price for all this: it has no ruins or buildings of any interest to the traveller!

The town of Ayios Nikolaos is comparatively new—largely built up since 1870—and somewhat artificial: a small creek was actually made into the harbour when it was decided to establish the city on the hillside. During the 19th century, many Sfakians, seeking employment and a new lease of life, settled here. The chief attraction of the town is the harbour, with its nonchalant activity: a naval patrol keeps guard, an occasional fishing boat puts in, and the cafés create what excitement there is. Across from the harbour is a promontory, making two small bays: this was the site of some ancient acropolis, as well as the Venetians' castle Merabello (there are only a few remains).

The most spectacular attraction is the dark, so-called bottomless pond, Lake Voulismeni, situated some 20 yards to the left, and back from, the harbour. It is not volcanic in origin; more likely, it is the aperture of some subterranean river that finds its escape hatch here after draining down from the mountains. It is known by some as 'the bath of Artemis'; there is also the legend that a secret passage connects it to Santorini, the volcanic island north of Crete. The pond's diameter is about 65 yards—and despite its reputation for being bottomless, certain sceptics have claimed that the water gets quite hard about 210 feet down. The Tourist Information Office is here by this lake.

Also to be seen is one of the three *almyros*—the brackish, salt-water springs found on Crete's north coast. This one is to the north of Ayios Nikolaos, a few hundred yards from the sea.

Gournia

Gournia deserves to be better known as one of the wonders of the archaeological world: here was uncovered, not another Minoan palace, but the almost complete remains of a Minoan town. It is a sort of 'poor man's Pompeii', and, although lacking the glamour of some of the great Mediterranean sites, should be visited by anyone who intends to go home feeling he has seen Minoan civilization.

The road to Gournia is the road to Sitia, leaving Ayios Nikolaos along the coast, with the Gulf of Merabello to the left. It is a pleasant winding road—occasionally rather dusty, but asphalt in stretches. In the far distance are the mountains of Sitia, with the sheer vertical rise of Thrifti in the middle distance. The road passes through a few straggling villages—including Kalokhorio—but it is the dramatic coastline that makes the trip: inlets, promontories, beaches. About 18 kms from Ayios Nikolaos is a road branch to the right: this leads to the Monastery of Faneromeni, which can provide overnight accommodation for five or six people. Another kilometre or so farther on you descend to the flatland beside a small bay, and almost before you know you are at Gournia with its ruins clustered against the hillside to the right. The buses to both Sitia and Ierapetra, incidentally, will put you off here.

The name 'Gournia' is a topographical name for 'basin': *gourni* is the trough from which barnyard animals drink, and the valley formed here as the land comes down to the sea resembles this trough. At this little bay on the narrowest section of Crete, sailors and traders of old probably beached their craft in order to take their cargo overland, thus avoiding the rough passage round the eastern end of the island. (Ierapetra, p. 154, was the other end of this commercial route.) A settlement grew up, prospered, and by 1600 BC must have been a flourishing town, self-supporting if not self-governing. Little is known of its exact relationship with the great Minoan powers to the west: certainly Gournia had some sort of ruler, whether an independent prince or a dependent governor. Undoubtedly its prosperity was linked with the wealth and influence of the great Minoan palace centres. But Gournia grew and functioned on its own terms, as a self-contained town with many of the features we see in Greek towns today. It made no impact on the times, and when Minoan power declined Gournia declined: probably it fell to marauders, was destroyed in a conflagration, and then abandoned. This happened around 1500-1450 BC. It was forgotten, and eventually disappeared from men's sight and minds. When the great age of Cretan excavation began, Gournia's whereabouts were not only unknown, its very existence was unsuspected. There were no traditions, no classical references, no remains.

Evans must be credited with arousing interest in discovering Gournia: It was his finds in the region which suggested there was probably some sort of settlement. An American archaeologist, Miss Harriet Boyd, directed by the find of a sealstone brought to her by a local Cretan, decided that the hypothetical settlement might be on the ridge where many potsherds had been discovered. Digging began in 1901, and by 1904 virtually the whole town was unearthed: the answer to an archaeologist's dream. Miss Boyd (who married the English scholar Hawes and so is often referred to as Boyd-Hawes) was assisted by her American colleagues, Miss Hall and Richard Seager—not to mention the local people who did the actual digging.

The site is a limestone ridge, and the town—its streets and structures—was built to conform to the lie of the land, so that Gournia sprawls rather gracelessly over the hillside. It was never fortified, and it lies quite exposed except for what protection the sea afforded. On top of the hill—we hesitate to call such an unclassical place the 'acropolis'—was the 'palace': a miniature Minoan palace, even less ambitious than Ayia Triadha. There were stairways, pillars, courts and the usual apartments; but nothing is particularly grand in comparison with the rest of the town nor is the palace particularly isolated from the community. There was an *agora*, or public market place, and a small sanctuary where cult objects were found, showing that the Mother Goddess was worshipped here: terracotta images twined with snakes, doves, tripods, the double axe. But none of these really add to our knowledge of Minoan life. It is as a revelation of domestic economy that Gournia is valuable, for within and around the houses and shops were found objects invaluable for the study of the life of the 'middle' and 'lower' classes: vats for washing oil; a forge with a mould for casting chisels, awls and nails; loom weights; a carpenter's kit, including saws, files, axes, chisels and nails; and many other artifacts now in Iraklion's Archaeological Museum.

Up and down the streets you may walk, stepping in and out of the houses. Stairways are still in place, low doorways must be guarded against, second storeys are clearly indicated. It is all very familiar to anyone who has strolled through a contemporary Greek mountain village: some of these houses at Gournia would need little except roofs to be habitable as modern peasants' homes. More than one visitor to Gournia has commented on how small the houses are: but think of other primitive settlements of this era and then look at Gournia as a whole. Here are block after block of dwellings where

men lived and worked, roads and steps they climbed, urns and implements they used, a square where they gathered to conduct their affairs,
altars where they worshipped. True, it is all rather crude, cramped
and basic. But it is basically familiar: Gournia is the prototype of
European civic life.

There is a caretaker who will guide you through: he knows only
Greek, but with a little imagination you will understand his expla-
nations. He knows the site, both in its general plan and in the details
of the excavation. But to get the best impression of Gournia you must
go down to the main road and proceed east some few hundred metres,
to where the road begins to climb up to the pass: halt halfway up
and look back: you will see Gournia spread before you, like a great
spider's web across the slopes.

Pakhia Ammos

Continuing along this road—the one climbing away from Gournia—
you arrive some 3 kms later at the little port of Pakhia Ammos. First
you go through the narrow pass, emerging to look down to the harbour.
To your right as you descend is a large stone villa: this was constructed
earlier in this century by Richard Seager, when he was excavating
in eastern Crete. A man of independent means, there are tales of grand
parties he threw in his villa with dozens of distinguished house-guests.
At the news of still greater 'finds' in Egypt he went there to dig, caught
some disease and died in 1925, still in his prime, shortly after his return
to Crete. (The Germans occupied the villa during the war: you can
still see signs of their occupation.)

Pakhia Ammos is a port of call for local coastal shipping. Tomatoes
and olives are cultivated on the rich plain behind the harbour. Minoan
cemeteries were found scattered over the plain but there is nothing of
interest to the non-specialist. In the town are several eating-places,
as well as Tourist Inns where you can get a bed for Drs. 15 a night.
On the route to both Sitia and Ierapetra, Pakhia Ammos allows you to
fit Gournia in to several possible excursions.

Kritsa

Only 11 kms from Ayios Nikolaos is Kritsa, the largest village of
Crete, and a place with several claims to fame. To get there, take the
road out of Ayios Nikolaos as though heading for Gournia or Sitia,
but at the edge of town take a sharp turn right and climb up into
the hills—eventually this road becomes the narrow winding main
street that leads into the main square of Kritsa, with its large shady

tree. The village has a fairly spectacular position, clinging to the steep mountainside, and with a superb view over the Gulf of Merabello: the houses that crowd the slopes all have balconies that look across the valley to the sea. The people of the region keep up the traditional arts and crafts and there is a small display of their work in the village square. (It was in Kritsa that the film version of Kazantzakis' novel, *The Greek Passion* (*Christ Recrucified*) was made: it was called *He Who Must Die*. The principal actors were French, but many local people appeared. Although the setting of the novel was Anatolia (Turkey), both history and the film make the Cretan setting quite legitimate.)

The main glory of Kritsa is the 13th-century Church of Panayia Kera (All Holy Lady). It is the white church on the right just before reaching the village: it stands in the middle of an olive grove, surrounded by white-washed walls. There are three naves, with corresponding apses: the central nave is the oldest: tambour and buttresses were added considerably later, The frescoes—dating from the 14th century—are accepted as one of the major triumphs of Byzantine art. They have been partly restored, but their strength and art derive from the originals. Scenes from the life of the Virgin are depicted on the vaults with some realism; saints and evangelists are portrayed along the walls, and with their rich gowns, muscular lineaments and intense eyes they make an overpowering impact. Frescoes such as these would make the fortune of a town on the main route: here in Kritsa they go almost unnoticed. There are notable frescoes, too, in the Church of St George Kavousiotis; and the 14th-century Church of St Constantine, with its tombs, is worth seeing.

Lato

About 3 kms north-west of Kritsa—(perhaps twenty minutes' walk) are the ruins of ancient Lato, or Lato Etera. The site is now known as Goulas. The path from Kritsa leads out through the cemetery—a villager will, if you wish, act as guide.

Lato was originally explored by Evans, but the French took charge of excavations there early in the 20th century. It was an Archaic-Hellenic settlement dating from the 7th century BC: in its day it must have been a fairly strong and prosperous city. The extensive remains rise in banks or tiers, with two acropolises, fortifications, houses, shops, doorsteps, cisterns and roads. The market place, the magistrate's residence and a temple have been identified. Most of the ruins date from the 3rd century BC. There is also a curious circle of stones, a rotunda of some kind—perhaps a ceremonial area.

The setting of Lato is one of its principal charms, with olive trees all around and a fine view across the Gulf of Merabello.

Elounda and Spinalonga

Elounda is a seldom-visited site, yet it has certain unique attractions that make it well worth an excursion from Ayios Nikolaos. There are three ways of getting there: one is by the extremely rugged back road via Dreros (see p. 143); another is by a road out of Ayios Nikolaos—not very good, but passable (and there is one bus daily); the third approach is to hire a boat in Ayios Nikolaos. This would be necessarily an impromptu arrangement, but the Tourist Police would assist: the fare would be round about Drs. 20 per person (round trip), with a maximum of Drs. 80 for a party of reasonable size. This is a pleasant way to arrive at Elounda, where there is a modest little hotel—the Nea Elounda (Class E)—where you can also get meals. This fishing village is an ideal place to pass a quiet evening—rather like being on some calm fjord.

Elounda is an insignificant port now but it has seen its share of history. The nearby site of Olous was a Minoan settlement originally, and since then the inlet has witnessed the coming of Greeks, Romans, Venetians, Turks, French, English and Germans. (Before the war, English hydroplanes used to land in the bay.) Under the Venetians it was an important trading port, and even now merchant ships lie off-shore.

The site of Olous is on a small peninsula, connected to Elounda by an isthmus. You walk out of the village—or rather, to the right of the harbour—and cross a canal by a bridge-walk: these were constructed by the French during the occupation by the Allied Powers in 1898. There is an old abandoned mill, and there are the salt flats: sea water is let in, the dykes are blocked, and the water evaporates leaving the salt. These are no longer worked to any extent. Once on the peninsula, follow the shore to the right. In the field to the left is a mosaic floor, the remains, probably, of some ancient Christian basilica: it has now sunk well below the level of the land, but is fenced off and protected. It depicts some lively fishes and is worth crossing the field to see.

Along the edge of the shore are the remains of Olous—now sunk beneath the water, owing to the island's shifting in the 6th century AD. What you see is not very impressive, but skin-divers might find it worth exploring further. Ship-berths are clearly visible: Olous was the port for Dreros. There were once structures on land, including temples to Zeus and Britomartis, but the stone was carried off and used in walls and other buildings.

Back on the dock at Elounda, you can look across the bay to the islet of Spinalonga. The Venetians constructed a most impressive fortress here; it was one of the last outposts of the Venetians on Crete, for it was 1714 before they finally surrendered it to the Turks. (There was also a church within the fort.) The Turks held it until early in the 20th century when, under the administration of Prince

George, the island was converted into a leper colony. This was dispersed after World War II and now the island is abandoned except for caretakers and the occasional tourists' party. (There is no risk of getting leprosy.) Your boat from Ayios Nikolaos could stop here or you can arrange with someone at Elounda to take you out, at least to circle the island.

Sitia

Sitia is a travel-poster version of a quiet little Mediterranean port, with cafés along the *quai*, fine bathing, and the air of an isolated terminal. It is also a port of call for the ship between Crete and Rhodes, and it is the starting point for several interesting excursions into the easternmost reaches of the island.

Sitia can be reached by bus from Iraklion or Ayios Nikolaos. The road follows the route to Gournia and Pakhia Ammos, but instead of cutting south across the isthmus to Ierapetra, you stay on the coast, passing through the valley of Kavousi, with the peak of Mt Thrifti rising above. The stretch from here to Sitia—some 51 kms from Pakhia Ammos—has been called 'the Riviera of Crete', with its slopes and tiers of orchards and villages clinging to the hills. Along the way you pass several sites of interest mainly to the experts: Kavousi, dating from post-Minoan times; Kamezi, with an oval house from the middle Minoan period; and Mouliana, with beehive tombs and finds of swords and bronze objects. To the left are the islands of Psira and Mokhlos. Mouliana—32 kms from Pakhia Ammos—is also famous for its red wine. Proceeding through the village of Skopi, you see the Bay of Sitia before you: in the distance stretches the north-east extremity of Crete—Cape Sidheros, with the islands known as the Dionysiadhes offshore.

Gently sloping to the sea, crowned by a few remains of the Venetian fort, Sitia has little of the glory that the Venetians projected for it: Sitia was to be the fourth of the great coastal cities but never quite made it. The Venetians themselves recognized its failings and dismantled much of the fort, carrying the cannons off to other cities. There was a small castle and a rector's palace, but when the Turks took over these fell into decay along with the fort. Two churches remain—one in the form of a Greek cross, and the other in Venetian style, with three naves. Perhaps Sitia's greatest claim to fame is as the birthplace of Vincenzo Cornaros, author of the master works of the 17th-century Cretan literary renaissance. (It is sometimes claimed that he was born in Petra, near Sitia.)

Today the chief source of income for the region is the *sultanina*—the raisin. The people are mild and genial—a far cry from their brawling relatives in Sfakia. (Incidentally, this part of Crete was occupied by the Italians during World War II.) There are several eating-places in Sitia and two hotels—the Krystall (Class C) and Mysson (Class D).

Sitia has provided the name of this region and Nome: 'Lasithi' is a corruption of La Sitia, the Venetians' name for their settlement. Before the coming of the Venetians, this eastern region had the reputation of being the home of the 'Eteocretans'—the 'true' or indigenous Cretans: it is claimed that with the arrival of the Dorians after the break-up of Minoan-Mycenaean civilization, the native Cretans retired to these eastern hills where they preserved their language and culture in some 'pure' form. As we shall see when we discuss some of these eastern sites, some traditional modes survived; but in general no modern scholars really believe that the 'pure Minoans'—whatever they would be—linger on in Lasithi.

Eastern Crete

With the exception of Itanos—which was excavated by the French both at the end of the 19th century and after World War II—the sites of this part of Crete were originally excavated by the English, in the early years of this century; some have since been developed by Greek archaeologists.

Monastery of Toplou

Some 20 kms east of Sitia is the isolated Monastery of Toplou, noted for its hospitality to strangers and wayfarers. It is also reputed to be one of the richest monasteries in Greece, as it owns much land in the region. Founded in 1300, the original building was burnt; it was rebuilt in 1718 and named Toplou—'the cannon'. It has the appearance of a fortified castle, and has indeed been an important centre for resistance and refugees from the occupation of the Turks to World War II. The Panayia Akrotiriani—'Virgin of the Cape'—is worshipped here. Above the façade of the chapel is an ancient plaque commemorating a treaty between Egypt and the Cretan realm of Itanos-Ierapytna, (circa 70 BC) and within are some valuable icons: one in particular, dating from the 18th century, depicts the creation of the world and scenes from the Bible—a masterpiece of miniature work, crowded with figures and scenes. What makes a visit to Toplou really worth while, beside the distinctive architecture of the Monastery (showing Venetian influence) is the primitive isolation of its situation. It may be reached by boat from Sitia or by car, with a short walk.

Itanos

Itanos is near the end of Cape Sidheros. The only way there is by footpath, overland from Toplou. It takes about two hours of hiking, and would be rather difficult to find without a guide. It is deserted—it is known by the natives as Erimoupolis: 'deserted city'—and has only a few ruins. It was originally a Minoan site and is one of Homer's '100 cities of Crete'. It was inhabited into Roman and Byzantine times. What are now to be seen are the wall of an Hellenic acropolis, the base of a Roman statue and parts of an early Christian-Byzantine church. As so often on Crete it is the setting—bleak, solitary headland—that makes the site impressive.

Nearby is a palm grove, known as Vai, one of the few on Crete, with a fine sandy beach.

Palaikastro

Some 20 kms due east of Sitia, along the eastern coast at the base of Cape Sidheros, is the village of Palaikastro, with the ruins of ancient Heleia near by. There is a good road from Sitia—about an hour's drive—and then a 20-minute walk to the ruins.

Palaikastro must have been an important commercial settlement— somewhere in the late Minoan period; it was larger than Gournia, but because it was more spread out the natives have carried off the stone over the centuries and the remains are not so impressive. The town lay close to the shore, at the foot of the hills; with its acropolis rising above it, the curving bay and lofty headlands, it must have been an imposing place. Excavations have revealed a well-paved main street, lined by houses and shops; in one were found weights, jars, a sink and a drain. There was a many-roomed palace of large stones, the seat of some local prince: Palaikastro was one of the few places on Crete to be rebuilt after the great disaster of 1400 BC.

Minoan cemeteries were found, dotted over the plain, and a Minoan sanctuary discovered in a rock shelter in the nearby hill of Petsofa. Among the most important finds are remains of an Archaic-Hellenic temple, with a fragment of a frieze, and the *stele* (memorial column) inscribed with a hymn to Dhiktian Zeus. (The carving on the *stele* only dates from the 3rd century AD, but the hymn itself is centuries older and reveals the religious sentiments of an earlier age.) Among other valuable finds were bronze tripods, shields, terracotta figurines, ivory plaques, and much pottery and vases.

Zakros

Almost 25 kms by road down the coast from Palaikastro is the Minoan site of Zakros. It was a port of call for ships bound for Libya and Egypt, and must have been fairly active. Some small houses have been excavated, with finds of potsherds and seal impressions.

From Zakros you could follow the road back to Sitia, or walk overland, due west, to Praisos.

Praisos

Praisos may be approached by taking the bus from Sitia to Maronia, and then heading farther south towards Khandras. (En route to Maronia, about 7 kms out of Sitia, to the right, is the site of Akhlada, a small Minoan settlement.) Praisos is at the summit of a conical hill and was perhaps the chief post-Minoan settlement: as such it was the centre of the so-called Eteocretans. Only jumbled stones remain, but tombs and an Hellenic acropolis indicate a fairly continuous settlement. Here at Praisos, as at Dreros, texts with Greek characters of the 6th to 3rd centuries BC—but using pre-Hellenic words—give evidence of some isolated, if not indigenous, people. A late Hellenistic house of some size and elegance hints at the enduring prosperity of the site.

Ierapetra

Ierapetra is the largest town on the southern coast of Crete, but it has long since lost whatever importance it knew as a port for trade with Africa and Asia Minor. Today it is noted largely for its sandy beaches, rich vegetation, wine and hospitality.

It is possible to approach Ierapetra from Iraklion by cutting down to the south-east via Viannos: (see p. 139, the trip to Arvi). Most people will probably come via Ayios Nikolaos. This is the bus route: leaving Ayios Nikolaos, you pass Gournia and Pakhia Ammos and then turn inland to the right, crossing the isthmus at the narrowest part of Crete. On this road, only some 2 kms south of Gournia, is a knoll where the early Minoan settlement of Vasiliki was excavated by Seager early this century. (The bus puts you off on the road: the site is a kilometre's walk to the right.) Graves were found here, but there are no remains of any interest now. What was found, however, was the extraordinary pottery that has come to be known as Vasiliki 'flameware': a mottled, red-and-black pottery, it is found elsewhere on Crete and even around the Mediterranean, but nowhere with such a brilliant quality as at Vasiliki.

Ierapetra is about 13 kms from Pakhia Ammos. It has a public garden, fine swimming, and a small collection of antiquities in the Municipal Building. There is a local wine that tastes something like sparkling Burgundy. The prosperity of the town now rests on the olive oil and tomatoes of the area. There are several good eating-places, particularly around the central square, and three hotels: Creta (Class C), Lyvikon (Class D) and Aigli (Class E).

The modern city is on an alluvial plain, with the city protruding into the sea, dominated by the remains of the Venetian fort: some of the towers are well preserved. It is situated on the site of ancient Ierapytna, a Minoan harbour town that grew to importance as a junction for trade between Crete and the African and Asian ports to the south and east. It must have been linked with Gournia as part of an overland route. The post-Minoan peoples kept up the port, and it is said to have been the last Cretan city to fall to the Romans under the Roman consul Metellus. It once had fine Roman buildings, including theatres, but little remains from that period. Then came the Venetians and the Turks: the former left the fort, a church and a fountain, the latter a minaret. You may also be shown a house where it is claimed Napoleon passed a night—en route either to or from Egypt: there is no evidence to support the claim, but it adds to the charm of the town.

From Ierapetra it is possible to go directly back to the main road along the northern coast and then continue either to Sitia or Ayios Nikolaos. It is also possible to take the route mentioned previously: an extremely poor road to Ano Viannos, over Pefko—with a side-trip to Arvi. For the adventurous, there is the route to the north-east, via Koutsouras and Khandras, and on to Sitia: this could take in visits to sites such as Praisos and Akhlada (p. 154).

Psira and Mokhlos Islands

With the help of Ayios Nikolaos' Tourist Office excursions could be made to both these islands, in the eastern reaches of the Gulf of Merabello. The ideal thing would be a cruise around the entire gulf, and this could take in Elounda, Gournia, Pakhia Ammos and even Sitia. It is, however, always possible to arrange a trip to the islands from one of the coastal villages.

The islets, which were excavated by Richard Seager during 1907-8, are barren now and without water, yet at one time they were harbours for trade through and around the gulf. Finds from various periods on Psira indicate close relations with Egypt, Syria and Palestine. Houses contemporary with those on Gournia have been found, yielding stone and pottery vases as well as fragments of painted relief.

Mokhlos is only about 200 yards from the shore and was once probably a peninsula. An early Minoan necropolis was excavated here and vases of alabaster, marble, breccia and steatite, some worked as thin as porcelain, were brought to light from a settlement that flourished in the Minoan Neopalatial period.

Iraklion to Rethymnon

Lying as it does, practically midway between Iraklion and Khania, Rethymnon is accessible by sea or road. Most will come by road from Iraklion—a distance of some 78 kms. (There are three buses daily, in both directions.) You leave Iraklion by the Khania Gate, following the same route for Fodhele—not the turn-off at 8 kms out of Iraklion, but the asphalt road that climbs the winding mountain route away from the coast. Once in the hills you pass the turn-off, left, to the site of Tylissos and the village of Anoyia; continuing, at 20 kms, you go through the village of Marathos; just beyond this is the turn-off, to the right, that is the alternative route to Fodhele. Going on through Dhamasta, you come to the village of Geni Ghave, noted for roasting suckling pigs—if you pass through at noon, you might even get a taste of one.

The Idha Range dominates the landscape of this part of the trip, with its waters accounting for the fertility of the region: the most prominent river is the Mylopotamos, winding about the valley on its way to the sea. Now, with the peaks of the White Mountains (Levka Ori) ahead as you proceed due west, you arrive at Perama (53 kms). In the nearby hills is the Cave of Melidhoni (p. 162); and on the coast to the north is the ancient Hellenic-Byzantine port of Panormos. Continuing to the village of Platanias (73 kms), there is a turn-off to the right, where it would be possible to detour some 18 kms to visit the Monastery of Arkadhi (p. 159). Continuing on the main road, though, you descend onto the flat and fertile coastal plain; left rises the Vrisinas Range, source of Rethymnon's water. Sprawled along the coast, with its minarets adding a distinctly exotic air, lies Rethymnon.

Rethymnon

Hotels

These are all centrally located; none are luxurious, but they suffice. (See list, p. 52.)

Restaurants

Rethymnon has the usual variety of eating places and cafés, clustered around the squares and along the harbour. The better-known ones are: Trekhantiri, Ionia, Panellinion, Possidonian, Khania, and Taverna.

Buses

Buses for the various villages and sites within Rethymnon Nome, as well as those to and from Iraklion and Khania, use the main square along the principal thoroughfare—the Platea of the Four Martyrs. As elsewhere on the island, schedules between the smaller villages are often inconvenient; for those without their own vehicles, taxi excursions should be considered.

Stores and Facilities

Rethymnon can provide for all normal needs, although it is certainly not to be compared to Iraklion. There are pharmacies, clinics, a Bank of Greece, post office and telephone exchange, and two cinemas. In the summer season, there are two well-known centres for dancing—the Romantzo and the Trekhantiri. There are several good sandy beaches, both west and east of the town. There is an active branch of the Hellenic Touring Club, making excursions to the natural sites and antiquities of the Nome: foreigners are welcome. (Contact Prof. Dafermos, or Mr Costas Mayouras, Secretary of the local Tourist Committee.)

Museum

Inside the Venetian Loggia is the small civic collection of finds from the Nome—including Minoan, Hellenic, and Roman artifacts. There is no official curator, but you could count on seeing the exhibitions during the same hours observed by Iraklion's Archaeological Museum.

Rethymnon is the third largest city of Crete, and enjoys the reputation of being the 'intellectual capital' of the island. Without getting involved in the city's credentials for this latter honour, it can be said at least to be a point of pride to the citizens. Travellers in Rethymnon—both the city and Nome—have claimed to see a little more pride in appearances, a little more order and cleanliness—none of which is necessarily an inducement to travel here. In any case, Rethymnon has its own modest charms; it is a delightful place to pass a few days while taking excursions into the countryside. The Nome lacks the extensive and spectacular sites of other parts of Crete, but there has been a fair amount of excavation—tombs, houses, minor settlements: the Germans, for instance, during the war, turned up quite an elaborate compound at Monasteraki, the westernmost Minoan ruins of any size. You need, however, a specialist's interest—and a guide—to find your way around to these sites.

The city of Rethymnon is on the site of ancient Rethymna, but nothing of interest to the amateur remains. Indeed little is known of its history. In the medieval period it is mentioned only in passing, with its fort and towers sketched as seen from afar. The town received its distinctive imprint from the Venetian period—with a slightly Turkish veneer to give it a special air: Venetian arches back up against wooden, overhanging Turkish balconies, creating a unique impression for the visitor strolling through the narrow streets. All in all, though, what interests the tourist is the evidence of the 16th and 17th centuries under the Venetians.

The principal architectural survival of this epoch is the elegant 17th-century Loggia, where the civic museum is housed. (Rethymnon had a fine clock tower from this period, but it fell into disrepair and was demolished by the local citizenry after World War II.) There is also the Arimondi Fountain, dating from 1623; Alvise Arimondi was the Venetian Rector and built several fountains around Rethymnon; this one has four original Corinthian columns, and a restored back wall from the Turkish period. There is also the Church of the Virgin of the Angels and the Church of San Francisco from Venetian times, along with many other arches and architectural fragments.

The most impressive structure left by the Venetians is the great fortress surmounting the rocky promontory on the coast: the city proper is actually built on the isthmus connected to this citadel. The first fort on this site was ruined by marauding Turks in 1571; it was rebuilt and greatly enlarged, with the Cathedral of St Nicholas (1585), the Rector's palace, and other public buildings within its walls. When the Turks finally occupied the entire place, the cathedral and other buildings went to ruin, intentionally or otherwise; the German bombardments of World War II finished the job. Its massive walls, though, are largely intact, and its main gate—as entered from the town—is most impressive. Within, all is neglected: the outer ramparts survive, walls and arches stand here and there, a great church with domes carries on, but it is a scene of desolation and rubble. It is the property of the animals—goats, rabbits, chickens, cats—and smells accordingly.

The other worth-while sights of Rethymnon are the minarets: most were simply attached to 'converted' Venetian churches. South of the city, though, is a mosque with minaret, dating from the early 18th century, that is fairly well preserved.

Monastery of Arkadhi

The Monastery of Arkadhi is the supreme symbol for Cretans of their ageless strife and dilemma: freedom or death. Like many other monasteries on the island—because of their isolated situations in the mountains—it has always served as a centre for resistance movements and revolts against foreign powers. Even under the German occupation, Arkadhi was used as a meeting place for partisans.

It was during the revolution of 1866 that Arkadhi achieved immortality. As usual, it had supported the uprising against the Turks—a battle was fought there in June of that year. Then, in the autumn, a sizeable group of Cretan fighters, as well as women and children, established themselves in the monastery, which was soon besieged by the Turks. Thousands of troops were called in, and when their overwhelming numbers made the fall and surrender of the monastery imminent, the Abbot directed that the powder stores be ignited. In the ensuing explosion, almost 1,000 Cretans lost their lives, and 1,800 Turks were said to have perished. This was on November 8, 1866, and the episode created a furore in the European press. The anniversary of the event is an annual festival attracting crowds and dignitaries from all over Crete and the mainland. (It is also marked in Rethymnon by athletic competitions, games, fireworks and dances.)

But even if you can't be there on that particular occasion, the Monastery is something to see. If you depend on the buses, you are forced to go out late in the afternoon and return to Rethymnon early in the morning—except on Sundays, when the schedule allows you to pass the day there. There is no problem about accommodation, however: the Monastery has a guest house that can sleep large parties, and there is a new Tourist Pavilion that can also handle some people on special occasions. Simple meals can be had.

The road to Arkadhi is picked up at the village of Platanias, about 5 kms east of Rethymnon, turning south from the main road. You pass through the villages of Adhele (home of Giamboudakis, who is credited with actually having set fire to the powder magazine), Kyriana, and Amnatos.

The church of the Monastery, although still bearing scars of the assault of 1866, has been greatly restored. Its façade, however, is of intrinsic architectural interest, being the most ornate of the Venetian period structures on Crete. It dates from 1587, and is a mixture of styles: there are Corinthian columns, classical arches, renaissance garlands, and baroque scrolls. Its light, almost fantastic impression is somewhat incongruous in the wilds of Crete.

The stairs and portals of the church date from the 17th century. The main (eastern) entrance and gallery to the monastery itself, although rebuilt after 1866, are worth inspecting. You may be shown the actual locale of the explosion—'untouched'; also, some survivors were said to have been beheaded in the refectory, and the bloodstains may be displayed. There is also a small 'museum', with mementoes of Arkadhi's history, in the great hall. In the courtyard is a cypress, said to have been planted when the monastery was founded, and a laurel tree planted by Venizelos in 1905 when he was leading the struggle for Crete's freedom.

About 6 kms north-east of Arkadhi is the post-Minoan site of Elevtherna. By the 8th century BC it seems to have been a prominent settlement, and remains of a classic-period bridge testify to its endurance. It is chiefly known, though, for the Archaic statue—late 7th century—one of the major specimens of 'Daedalic' art.

Monastery of Preveli

Although hardly as dramatic either in history or appearance as Arkadhi, Preveli has seen its share of history and makes for a rewarding excursion. Some travellers have found its position one of the most impressive of all the many sites on Crete.

The bus service goes only to the village of Levkoyia; from there it is a half-hour's walk (2½ kms) to the Monastery. The road passes through the villages of Armenoi, Balli, and Koxares (with connections to Ayia Galini); also through the Gorge of Kourtaliotiko, emerging with a fine view of the southern coast and the Libyan Sea.

The Monastery is not far from the sea and commands a handsome view across rugged slopes. It has been plundered on several occasions, but most of it is intact. Inside, there is a fragment of the True Cross, and a small 'museum' of religious articles, priests' costumes, and weapons. The icons and frescoes are not especially noteworthy.

Rooms and meals are available for guests.

Ayia Galini

Since there are several ways of approaching Ayia Galini, it is best to describe what awaits you at the destination. It is nothing spectacular, but for those with a little time and curiosity, Ayia Galini is a picturesque corner of Crete. (Its name means 'holy serenity'.)

It is, essentially, a small fishing port clinging to the southern coast—a cross between a pirates' cove and the Italian Riviera. Its main attraction are the grottoes that can only be approached from the sea. In addition to hiring a boat to see these, you might be able to get it to take you somewhere farther down the coast. There are two small inns at Ayia Galini—the Pantheon and the Libya—with beds for about Drachmas 15; meals are available. Don't expect anything too elegant.

Now for the ways of getting there—each of which can be combined with some other site or excursion. There is the bus direct from **Rethymnon**—the one that could be picked up at Koxares, after a visit to Preveli. This is a lovely drive through the centre of Crete. Among other places, you pass through the village of Spili, renowned for its cascades of water and shade trees. There is also the bus service to the village of Fourfouras (see below): Ayia Galini is 20 kms overland from Fourfouras, via some rugged terrain, and this will not attract many people. Likewise, Ayia Galini might be taken as the starting point—or end—of an ambitious hike along the southern coast to Sfakia and points west: leaving Ayia Galini on the Rethymnon road, you come to the village of Melambes where you pick up the trail west, along the southern slopes of Mt Sidherota; eventually you come to Preveli; pushing on via such villages as Mirthio, Phinikia, Rodakino, Aryoulis, Patsianos, and Vraskas, you finally arrive at the village of Sfakia—a trip of some 60 kms, and recommended only to professionals.

Of more general interest is a trip combining Ayia Galini with Phaestos and its environs. Should you spend the night at Ayia Galini, an early bus would take you on via Timbaki and leave you on the road below Ayia Triadha or Phaestos; this would give you the day to visit these sites, and you could go on to Iraklion in the afternoon. The trip could also be worked in reverse: Iraklion—Phaestos—Ayia Galini—Rethymnon.

Province of Amari

Throughout the hills and valleys of this province there are some delightful scenic pleasures; just as remarkable, though, are the many churches and chapels, some with first-rate Byzantine icons and frescoes. Wherever you chose to spend the night you could be sure of finding some sort of accommodation. If you are dependent on the bus, your destination is the village of Fourfouras: this is a possible starting point for an ascent of Mt Idha, for the village lies directly at its foot. From here, too, you could walk overland to Ayia Galini.

The road from Rethymnon to Fourfouras passes through the villages of Prasses (11 kms) and Apostoloi (30 kms). Some 5 kilometres later you reach the Monastery of Asomatos—now an agricultural school: the Venetian influence in its architecture is evident, and it would be worth getting off here and continuing the last few kilometres by foot. En route to Fourfouras you pass Visari, where there are remains of an old Byzantine church.

Melidhoni Cave

Another site that is both a natural attraction and an event in Crete's history. As it lies just off the road between Iraklion and Rethymnon, some people will find it convenient to visit while travelling between these two points; others can get the bus from Rethymnon.

The cave is quite large, with stalactites and many chambers. During the classical period it was dedicated to Hermes Talaios—this last name in honour of the mythical monster, Talos, a giant of bronze: the cave was his dwelling place when he was not striding around Crete —thrice daily!—and hurling boulders at any strangers who might approach the island.

But it is its historical associations that make the cave a shrine today. In 1824, several hundred Cretans from neighbouring villages had taken refuge here from a troop of Turkish soldiers ravaging the land. When the Turks discovered that the Cretans were in the cave, they piled brush at the mouth of the cave and set fire to it. The Cretans within were suffocated. For decades afterwards, visitors to the cave report seeing the bones and skulls in the crevices and corners where the people had scrambled for air.

This is not everyone's idea of a pleasant outing, but the cave is interesting and some people will wish to fit it in to round out their picture of Crete.

Rethymnon to Khania

This trip can be made by ship, but most travellers will probably go by the main road. Heading west along the coastal plain, you pass through Ghonia (10 kms) and Episkopi (22 kms)—the last village of any size in Rethymnon Nome. Several kilometres into Khania Nome, you pass the few remains of the ancient Hellenic site Idhramia, near the village of Dhramia. From here there is a turn-off south-west to the only fresh-water lake on Crete—Lake Kournas (the ancient Korion or Korisia). It is surprising to run across such a lake—although you must actually leave the main road to find it—and travellers have always commented on its special atmosphere, tamer, and so refreshing, compared to the more rugged attractions of the rest of Crete. It is roughly 900 metres wide—and you may be told it is bottomless. Other legends have grown up about it: if you shoot across it, the bullet will never reach the opposite shore; and it was once the site of a village, and the ghost of a young girl who was raped on the spot by her father haunts the lake. The real mystery is just what such a body of water is doing here; but in any case, it can be appreciated.

Moving on a few kilometres, you arrive at Georgiopolis, named after the Prince George who once acted as High Commissioner of Crete. (Nearby is the ancient Hellenic site of Amfimalla.) Continuing, the road crosses the Almyros river; to the north-west extends the small Cape Dhrapanon, an especially fertile region; the road passes through a well-wooded countryside—noted for cypress trees—and then arrives at Vrises, before beginning the long descent to Soudha Bay.

Soudha Bay is the largest and best-protected natural harbour of Crete —and a candidate for the most remarkable land-locked harbour of the entire Mediterranean. About 15 kms long, and 3 to 6 kms wide, its deep waters—10 metres—can take even today's great ships. In fact, it is a NATO naval base, and you are likely to see ships and sailors of several nations as you drive past the docks. More important than sheer size in ancient times was the fact that the entrance could be easily defended: the Akrotiri promontory is on the northern side, and there are three small islands—once known as the Levkai Islands—at the narrows. The one that actually commands the bay is Soudha Island: Soudha means 'ditch' —a translation of the Saracens' name for the place—Khandax, most likely referring to the ditch around the fortifications. The Venetians built extensive fortifications: these still exist—along with the church—and give a good idea of the importance of this outpost: it was one of the last three forts held by the Venetians, only surrendering to the Turks in 1715. Eventually British troops were quartered there at the turn of the century, when the Great Powers were running Crete. (Looking down over Soudha

Bay is a large cemetery of the Allied Forces—mostly British Commonwealth troops—who lost their lives on Crete during World War II.)

Driving along the edge of the Bay, you come to the village of Megala Khorafia: a 20-minute walk from here brings you to the site of the Hellenic city of Aptera (excavated early in the 20th century.) Aptera means 'featherless': it derived its name from a contest between the Muses and the Sirens at the Museion (a spot near the site): after the Muses triumphed with their music-making, the defeated Sirens plucked off their feathers and cast themselves into the sea, becoming the islands in the Bay. In its day, Aptera was one of the chief commercial cities of Crete, and it was well known right into the early Christian era. There are fairly extensive remains: cyclopean walls of the early settlement, a theatre, the temple of Demeter, a Dorian temple, the Roman cisterns, many other Roman and Byzantine structures, bas-reliefs and inscriptions. The view across the Bay is rewarding.

Continuing along the shore of the Bay, you pass the old Turkish fort of Izzedine at Kalami—now the site of a prison. Then, descending to the water's edge, you arrive at the modern harbour installations of Soudha: here is where the NATO facilities have left their mark—great walls, housing developments, and all the paraphernalia of contemporary commerce. Soudha is the port of call for Khania and has grown rapidly since the war. The main square is dominated by a statue of Prince George of Greece, who arrived in 1898 to govern Crete.

From Soudha, it is about 6 kms across a fertile plain to the city of Khania. Olive trees, vines, plane trees and, above all, orange trees, make the landscape unusually green and lush. This is the chief orange growing region of Crete, and Khania is the centre for export. (The orange, by the way, is called 'portokali', as it was introduced here from Portugal.) The approach to the centre of Khania is by a shady street lined with trees and flowers—all quite suburban.

Khania

Hotels

See list p. 52.

Restaurants

There are numerous restaurants and cafés in Khania; some of the best are near the harbour. Among the restaurants are: Hellenikon, Aptera, Averoff, Hellas, Nylon, Rex, and Panellinion. The Tavernas include: Ta Kavouria, Brokali, Bouzounieri, Anitsaki, and Honolulu.

Entertainment

There are several cinemas—some are open-air in the summer. Several eating places around town and road houses on the outskirts feature music and dancing—in the modern vein: the Kipos (in the Municipal Gardens), the Prassini Paparouna ('Green Poppy'), Gerakina, Honolulu, Neraida, Asteria, Kalamaki, and Nikhterida.

Buses and Cars

Khania is the terminal for all buses within the Nome: they leave from various points—the Municipal Market Square, the New Shops, the Conservatory, 1897 Square. Inquire at the Tourist Information office or from the Tourist Police about any particular trip. There are daily connections to almost any place a tourist would want to go—with the usual inconvenience in the scheduling. The tourist agencies can arrange private excursions; there are taxis; and it is possible to rent cars.

Consulates

Only France and Sweden now maintain consulates in Khania.

Post Office and Telephone and Telegraph Office

The central post office is at 11 Tzanakaki Street: it is open on weekdays from 8 a.m. to 12 p.m. and from 3 p.m. to 5 p.m., on Sundays and holidays it keeps morning hours only. The telephone and telegraph office is located above the post office and is open 24 hours a day.

Stores and Facilities

The shops of Khania offer a complete line of goods and services and can handle all normal needs of the tourist: there is not the selection of Iraklion, however. There are clinics. There are several banks, including the Bank of Greece, to handle any special transactions.

Khania offers a fine selection of native handicrafts in many shops: textiles, jewellery, costumes, needlework, embroidery, wood carving, and musical instruments are among the items. Travellers are reminded that handwork may occasionally be bought in the villages.

Swimming and Sports

There are several fine beaches outside Khania: two favourites are Galatas and Platanias.

For information about sporting events in Khania, contact the office of the National Stadium on King Constantine Street.

There is good hunting—hares and partridges—and fishing in the region: inquire at the Tourist Police about seasons and regulations and for information of the local associations devoted to these sports.

Mountain Climbing and Excursions

Khania is the centre of much activity in these lines: there are three groups that go on excursions to visit antiquities or to make ascents of nearby mountains—the Greek Mountain Climbing Association, the Alpine and Nature Worshippers' Union, and the Touring Club of Khania. Foreigners are welcome on any of their trips.

Other Possibilities

Roman Catholic services are held at 46 Halidou Street (by the harbour, near the Orthodox Cathedral).

There is a library, a music conservatory, and a broadcasting station. The local branch of the Greek-American Cultural Institute—a private organization—teaches English and welcomes visitors. The French Institute teaches French. (There is also an order of French nuns.)

There are many professional associations in Khania—everybody from doctors and pharmacists to raisin growers and fishermen. There are several intellectual and artistic organizations. Anyone desiring to contact any of these groups could get help at the Tourist Organization Office, Nomarchy Building.

Museums

Archaeological Museum

Although it can hardly rival the great Minoan collection of Iraklion, Khania's museum has an interesting little collection of art and artifacts from the Nome, including pottery, sculpture, coins, mosaics, inscriptions, utensils, and arms. The museum is located in the Church of St Francis. It keeps the same hours as Iraklion's Archaeological Museum.

Historical Museum

One of the major archives of all Greece, this collection covers the later Byzantine, Venetian, Turkish, and contemporary periods of Crete's history. There are many rare documents and books, as well as icons, armaments and other historical objects. The museum is at 20 Sfakianakis Street, not far from the harbour, and is open daily from 8 a.m. to 1.30 p.m. except Sundays.

City of Khania

Khania is not only the capital of its Nome but also the administrative capital of the island, and has all the bustle befitting its position. At the same time, it has a rather more relaxed air than Iraklion—due, perhaps, to the abundance of greenery and flowers in and about the city. And on an island noted for its hospitality, the people of Khania take a special pride in the gracious face and manner they offer strangers.

History of City

Khania is the descendant of ancient Kydonia—home of the Kydons, one of the early peoples of the island. They took their name from King Kydon, son of Hermes, and inhabited the plain in and about the modern city. From prehistoric times down to the Roman conquest, Kydonia seems to have been an independent city-state; and if it never achieved the fame or greatness of certain of the other sites, Kydonia played a prominent role in the various inter-island wars and alliances during the post-Minoan era. It was besieged in vain by the Athenians in 429 BC, and led the fight against the Romans. After the Romans took over, and on into the Byzantine period, Kydonia continued to be of some importance, but by the 7th century AD it had declined along with the rest of the island. From the time of the first brief Arab occupation in the 9th century up to the coming of the Venetians, Kydonia was a small town, noted for little else than its cheese. But when the Venetians chose to rebuild the city, naming it La Canea in 1252, a new era of prosperity began. The Genoese seized it from 1267 to 1290, but the Venetians took it back and turned it into a centre for the whole western end of Crete. By the 16th century, the Venetians had constructed the Kastelli—covering the old city on the hill above the harbour—the outer fortifications and harbour installations, and many churches and other public and private structures. La Canea briefly enjoyed the reputation of being 'the Venice of the East'. But after a two-month siege, it fell to the Turks in 1645. They converted the churches into mosques, repaired the fortifications, and settled in: in the 19th century they located the capital of the whole island in the former Venetian Kastelli. (The Pasha's seraglio was also here. And travellers in the 19th century report a whole community of Africans and Arabs encamped at the edge of Khania, which must have added to its exotic atmosphere.) In 1898, the Turkish troops had to withdraw, and international forces moved in under the aegis of the Great Powers. Prince George came as the High Commissioner, and Khania was kept as the island's capital—an honour it retained when Crete united with Greece in 1913.

Sightseeing in Khania

There are no particular remains of ancient Kydonia, although tombs have been found in the area, and many relics turned up over the years attest to the history of the site. Most of these finds are now on exhibition in Khania's Archaeological Museum.

Although the once magnificent Venetian structures have largely disappeared, the main historical interest of a tour through Khania is to see how much does remain from this period. Enough survives to hint at what must have been its days of glory.

Khania may be divided into two parts—the new city and the old. The new Khania has grown up along the plain behind the harbour, gradually absorbing the suburbs such as Khalepa (see p. 171). This new city has most of the facilities for the tourist—although the cafés and restaurants by the old harbour are the most popular. The new city has the bus terminals, for example—and the Central Market: near the 1897 Square, this is a large structure in the shape of a cross, modelled after the great market at Marseilles. Here is brought the produce of the region, and it can be quite a heady experience to stroll through the crowded lanes. More restful are the Public Gardens, in the heart of the city: a bandstand, cinema, and restaurant add to the attractions of these gardens—at least for the native Khaniots. The old city clustered around the Kastelli, down by the harbour, and spread back through the narrow streets where the Venetians erected town houses and churches. We describe the principal points of interest.

Kastelli (Inner Wall)

This name is applied to the actual fortifications above the harbour as well as to the quarter of the city. The Venetians started constructing in the 13th century, erecting the walls on the older Byzantine foundations and using, probably, materials from the ancient ruins of Kydonia's acropolis. Little remains of the fortress proper except fragments of the bastions. Within the Kastelli there was once a loggia, a palace, a cathedral, and a monastery: little remains. There was also the Venetian Archive: a fine portal survives (at 37 Lithinon Street), with an inscription dated 1623. The columns and pilasters are side by side, with the orders superimposed. Also within the Kastelli Quarter are the Arcade of St Mark and the marble portals of the Zangarola Mansion.

Outer Venetian Wall

The Venetians erected this during the 15th and 16th centuries to embrace the entire city. The total circumference is some 3,000 metres; alongside the wall was a moat, 50 metres wide and 10 metres deep in places. Much of the wall, especially on the eastern and western sides, is intact; there are also the remains of the Sabionara Bastion, decorated with the Lion of St Mark.

Venetian Breakwater and Habour Facilities

The Venetians had great plans for La Canea, but no matter how much

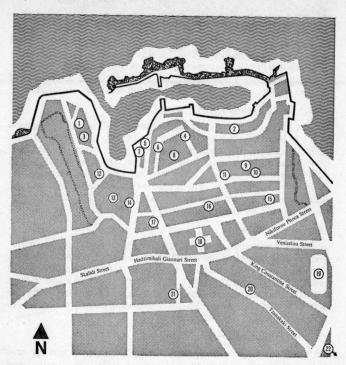

Khania

1 Church of The Saviour
2 Dockyards
3 Tophanas Quarter
4 Arcade of St Mark
5 Cretan Historical Archives
6 Venetian Archive
7 Turkish mosque of Janissaries
8 Kastelli Quarter
9 Splanzia Quarter
10 Church and Venetian arcade of
   St Nicholas
11 Venetian church of St Rocco

12 Renieri Gate, Venetian chapel
   and Powder Magazine
13 Old Jewish Quarter
14 Khania Museum Venetian
   church of St Francis
15 Church of Ayia Anargyri
16 Mosque
17 Cathedral church of the Virgin
18 Public Market
19 Stadium
20 Post Office
21 Tourist Police
22 Historical Museum

they dredged, the harbour was never really successful. They built a
breakwater by carrying rocks out on rafts and dumping them. (In the
middle of this they erected a small Church of St Nicholas and a fort
—used by both the Venetians and Turks as a place to execute convicts.

No remains.) Along the harbour the Venetians also constructed great *arsenali*—great domed dockyards for shipbuilding and storage. There were two main projects—one in the 15th and one in the 17th century—but of the original two dozen *arsenali*, only seven remain. The tops of the arches were once covered with lead, but the Turks removed this.

Church of St Francis (Idhaon Andron)

One of the finest of the Venetian structures on Crete, and the largest of the 23 Venetian churches in Khania. It has three vaulted naves, with gothic windows; its façade is disfigured, but is otherwise well preserved. The Turks converted it into a mosque, naming it after the Youssouf Pasha who conquered Canea: they left a legacy—a lovely Turkish fountain in the enclosure. (The church is on Khalidon Street, near the waterfront, by Sandrivani Square. 'Sandrivani' is Turkish for 'fountain.') The Archaeological Museum of Khania is located here.

Church of St Nicholas

Built by the Venetians, it served as a Dominican monastery; the Turks converted it into the Imperial Mosque of Sultan Ibrahim, which it remained until 1912, when it became an Orthodox church. As a result of its various conversions, the tower now looks like a cross between a minaret and a campanile. (It is the tallest minaret in Khania.) It is on Splanzia Square—a delightful place to sit and enjoy a cool drink under the shade of a giant plane tree.

Church of Ayia Anargyri

An Orthodox church dating from the 16th century: it was the only Orthodox church allowed to hold services under the Venetian and Turkish occupations of Khania. Its icons are of considerable age and artistry.

Mosque of Djamissi (Janissaries Mosque)

It was built in 1645, following the conquest of the city: the original dome survives, supported by later exterior arches. The graves of some Turkish priests are at one side. Located by the harbour.

These are the major monuments of Khania. There are, however, several other buildings and remains to be viewed by anyone desiring to cover the ground thoroughly. These are principally Venetian structures, and may be found in two quarters of the city:

Tophanas Quarter

Gate of Renieri: Off Zambeliou Street, on Theophanous Street. The portals bear an inscription from 1608 and the escutcheon of the Renieri family. Beyond, to the left, is a small Venetian chapel; past this are some old powder magazines and a house that probably served as headquarters for the arsenal. (Behind this is a Turkish house.)

Church of the Saviour (San Salvatore): At the end of Theotokopoulos Street. As with many other churches, it was once used as a mosque by the Turks.

Venetian Mansions: At 43-45 Zambeliou Street and 16-18 Angelou Street. Note the architectural details and other Venetian remains.

Venetian Portals: Within the enclosure of the Firka Tower, near the port, there are stairs and a balcony. Note the 17th-century inscription and the Venetian lion.

Splanzia Quarter

Church of St Rocco: On Splanzia Square, it bears a Latin inscription from 1630.

There are also narrow Venetian lanes between St Nicholas and Minos Streets, Venetian Portals near 14 Hadzimihali Giannari Street, and a Venetian mansion at 30 Rianou Street.

Turkish Monuments

In addition to the Turkish structures mentioned, there is a fine minaret on Hadzimihali Giannari Street, and the Mausoleum of Hamit Bey on Koubes Square.

Khalepa Quarter

There is still one other part of Khania that should be seen—the Khalepa Quarter, a pleasant, hilly suburb on the sea at the base of the Akrotiri. It is approached by driving along the Khalepa Boulevard—there are frequent buses—and might be combined with an excursion to the Akrotiri. When Prince George moved to Crete, he settled in Khalepa, and his mansion and the former Palace of the Governors are to be seen. Khalepa had always been something of a prosperous residential section, and it has many fine villas—some of which have served as national consulates. There is also the Convent of the Sisters of St Joseph, French nuns who have been influential in keeping French culture alive in Khania. There is the Church of St Mary Magdalene, built by Prince George's sister, the Grand Duchess Maria: it is in the Russian manner, a sort of Gothic-Byzantine style. The famous Cretan-Greek statesman, Eleftherios Venizelos built a house here, too: it is kept by his family, and across the street is a small park with his statue.

There are several restaurants in the neighbourhood.

Speaking of Venizelos, those interested in following his traces can visit what is called 'the house where he was born' in the village of Mournies, about 5 kms south of Khania. (In any case, Mournies is a delightful spot, with its trees and springs: there is a hotel, the Koukounara (Class B).) And some 17 kms south-west from Khania is the village of Theriso, Venizelos' mother's home village. Having formed a party in 1901 that was pledged to seek union with Greece, he convened a Revolutionary Assembly at Theriso in 1905 and ended up by resorting to armed rebellion. The trip goes through an impressive ravine; Theriso has two fine churches and a nearby cave where ancient vessels were found.

The Akrotiri

Akrotiri means 'The Promontory', and a glance at the map reveals how it acquired this name. It is a region rich in history, from earliest times to contemporary Crete, and is visited every year by thousands of people, from native Cretans to international travellers. There are two main destinations for most visitors—the Hill of the Prophet Elias (only a few kilometres outside Khania) and the Monastery of Ayia Triadha (some 16 kms into the hills). Buses take you to both places—as well as to one or two other sites on Akrotiri: only feet will take you to some parts.

Hill of Prophet Elias

The ride to the Hill of Elias is east out of Khania, through Khalepa; at about 6 kms, you arrive at the top of a ridge, with a superb view across the water and down on Khania. This hill is a symbolic peak of Crete's long struggle for freedom, and a statue to Eileithyia, Goddess of Liberty, commemorates this. For it was here, in 1897, that Cretan insurgents raised the flag of Greece, despite the injunctions of all the Great Powers and the Turks: when the flagpole was broken by the subsequent bombardment from the fleet offshore, a Cretan stood up and held the flag in his own hands. Many legends have accrued to this incident: one is that the sailors of the fleet stopped firing and cheered the valiant Cretans; another claims that an explosion occurred in one of the Russian ships taking part in the shelling—and this was attributed to divine anger, because the shells were destroying the Church of the Prophet Elias. If any further associations with Cretan aspirations are needed, there is the grave of Venizelos close to the statue of Eileithyia.

There are restaurants—the Nikhterida, the Neraida, and the Asteria —which enjoy a fine view: favourite gathering places in the evening.

Ayia Triadha

This is one of the principal monasteries of Crete, although like all of them, it has declined since the 19th century. It is situated in the centre of the promontory, in a sheltered position at the foot of limestone hills. It was founded in the 17th century by Jeremiah Zangarol, a Venetian converted to Hellenism. There is a strong Venetian influence in its architecture: a monumental entrance in the classic style dates from 1632, and a campanile from 1650. It has an especially rich treasury.

Gouverneto

About one hour overland to the north of Ayia Triadha, a hike across the hills brings you to the Monastery of St John of Gouverneto, a local hermit-saint who lived and died in a nearby cave. The monastery shows Venetian influence. Above it rises Mt Skloka, with an excellent view. In the cave is a strange formation in the shape of a bear. The saint's day is observed every October 7, when hundreds of pilgrims and visitors come out to Gouverneto.

Katholiko

Behind the cave of Gouverneto, a path leads down to a narrow gorge: there, wedged in between rocky precipices, is the deserted Monastery of Katholiko. It is one of the older monasteries on Crete, but in the late 16th century it was pillaged by pirates from Africa, and the monks began to abandon it, most moving to Gouverneto. Near by is the cave of Katholiko—150 metres wide and up to 20 metres high, with many stalactites: it is quite spectacular.

Minoa

On the southern coast of the Akrotiri, along Soudha Bay, are some remains from the ancient Hellenic harbour town of Minoa: a wall and tower may be seen—perhaps a lighthouse. (Across the Bay is Aptera.) Near by is the modern village of Sternes, with ruins of the old church of Ayii Pantes: around Sternes are remains of other buildings and catacombs from the early Christian era, as well as several caves.

Other Points

The Akrotiri is especially rich in caves, many of which have yielded important finds to archaeologists and anthropologists during the 20th century. To name only a few: in the Koumarospilios, the German Jantzen discovered human skulls at least 5,000 years old; above the small port of Stavros is the Cave of Lera; and east of Rizoskloko is the Cave of St Spyridos, with a church dedicated to this saint.

In the south-eastern corner of the Akrotiri, along Soudha Bay, is Korakies, with a fine view over the Bay. It is only 8 kms from Khania and can be reached by bus. There is a convent here, noted for its embroideries.

Sfakia

On an island where nature and history have conspired to create a tangle of legends and mysteries, perhaps no part of Crete has quite such an aura of myth as the Province of Sfakia. Among those who know, the very word 'Sfakia' conjures up visions of almost superhuman mountainmen—staunch fighters for their independence, marauding brigands, clambering over stark gorges, tending their flocks, hunting the wild goat, striking down their enemies. Inevitably, too, Sfakia prompts visitors and writers to superlatives: the land is the most rugged, the people are the most fearless (or lawless!), the flora and fauna are even unique. In brief, it is a region that will attract some and repel many. Some background is desirable, in any case, for the uninitiated.

It is hard to say whether the land made the men—or the men chose the land. Now they are inseparable in their rugged isolation. Although the population has declined drastically, this cannot really be blamed on the terrain. One theory has it that the Sfakians are pure descendants of the Dorians who moved into Crete after the breakup of the Minoan-Mycenaean empire; other theories claim them as Achaeans, as the Eteocretans—as Saracens, even! Whatever their origin, the Sfakians did not make much of an impress on history: they were left to their own resources, and over the centuries came to be feared by native Cretans as well as by invading foreigners. The Venetians had the intention of subduing the Sfakians and built the impressive Frango-kastello on the coast, but little came of this. When the Turks divided up the island among the Pashas at the end of the 17th century, the Sfakians still held their own. They not only continued their autonomous affairs, but actively harassed the Turks—again, to the great discomfort of their less belligerent fellow-Cretans, who lay exposed to the vengeance of the Turks after the Sfakians withdrew to their mountain stronghold. By the end of the 19th century there was hardly a patch of Sfakian soil that was not coloured by the blood of some incident. During the German occupation, this region once more became the centre of resistance. It is fair to say that Sfakians have remained a law unto themselves throughout their history.

Then, too, they have this not entirely undeserved reputation of being lawless—pirates, smugglers, brigands, revolutionaries, brawlers, what you will. That day is largely past, except for a bit of sheep stealing or petty smuggling. And to give them their due, they have always fought and killed as much among themselves as against outsiders: vendettas have taken the lives of many Sfakians. As with those other island outposts, Sicily and Corsica, family blood runs thick, passions run high, and quarters are close. But none of this involves the visitor to Sfakia. What the visitor notes, rather, is a land inhabited by mere hundreds, where once thousands lived and worked and fought. Ports sit idle. Flocks and trade have dwindled. Decimated by rebellions and vendettas, by-passed by history, many Sfakians have emigrated in search of a livelihood. The remaining people still hold to the old ways —in fact, Sfakia is noted for the pure tradition of its handicrafts. There are the ruins and sites of its past that may yet draw tourists. There will always be the spectacle of the land. But Sfakia's energy is slipping. Perhaps it is because there is no longer any serious challenge to their existence, no tension in their lives: Sfakia thrived on resistance. A bastion of independence, Sfakia is now independent—and ignored.

You will still hear Sfakia and its people described as 'savage' or something to that effect, but this is not true. Certainly the foreigner need not fear for his safety or property. They are a rugged, proud people, and if you go there with respect for their integrity, they will respect yours.

Exactly how much time is needed for a trip through these parts? Well, you can be in the village of Khora Sfakia in a few hours by bus. But to see the land properly, to go from one site to another, taking things as they come, would require several days at least. We have tried to indicate the possibilities.

If you set out from Khania, head east on the main road to Rethymnon; at 33 kms you come to the village of Vrises, a well-known spot for excursions. There are an inn and eating-places, as well as a monument to the Post-Constitutional Committee of 1897. Here at Vrises you take the road to the right, south and inland: it is often blocked in winter by snow. After 18 kms you arrive at the village of Askifou, on a plain of the same name. The plain is at 730 metres and is surrounded by hills and villages; the whole region is popular both as a summer and winter resort. In this area, too, is the ravine of Katrai (named after a son of Minos), extremely narrow and steep, but only about 2 kms long. This ravine was the scene of two bloody massacres : in 1812 thousands of Turks were trapped and slain here; and decades later, the troops that had occupied Arkadhi were destroyed.

Some 10 kms past Askifou is the village of Asfendou, in the midst of another plain on a hilly site. There are several interesting old churches, including that of St George. Nearby is the ravine of Kapni, and the cave of Falangari, with stalacites and water. Also close by is Kalikratis, noted for its spring with curative waters and a subterranean brook. Asfendou is not on the main road and a detour is necessary.

The main road winds down towards the Libyan Sea, with a dramatic view of the barren landscape and distant coast. Finally (74 kms) you arrive at the village of Khora Sfakia, with its imposing sheer cliffs. In its day, Khora Sfakia was the largest town on the southern coast—with 3,000 inhabitants, a prosperous commercial life, and, it is claimed, 100 chapels and churches! (This was in the 16th century: they were built by individual benefactors and neighbouring villages: almost all are in ruins.) It is a sleepy little village with only a few hundred inhabitants: it seems to have tumbled into the sea down the rocky slopes. It is possible to get overnight accommodation and meals.

Khora Sfakia was always a rallying point for revolutionaries, and the whole area has many buildings and sites associated with various uprisings. In the village, among the many churches, note especially the Church of the Holy Apostle; several others also have frescoes of the Byzantine period. The nearby village of Komitadhes has another old church, dedicated to St George: it dates from the early 14th century and has extremely fine frescoes. Also near by is the Thymniani Panayia Church, where the self-governing Sfakians held their assemblies during the years before 1821.

There are several caves in the region, but the most famous one is called the Cave of Daskaloyiannis—'John the Clerk' or 'Educated One'. Daskaloyiannis is one of the best known of the many revolutionary leaders of Crete—thanks largely to the ballad, *The Song of Daskaloyiannis*, set down some 16 years after his death and recounting his bloody fate: he had taken the lead in the uprising of 1770, and when he finally delivered himself over to the Turks to discuss surrender terms, they disagreed, and he was seized, tortured in the fort at Iraklion, and then skinned alive. It was in this cave that the revolutionaries of 1770 established their own mint.

From Khora Sfakia it is possible to make several excursions, by boat or by foot. An ambitious one would be an overland hike east to the Monastery of Preveli or to Ayia Galini: (see p. 160). From these points you could get buses back to Rethymnon or Iraklion, and in general you would be on the edge of central Crete. Local boats make frequent trips between Khora Sfakia and Ayia Roumeli; the fare depends on the number of passengers. This would allow you to make the trip north through the Gorge of Samaria (see p. 177).

Frangokastello

A more reasonable side-trip would be to Frangokastello, about 10 kms east of Khora Sfakia. Patsianos is the village to aim for—the castle itself is in an isolated situation on the coast. The Venetians thought they could subdue the Sfakians, so in the 14th century they erected this impressive fort—using, in part, stone from some ancient site. It is a sizeable, square fortress, with four corner towers—and still fairly well preserved, with the Lion of St Mark on guard. But the Venetians never really succeeded in taming the Sfakians, despite the many bloody battles fought in this area. It is said that the Cretans used to dance on the flat land by the castle—doing the Pyrrikhios, the soldiers' dance of war, as taught by Rhea to the Curetes who had protected the young Zeus. Nowadays, in place of battles and dances, the Cretans claim to see the ghosts of the hundreds of Sfakians who died defending the fort against the Turks in 1828: only in early May, at dawn, do these *drossoulites*—'dew shades'—appear: evidently a mirage of some sort, due to peculiar weather conditions.

Khora Sfakia to Ayia Roumeli

Still another possibility for the ambitious is to go west to Ayia Roumeli —or even farther. You might get a boat to take you all or part of the way, putting in at various sites; and some hardy souls might walk overland. We describe that route here.

Cutting north-west, well above the coast, a good two-hour walk brings you to the village of Anopolis. Because of its position and the nearby harbour of Loutro-Phoenix, Anopolis flourished under the Romans and into the Byzantine period: with its suburbs and dependencies, it is claimed to have numbered 70 thousand inhabitants at its peak. It was an autonomous city, with its own mint. There are some ruins to be seen, including cyclopean walls. There are also remains of a house said to have been the residence of Daskaloyiannis.

Below Anopolis, on the coast, is Loutro—the ancient port, Phoenix, recommended by Strabo. There are a few scattered remains from the Roman period, as well as early Byzantine ruins. During early Christian times it was the See of a Bishop. The Church of the Transfiguration of Christ has frescoes from the later Byzantine times. Loutro stands on a steep, bare hillside on a peculiar promontory: it is shaped like a spade, with shelter on both sides. There are subterranean vaults—Venetian structures—indicating that it was once a thriving port. There is also a building, in a fair state of preservation, where the first government of the revolution of 1821 met: it is called the Kangelaria Kivernion—'the chancellery'.

Another 2-hour walk overland, north-west from the coast and across the ravine of Aradin, is the village of Ayios Ioannis. Its Church of the Arkhistratighos Michael dates from the Byzantine period—although it is probably built with material from ancient ruins: the frescoes are worth examining. There is the deserted monastery of Ayios Ioannis, which gave the village its name. There are several caves in the vicinity: the most involved one is Dhrakolaki (*drako* means 'dragon'), quite large, with water and sandy ground: no one is advised to explore unless properly equipped. Near by is the site of ancient Aradin: its name is Phoenician, and it is mentioned in an ancient military alliance with the King of Pergamon in Asia Minor. The ruins include a structure called 'the dance of the Hellenes' and prehistoric dwellings carved in the rocks.

From Ayios Ioannis, the trail descends to the sea coast, passes the church of St Paul, and arrives at Ayia Roumeli.

Gorge of Samaria

Probably the most spectacular locale and adventure Crete offers is a trip through the Gorge of Samaria. People who have made the excursion—and there have not been very many apart from natives of the area—resort to all sorts of extravagances in their descriptions, and even allowing for travellers' tales, it is a moving experience. To do it properly you must allow from 3 to 5 days, starting from Khania, not because it takes that time just to walk through the gorge—if you press, you can get through in a day—but because the total excursion (the approach, the gorge, adjoining sites, and the return) consumes several days. And if you were to combine several of the sites along the southern coast with a stay at Ayia Roumeli, then still more time could be profitably spent.

There are two ways to pass through the Gorge: one is to descend from the north, emerging at Ayia Roumeli on the southern coast; the other way is to start at Ayia Roumeli. To get to Ayia Roumeli presents certain problems, as there is no road for vehicular traffic there. (Indeed, the whole Gorge is not to be approached during several winter months when snow and torrents isolate it.) One way is to take a small boat from any of several ports along the southern coast; another possibility is to get a bus to Khora Sfakia, Souyia, or Palaiokhora, and then walk overland. Here we describe the approach to the Gorge from the north.

The road cuts south from Khania, and at 12 kms passes through the orange groves of the village of Alikianos. Here is the Byzantine Church of St George, with 15th-century frescoes; near by is the cave of Hellenotrypa as well as ruins of an ancient site now called 'Kastellos'. Here, too, is the tower of the Venetian overlord, DaMolin, where the *pallikares* ('mountain chieftains') were killed by a trick: they were all invited to a wedding, and then surrounded and slaughtered. Proceeding south from Alikianos, the main road goes on to Lakkoi—the end of the line for the bus, and the starting point for the Gorge. But if you bear left after Alikianos, you come (8 kms) to Meskla, known as Crete's 'Garden of Green', thanks to its well-watered fields, orange groves, and fine trees; watered by the Platanos River, it is a fairly prosperous village. The Venetians used Meskla as an administrative centre; it was also the headquarters of the native chieftain, Kantanoleon, a leader in the struggle against the Venetians. The Byzantine Church of the Transfiguration of the Saviour has 14th-century frescoes of unusual beauty and value. There is another Orthodox church built over the mosaics of an ancient temple of Venus; and the Church of Our Lady has a column of heavy stones said to be from some ancient sanctuary. Near by is the site of the ancient settlement of Rizinia: little is known about it, but judging from the cyclopean walls and chambers carved out of the rocks, Rizinia was settled very early. It is on the Platanos River, at the foot of a mountain; the ancient acropolis was on the site called *Poulai*—ruins of walls and towers remain—and on the spot called *Zagre* (probably after Zagreus Dionysus) are more large stones.

Meskla and Rizinia, then, are side-trips for those with time to spare. Most will proceed directly to Lakkoi. (There is a trail overland between Meskla and Lakkoi—only 2 or 3 kms.) Lakkoi is another of the idyllic mountain villages of Crete, surrounded by green slopes and fields. Unless you have your own transport, you now face a 10-km hike to the Omalos Plateau. At 1,050 metres elevation, and some 25 kms square, it

is one of the most impressive of the Cretan upland plains: it almost seems to be a great drained lake—and indeed gets quite marshy in the centre. It is not nearly as thickly populated as the Lasithi Plain, but is very fertile and produces potatoes and tomatoes. At the edge of the plain is the house and grave of Hadjimichali Daliani—one of the leaders of the rebellion of 1866. (He later wrote his memoirs.) There is a well and a refreshment spot near by. In the middle of the plain is the cave of Dhigenis (or Honos). Some 3 or 4 kms across the plain is the actual entrance to the Gorge—the Xyloskalon ('ladder of wood'): zig-zagging down the path, you descend into the Gorge.

The Gorge of Samaria is said to be the largest true gorge in Europe. It is 18 kms long, and varies in width from 2 to 40 metres; the steep walls rise from 300 to 600 metres, at some points so sheer that there is barely any sunlight, and at the *sideroportes* ('iron gates') you walk between a narrow pass of steep rock. Thousands of years of torrents have eaten away the rocks, creating such a gorge. Even now there is a sizeable stream during the rainy season and after the thaw: in 1955, Ayia Roumeli was inundated, due to unusually heavy rains in the White Mountains. Throughout the trip you will see flowers, herbs and shrubs clinging to the crevices: dittany and cypress are especially notable. And if you are really lucky, you may see the famous Cretan wild goat —the *agrimi*, now confined to this gorge. It is so elusive that it is unlikely that the casual visitor will spot it; but those who have confirm the tales of its prodigious leaps and agility.

All who have been through the gorge describe the experience in awesome terms—like some descent into the underworld or back into some past millenium. But there is no real risk involved, either from nature or man. The fact is, you are not likely to see anyone during the passage—at most, some shepherds. For experienced hikers and campers, no more need be said. Less experienced travellers are advised to go in groups, and if you have any doubt about your ability to make your way, arrange for a guide—either in Khania or at one of the villages at the edge of the Gorge. You can get through it in a long day; spending a night there is considered a unique adventure. Wear warm clothing, in any case: there is not much sunlight during the day, and evenings can be very cool. Take along light camping gear if you plan to spend any time there. And be prepared to feed yourself for the hours you will pass in the Gorge.

Although we said that you won't see many people, the fact is that at about the halfway point you pass close by the settlement of Samaria, with the Venetian church of Holy Maria (1379) from which the gorge gets its name. (Before Samaria you pass the little chapel of St Nicholas in a lovely stand of cypresses.) Pashley, the famous 19th-century classicist-traveller, placed the site of the ancient Dorian city of Kaino near Samaria. There was an Oracle of Apollo; here, too, according to myth, was born the nymph Britomartis, daughter of Zeus—the Cretan Artemis or Dictynna. And the nereid Acacallis, wife of Hermes, was said to have been worshipped in this region. All in all, it is most atmospheric: it is easy to believe in the gods and goddesses of nature as you pass through such a gorge.

The Gorge ends quite abruptly at Ayia Roumeli, on the sea: the settlement is on a small alluvial plain, where the river emerges from the gorge. (There is a sudden drop-off at the shore, so no delta forms.) The village of Ayia Roumeli offers nothing spectacular: it is noted largely for its inhabitants—Sfakians—who make their living tending flocks, hunting wild game, and somehow subsisting off the gorge. There is one church of note: Our Lady of St Roumeli, built by the Venetians early in the 16th century. It has mosaics dating from the pre-Christian era and would seem to have been built over the ruins of a temple to either Apollo or Artemis—relic of the ancient city of Tarrha.

Tarrha was situated a little to the west of Ayia Roumeli, at the outlet of the gorge. It was settled at least from the 5th century BC, through the Roman period, and on to the 5th century AD. It was probably abandoned because of the decline of the trade routes and the resultant attacks by pirates. A few Hellenic remains have been turned up in recent years, as well as some Roman structures and fortifications. Tarrha was important enough to have its own coinage; it is also surmised that there was a glass factory, as a distinctive type of glass vessel has been found in the area. (The latest excavations have turned up tombs with jewellery and pottery.) Tarrha was particularly noted as the site of a temple-sanctuary of Tarrhanean Apollo; its inhabitants had a flourishing religion and mythology, involving not only Apollo, but Acacallis (daughter of Minos and wife of Hermes) and the Cretan virgin-goddess, Britomartis. The presence of the gorge, with its magnificent and mysterious natural setting, obviously stimulated the pantheism of the people living on this isolated coast.

From Ayia Roumeli, you face the same problem of moving on as you do in getting there: either you must take a boat or walk overland to one of the other towns on the coast serviced by buses. If you go up through the gorge, you must take care to bear left after the village of Samaria, otherwise you will get onto the mountain of Mavri.

Chapel of St Paul

Just a few kilometres to the east of Ayia Roumeli is a delightful chapel on a little clearing some 10 feet above the shore: it is known as the Chapel of St Paul, for he is said to have come ashore here and christened converts in a nearby spring (now only a trickle). The chapel is in the free cross form; its façade has an arcade of the Byzantine style from the 12th century. It is not particularly spectacular, but is well worth a side-trip from Ayia Roumeli, and could be taken in on a hike down the coast to the east—a trip described in some detail, starting from Khora Sfakia.

Selinou Province

Tucked away in the south-western corner of Crete is the Province of Selinou, probably the least visited area of the island. Today it is noted for its fine olives and oil, but it has many ancient sites and historical monuments that deserve to be better known. Not one of them is very spectacular in itself, but taken as a whole they provide an interesting glimpse into the post-Minoan, Byzantine, and Venetian periods of Crete. It is difficult to imagine that such isolated settlements could ever have 'made' history, but in their time they were involved in the power struggles of the Mediterranean: around 300 BC, for instance, several of them—Elyros, Lissos, Hyrtakina, Tarrha, Syia, and Poikilassos—formed the Confederation of Oreioi with Gortyne and King Magas of Cyrenaica. Remains of all these places are to be seen. Elyros was an especially strong post-Minoan power. Under the Romans,

some of these prospered; in the early Christian centuries, still others—
Syia, in particular—came into their own. Later, many Byzantine
churches and frescoes flowered, and the Venetians saw fit to develop
some of the sites. What remains today is fragmentary and only partially
explored: the definitive excavations and identifications have yet to be
made.

For the amateur traveller, this region has few attractions. Anyone
who wants to explore it should consult *The Tourist's Guide to Khania*,
Anestis Makridakis, the only available source of information on these
sites.

There are two basic approaches to Selinou. One would be to hike
overland from Ayia Roumeli, following the trails along and above the
coast all the way to Palaiokhora. This is only 25 or 30 kms as the crow
flies, but it would be at least twice that in actual hiking—especially
if you were to try to move up and down, from the port sites to the
highland settlements. Two or three days should be allowed. Another
possibility—probably appealing to more—would be to ride down to
Palaiokhora, either by bus or private vehicle, direct from Khania.
Palaiokhora is a lovely town, known as 'the bride of the Libyan Sea'.
There is an inn, and several eating-places, which make it a convenient
spot to pass some days while making excursions in the region.
(Palaiokhora is also known as Selinou Kastelli—after the Venetian
fort on its promontory.) Either en route to or as a side-trip from
Palaiokhora, you could visit Kandanos, famous for its Byzantine
churches and frescoes.

Gavdhos Island

One interesting excursion is to the island of Gavdhos, some 50 kms
offshore from Palaiokhora: it has the distinction of being the southern-
most territory of Europe—once you concede that Crete belongs to
Greece and Greece belongs to Europe. A boat leaves every Wednesday
from Palaiokhora, but with luck you might get one almost any time.
(You might also catch a ride from Ayia Galini, Khora Sfakia, or some
other port along the south shore.) Little is known of its exact history:
there are some ruins to be seen. and although surface finds from
neolithic times have been made, probably it was only settled in post-
Minoan times. Some have claimed it as Calypso's island: if so, it is
not hard to see why Odysseus kept moving. In *Acts* XXXII: 16, it
is mentioned by its ancient name, Klauda (or Kauda). And by the
Middle Ages it was actually the See of a Bishop. It has probably seen
its share of pirates come and go, too. Today, only a few hundred
people inhabit the island, supporting themselves by their flocks. It
rates a capital—Kastri—but the general effect is of a weird, desolate
landscape with many deserted houses. (A few kilometres north-west of
Gavdhos is the islet of Gavdhopola, a barren spot used for pasturing
sheep.) Simple accommodation is available on Gavdhos.

North-western Crete

This part of Crete reveals another, practically unknown island: rough, rocky terrain; a primitive landscape of valleys, mountains, and isolated villages; unexplored ruins. For the traveller with two or three days to spare, an excursion into this region can be a unique experience.

The bus only goes to Kastelli-Kissamos, but the other sites can be reached by a series of hikes. Once again, private transport would be a great help.

Heading west along the coast road, some 5 kms from Khania you come to Dharatso, where the Germans erected an imposing bronze eagle—a memorial to their parachute assault on Crete. The Cretans have chosen to leave it standing—as their own memorial. About 4 kms later you pass through Ayia Marina, a village with several old Venetian and Turkish houses now largely in ruins. Offshore is the island of Theodhoro, the ancient Akytos. It has a cave that seems to have been used as a place of worship around 2000 BC: its mouth looks like the gaping jaws of some beast, and legend has it that the island was once a wild animal that tried to devour Crete but was petrified by the gods. The Venetians and Turks used the island as a fortress, and now it is a sanctuary for the *agrimi*—the Cretan wild goat. (There are two or three dozen at present.)

About 8 kms farther, you pass through Maleme, where Khania's airport is located. Then, climbing up through the valley of the Tavronitis River (from *taurus*—'bull') and past the village of the same name, you arrive at the village of Kolymvariou (23 kms), just within the curve of the Rodhopou Peninsula. Kolymvariou has an inn and restaurant and is noted for its wines.

Rodhopou Peninsula was known in ancient times as Cape Tityros; today it is sometimes called Cape Spatha, after its outermost reach. It is one of two peninsulas that crown this end of Crete—like bulls' horns; the western peninsula is Cape Vousa, and between them lies the Gulf of Kissamos. At its widest part, Rodhopou Peninsula is only some 8 kms, but its central ridge rises to 2,500 feet. On the eastern side of the peninsula, just off the mainland, overlooking the coast and the Gulf of Khania, is the Monastery of Ghonia. Founded in 1618, burnt down by the Turks in 1645, re-erected in 1662, restored in 1798, and raised by one storey in 1874-84, it remains a fort-like structure. Venetian influence is evident, especially with the 'baroque' decoration of the refectory door. It has a handsome main gate, an extremely rich treasury, frescoes, and several fine icons of the 16th and 17th centuries—particularly a Crucifixion by Paleokapas.

Along the eastern coast, farther out, is the cave Hellenospilios: it is quite long, with many corridors and pools, stalactites and stalagmites, and many archaeological finds have been made here; and still farther out, near the little port of Ayios Georgios Kanzilieris and the tip of Cape Spatha, is the site of Dhiktinaia, named after the goddess Dictynna. It was from this spot that the nymph Dictynna (alias Britomartis, alias Artemis) threw herself to escape the lustful Minos: she was saved by the nets of fishermen—her name is derived from 'net' —and has since been venerated in western Crete as everything from a goddess of nets to a moon goddess. At times the whole peninsula was called after her—Dhiktinaion. There was a Hellenistic temple to her on the site; this was replaced by a Roman temple in the 2nd century AD, and it is mainly the remains of this that are to been seen. Cutting inland, more into the centre of the peninsula, you reach the village of Rodhopou: in this mountainous region, where stands the Church of St John, 'Giona', a festival is held each August 28-29. It is probably the largest religious festival in the entire Nome of Khania, and crowds from the whole western part of Crete gather here.

Back on the main road to the west, just after Kolymvariou, there is a turn-off left to the village of Spilia, noted for its Byzantine art. The 14th-century frescoes of the Church of Our Lady are superb examples of the 'Cretan school' of painting; and the altar of the Church of Michael Archangelos is a fine example of wood carving. Above the village is a cave with a natural interior amphitheatre.

Proceeding by the main road, you pass through the distinctive landscape of red earth, limestone slopes, olive trees and vines, approaching the village of Kastelli, on the site of the ancient Kissamos, port for the ancient Polyrhinia. Kissamos was an autonomous post-Minoan settlement; the Romans took it over—remains of their aqueduct are in place; and in the early Christian era it became an episcopal seat. The Venetians chose to develop the site: they made it the See of a Catholic Bishop, encouraged trade, and constructed walls in the mid-16th century (of which vestiges remain). A Venetian church also survives, as do remains of an ancient theatre and temple. The walls of modern Kastelli are doubtless made from material of ancient Kissamos. Present-day Kastelli is quite rural in appearance, but it is a centre for the production and trade of the district's wines. It has an hotel and restaurants. A nearby nunnery, Parthenonas, is noted for its woven fabrics. There is a fine little collection of archaeological finds from the region.

About 6 kms south of Kastelli-Kissamos, some 900 feet above sea level, is the village of Ano Palaiokastro at the site of ancient Polyrhinia —'town of many flocks'. It enjoys an excellent view over the Gulf of Kissamos. Founded during the 8th century BC, Polyrhinia was one of the chief settlements of Archaic Crete. Statues, bas-reliefs, and coins contribute to the image of a once-influential city that probably dominated much of the area because of its strategic position. (The worship of such familiar gods as Apollo, Hermes, Dionysus, Dictynna-Artemis, and Zeus is indicated by the coins.) Cyclopean walls, aqueducts, reservoirs, temples, and some graves carved in rock-caves are to be seen, but the inhabitants of the area have used much of the material over the centuries: the Church of the 99 Holy Fathers, for instance, has probably utilized parts of older temples.

Back on the coast, and proceeding west some 10 kms, you arrive at the post-Minoan city of Phalasarna. The site was first explored early in this century, but not much in the way of a conclusive history has yet been provided. It probably served as a port for Polyrhinia It seems to have had its temple to Dictynna-Artemis, but no particular palace—although there is a throne of sorts carved out of the rock. The bulk of the remains—remnants of walls, reservoirs, quarries, houses, storage rooms, and tombs—probably date from the Hellenic and Roman periods. With the great shifting of Crete—placed in the 6th century AD—Phalasarna's port installations were left high and dry and are now some 150 yards inland. Phalasarna sits on its promontory, in all its megalithic, isolated splendour, looking out across the Mediterranean to the west.

Above it protrudes Cape Vousa—the ancient peninsula of Korykia. The village nearest to Phalasarna is Platanos, with a frescoed church of uncertain date. Most of the peninsula is deserted. Off the outer tip of the peninsula are two islets—Gramvousa and Agria Gramvousa. The former, situated slightly to the south-west of the other, is a precipitous, almost unassailable island that is probably one of the oldest Mediterranean pirate lairs. The Venetians constructed a fortress on Gramvousa, and it was one of the last three holdouts against the Turks, capitulating only in 1692. Eventually the Christian Cretans managed to get it back, and marauders operating from there were a nuisance to all parties. The fort is in fair condition, and there are caves, a frescoed Byzantine church, and some Venetian structures.

Holidays and Festivals

Hardly a day passes on Crete without a celebration in honour of somebody or something—a saint, a village festival, a harvest, a national event. Each Nome has one place—either a chapel, a monastery or a village—where on major saints' days the people bearing that name gather. These 'namedays' are far more important to Greeks than their birthdays. Almost always dancing and general celebration take place on the night preceding the actual church observances, and extra services are run on the regular bus routes. Sometimes festivities are extended over two or three days, and the lavish Cretan hospitality sets itself no limits at all. You have been warned.

The asterisk beside certain dates indicates the official Greek holidays, when banks, museums, and many stores are likely to be closed.

Date	Occasion	Where and How Observed
Dec. 30 *-Jan. 1	New Year	In homes, cafés, hotels and public assemblies: observed by feasting, card-playing and gambling, and rituals such as opening the windows at midnight to let the evil spirits out.
*Jan. 6	Epiphany	At harbours and sea-shores: a cross is thrown into the sea to bring luck and blessings.
3 weeks before Lent	Carnival	Cities like Iraklion and Rethymnon make the biggest display, but eating, drinking, and good spirits are general throughout the island.
	*Clean Monday	This marks the end of Carnival: no meat is eaten—but a feast is contrived all the same. Kites are flown—by all ages.
	Lent	Observed by everyone to a certain extent, but a Holy Week of almost total fasting is the culminating feature of Lent.
*Mar. 25	Greek Independence Day	Not much celebrated on Crete.
	Annunciation of Our Lady	Church of Prassa (Iraklion) and Apokorona (Khania).
See note below	*Good Friday to Easter Monday	On Friday, there is a funeral procession through the streets. On Saturday evening, a long church service ends with rejoicing at midnight, lighting of candles, and fireworks. Easter Sunday is celebrated with eating, drinking, dancing. Many flock to military installations to celebrate.

Note on Greek Easter: The Greek Orthodox Easter is calculated in a way which baffles all but the initiated. As with the Western Christian churches, it must fall after the first full moon following the first day of spring, but it must also fall *after* the Jewish Passover. Holidays dependent on Easter, of course, must also be based on this fluctuating date.

Date	*Occasion*	*Where and How Observed*
1st Sun. after Easter	St Thomas	Monastery of Vrondisi, Ayios Thomas (Iraklion) and at Neo Khorio of Apokorona (Khania).
April 23	St George	Monastery of Epanosifi: religious feast with Archbishop celebrating Mass (Iraklion). Selinaris Monastery: religious feast (Lasithi).
	Ascension	Almyros Church: service and feast (Lasithi). Local dances and fireworks.
May 1	Spring Festival	Throughout the countryside people picnic, dance, and weave flower-wreaths.
May 5	St Irene	Village of Kroussona: religious feast (Iraklion).
May 20-27	Anniversary of Battle of Crete (Second World War)	City of Khania celebrates with athletic events.
May 21	St Constantine and St Helena	At various chapels named for these saints.
June 1-7	Amateur fishermen's week	Arranged by local Hellenic Club in in Ayios Nikolaos.
June 24	Birthday of St John the Baptist	With bonfires (which actually are observing the summer solstice); if lucky, you may see people jumping over them.
*June 29	St Peter and St Paul	Name day of the present King, so a national holiday.
July	Wine Festival	The city of Rethymnon has instituted a modern festival, with several days of wine-sampling. Dances in Cretan costumes.
July 17	St Marina	Village of Voni: major religious feast (Iraklion).
July 26 and 27	St Paraskevi and St Panteleimon	Observed at villages of Kounavoi (Iraklion) and Fourne of Kydonia (Khania).
Aug. 6	Feast of Trans-figuration of Saviour	At a small church on Mt Iouktas (approached from village of Arkhanai) (Iraklion). Religious feast. Also observed at Skine of Kydonia (Khania).
Aug. 8	St Myron	At the village of Ayios Myron (cave where saint lived, with sacred water) (Iraklion).

Date	Occasion	Where and How Observed
*Aug. 15	Dormition (Assumption) of Our Lady	At the town of Neapolis: feast starts on 14th with local dances, athletic sports; ends on 16th (Lasithi). At the village of Mokhos: festival organized by Greek Touring Club, with Cretan food, local dances in Cretan costumes, exhibitions of local hand-weavings and embroidery, fireworks (Iraklion). Religious feasts at villages, convents and monasteries throughout Crete.
Aug. 25	St Titus	Iraklion: religious procession from Church of St Titus, at 10 a.m.
Aug. 27	St Fanourios	Monastery of Vrondisi: religious feast (Iraklion).
Aug. 29	Beheading of St John the Baptist	At Giona, near village of Rodhopou of Kissamos (Khania). Also at various churches named after St John.
Aug. 31	Holy Sash of the Virgin Mary	Village of Psykhro: religious feast and local dances, hundreds of people descending to the plain on mules. (Lasithi).
Sept. 14	Raising of Holy Cross	Observed in city of Iraklion and villages around Mt Idha. Also at Alikianos of Kydonia (Khania).
Sept. 20-25	Sports	Swimming and athletic events organized by local clubs of Ayios Nikolaos (Lasithi).
Oct. 7	St John the Hermit	At the monastery of Gouverneto, and the nearby cave where the saint died (Khania).
Oct. 26	St Demetrios	Observed at many chapels, as this is a popular name.
*Oct. 28	'Okhi' Day	Observed all over Greece to commemorate the occasion when the Greek Premier defied the Axis.
Nov. 7-9	Anniversary of Explosion of 1866	Monastery of Arkadhi and at Rethymnon: Crete's own 'national' holiday, with people from all over the island gathering at the monastery.
Nov. 11	St Menas	City of Iraklion: Religious procession in morning for Patron Saint of city.
Dec. 4	St Barbara	Village of Ayia Varvara (Iraklion).
Dec. 6	St Nicholas	City of Ayios Nikolaos. (Lasithi).
*Dec. 25 and 26	Christmas	This is less important to the Orthodox than Easter, but the whole season of Twelve Days is marked, here and there, with singing on Christmas Eve. Popular diversions are gambling and fortune-telling. Fear of evil spirits —the *Kalikantzaros*—prevails.

Weights and Measures

The international metric system is used, officially and generally. The few exceptions that linger among the older folk are noted below.

Weight
Kilo (1,000 grams): approx. 2·2 lbs
Half-kilo (*misso kilo*): 500 grams
Quarter-kilo (*tatarto*): 250 grams
(The *oka*—1,282 grams or 2.8 lbs—has been officially banned, but is still sometimes used by older people.)

Volume
1 Litre: approx. 1·06 liquid quarts. 1 quart: 0·946 litres
Most commodities are sold by weight. Petrol is sold by the gallon. Liquids are generally sold by the litre. In restaurants wine is sold by large or small bottles or by glass; but in the wine taverns, wine is often sold by the kilo measure—with one kilo equivalent to one litre.

Length
1 metre: 39·37 inches
1 kilometre: 0·62 miles
Roughly speaking, one kilometre equals 5/8 of one mile.
The English yard may occasionally be used by men's tailors or by yard-goods dealers.

Temperature
The Centigrade scale is used.
To convert F. to C., subtract 32 and multiply by $\frac{5}{9}$. To convert C. to F., multiply by $\frac{9}{5}$ and add 32.

Time
Crete, like the mainland, lies in the Eastern European Zone, two hours ahead of Greenwich Mean Time and about 7 hours ahead of New York. Officially, Greece uses the Continental 24-hour system, where 1 p.m. is '13 o'clock', 2 p.m. is '14 o'clock', etc. But in actual practice people say 'One this noon', or '8 this evening'.!

All Greece—except Mt Athos—uses the Western Gregorian calendar; with the exception of Easter and its dependent holy days (p. 186), many Greek religious holidays and festivals coincide with those of Europe.

Currency

The Greek drachma has been fairly stable for some years now. As with all currencies there may be minor variations in the exchange rate according to where you make the transaction—in banks, travel agencies, hotels, etc.

The maximum amount of drachmas that a foreigner is allowed to bring in or take out is 2,000. If you should overstock, it is possible to buy back your own currency, but only at the Bank of Greece. You must produce the receipts of your original purchase of drachmas, and you will lose about one per cent on the transaction.

If, for any reason, you have to send money out of Greece to some other country, this may also be done through the Bank of Greece, and here again you will need to take all your documents and receipts.

Above all, the traveller should work out his own personal system for making conversions and relating values. For example: with the English £ at about Drs. 84, one drachma is about 3d., Drs. 10 about 2s. 5d., Drs. 50 about 12s. and Drs. 100 about £1 4s.; with the U.S. $ pegged at about Drs. 30, Drs. 10 are about 35 cents, one drachma about 3 cents, Drs. 100 about $3.33.

The Greek drachma—often known colloquially as a 'franc'—is made up of 100 lepta, which makes 50 lepta worth about a penny-halfpenny, The coins now in circulation include: 10, 20, and 50 lepta pieces, and 1, 2, 5, 10 and 20 drachma pieces. And beware: several of these are almost the same size and are easily confused. There are also notes to the value of Drs. 50, 100, 500, and 1,000.

Post, Telephone and Telegrams

Every village on Crete has some place where it is possible to buy stamps and send and receive mail. In the main cities you can sometimes buy stamps at kiosks as well as at the post offices (the word for stamp is *grammatóssima*). Postal rates on Crete are the same as on mainland Greece, but it is worth remembering that there is a special rate for postcards with less than five words of message.

Registered Mail
If you intend to send a registered letter, this should not be sealed until the post office official has approved its contents.

Parcel Post
If you are sending a package out of Greece you must be prepared to show the entire contents to the postal authorities: this means undoing even gift wrappings—often for each individual item. There is also a considerable amount of form-filling, stamping, etc. The Greeks themselves take their various gifts and items to the post office, get them inspected, and do all their wrapping-up there, and this seems to be the easiest way.

Air Freight
Olympic Airways has a surprisingly cheap service for light freight and packages—but only within Greece. It is worth while if you have to get things to and from the mainland while on Crete.

Telephone and Telegrams
There is at least one telephone to be found in every village on Crete and both local and long distance calls may be made. In the main cities telegrams may be sent from the central exchanges. In other places this may be done by telephone. (From midnight Saturday/Sunday till midnight Sunday/Monday telephone and telegram rates *within* Greece are doubled.)

Selected Reading

Most of these books are readily available, some in paperback editions.

General

*La Crète au cours des Siècles,*Raymond Matton (Athens 1957). Probably the best and most complete survey of all aspects of Crete's history and life.

The Greek Myths, Robert Graves (Penguin Books, 1957). This is required reading for a true understanding of Crete.

Mythology, Edith Hamilton (1940). The simplest and clearest guide to Greek mythology.

The Iliad and *The Odyssey*, Homer. Now and again one has a glimpse of Crete as part of the Aegean world of that time.

The King Must Die (1958) and *The Bull From the Sea* (1962). Although modern historical novels, these imaginative reconstructions of the Theseus legend and the Minoan world are like a voice from the past.

The Bible: Acts XXVII and Epistle to Titus.
A glimpse of Crete as it appeared to contemporaries.

Zorba the Greek, *Freedom and Death*, *The Greek Passion* (*Christ Recrucified*), *The Odyssey: A Modern Sequel*, Nikos Kazantzakis. Novels and an epic poem that have secured a place in the post-war literary world, they are as authentic a Cretan 'voice' as we are likely to have for some time.

The Palace of Minos, Arthur Evans. The great work on Crete—four volumes that represent the sum of his labours in the field. Evans wrote other works—*Cretan Pictograms and Pre-Phoenician Script*, *Mycenaean Tree and Pillar Cult*, *Prehistoric Tombs of Knossos*—but these are mainly for the specialist.

The Archaeology of Crete, J. D. S. Pendlebury (1939). In many ways this is still the best objective account of what has been found on Crete—before and through Roman times.

Minoan Crete: History and Archaeology

Greece before Homer, E. J. Forsdyke (1956).

The Aegean Civilization, Gustave Glotz (1925). There is a later edition —1952—of the original French version.

Mycenaeans and Minoans, L. R. Palmer (1961). This embodies the latest scholarship as well as some controversial conclusions.

Crete, the Forerunner of Greece, C. H. and H. B. Hawes (1909).

The Decipherment of Linear B, John Chadwick (1958). An excellent account of the deciphering of the Minoan script, by one who was directly concerned.

The Bull of Minos, Leonard Cottrell (1953).

The House of the Double Axe, Agnes Carr Vaughan (1959).

History of Crete after the Minoans

Aristocratic Society in Ancient Crete, R. F. Willetts (1955).

Numismatique de la Crète Ancienne, J. N. Svoronos (1890).

'The Arab Occupation of Crete', E. W. Brooks, in *The English Historical Review* (Vol. XXVIII, No. CXI, July 1913).

The Byzantine Empire, A. A. Vasiliev.

'Crete under the Venetians', William Miller, in *Gentlemen's Magazine* (March 1903).

La Crète sous la domination et la souveraineté ottomane, Ahmed Softazadé (1902).

A Short History of Modern Greece, Edward S. Forster (New Ed. 1958).

The Cretan Insurrection of 1866-68, W. J. Stillman (1874).

Les affaires de Crète, Victor Bérard (1898).

The Cretan Drama, H.R.H. Prince George of Greece.

Greece and Crete 1941, Christopher Buckley (1952).

The Cretan Runner, George Psychoundakis (1955).

Crete: A Case Study of an Underdeveloped Area, Leland Allbaugh (1953).

Crete and Religion

Prolegomena to the Study of Greek Religion, Jane Harrison.

The Minoan-Mycenaean Religion and its Survival in Greek Religion, Martin Nilsson (2nd rev. ed. 1950).

'The Cult of the Cretan Caves', S. Marinatos, in *Review of Religion* (V, 1941).

Greek Calendar Customs, George A. Megas (Athens 1958).

Crete and the Arts

Crete and Mycenae, Marinatos and Hirmer (1960); *Crete in Colour*, Reverdin and Hoegler (1961); *L'art de la Crète neolithique et minoenne*, Christian Zervos (1956). Three large and expensive volumes, lavishly illustrated with the masterpieces of Crete's great days.

Archaic Greek Art, Gisela Richter (1949).

Early Hellenic Pottery of Crete, Doro Levi (1945).

Byzantine Art, D. Talbot Rice (Penguin Books).

'La peinture murale byzantine de l'Ile de Crète', Constantine Kalokiris, in *Kritika Chronica* (1954). This is a Greek publication, but the essay is in French. The author has also written the standard work on the subject, in Greek.

'The Greek Drama in Crete in the Seventeenth Century' and 'The Cretan Drama: A Postscript', John Mavrogordato, in *The Journal of Hellenic Studies* (Vol. XLVIII, Parts I and II, 1928).

Monumenti veneti nell' isola di Creta, Guiseppe Gerola (Venezia 1905-32).

'Homer and Cretan Heroic Poetry: A Study in Comparative Oral Poetry', James A. Notopoulos, in *American Journal of Philology* (Vol. 73, No. 3, July 1952).

Travels on Crete

Relation d'un voyage au Levant, Joseph de Tournefort (Paris 1717). An English translation appeared in 1718.

Travels in Crete, Robert Pashley (1837).

Travels and Researches in Crete, Capt. T. A. B. Spratt (1865).

Description physique de l'Ile de Crète, Victor Raulin (1869).

Camping in Crete, Aubyn Trevor-Battye (1913).

The Island of Zeus: Wanderings in Crete, Ralph Brewster (1939).

The Colossos of Maroussi, Henry Miller (1941).

In the Wake of Odysseus, Göran Schildt (1953).

The Stronghold, Xan Fielding (1953).

La Crète vivante, Claude Dervenn (1957).

Minotaur and Crete, Robert Grantham (1960).

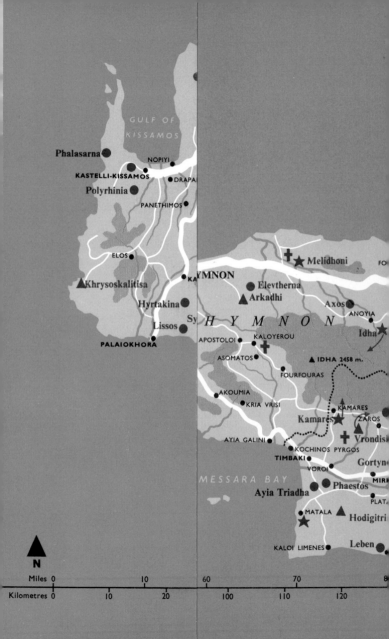

GULF OF
KISSAMOS

Phalasarna
NOPIYI
KASTELLI-KISSAMOS
DRAPAI
Polyrhinia
PANETHIMOS

ELOS
Khrysoskalitisa
KA   YMNON   **Elevtherna**
Hyrtakina   ▲ **Arkadhi**
Lissos   Sy   H Y M N O N
PALAIOKHORA   APOSTOLOI   KALOYEROU
ASOMATOS
FOURFOURAS
AKOUMIA
KRIA VRISI   **Kamares**
AYIA GALINI   **Vrondis**
KOCHINOS PYRGOS
TIMBAKI   **Gortyn**
VOROI   MIRR
Ayia Triadha   **Phaestos**
MESSARA BAY   PLAT.
MATALA   ▲ **Hodigitri**
KALOI LIMENES   **Leben**

✝ ★ **Melidhoni**   FO
Axos   ANOYIA
Idha ★
▲ IDHA 2458 m.
Kamares ★ ZAROS

▲ N

Miles 0 .... 10 .... 60 .... 70 8

Kilometres 0 .... 10 .... 20 .... 100 .... 110 120

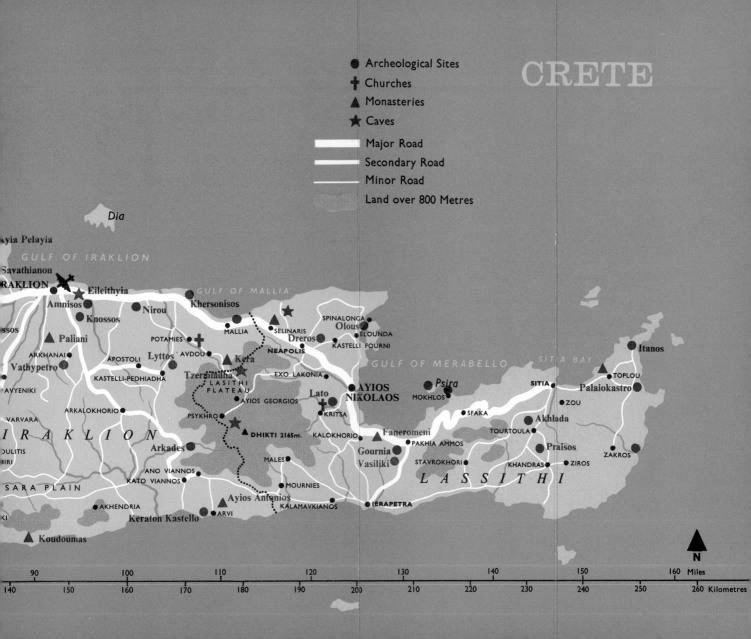

CRETE

Archeological Sites
Churches
Monasteries
Caves

Major Road
Secondary Road
Minor Road
Land over 800 Metres

Dia

Ayia Pelayia
GULF OF IRAKLION
Savathianon
IRAKLION
Amnisos   Eileithyia
Knossos   Nirou   Khersonisos
ssos   GULF OF MALLIA
Paliani   POTAMIES   MALLIA   SELINARIS
ARKHANAI   APOSTOLI   AVDOU   Dreros
Vathypetro   Lyttos   Kera   NEAPOLIS
AYENIKI   KASTELLI-PEDHIADHA   Tzerniadha   EXO LAKONIA
Varvara   ARKALOKHORIO   LASITHI
                                                        PLATEAU
I R A K L I O N   PSYKHRO   AYIOS GEORGIOS
OULITIS   Arkades   DHIKTI 2165m.
MIRI
SARA PLAIN   MALES
                              AKHENDRIA   ANO VIANNOS
KI   KATO VIANNOS
                    Koudoumas   Keraton Kastello   Ayios Antonios   MOURNIES
                                                        ARVI   KALAMAVKIANOS

SPINALONGA
Olous   ELOUNDA
KASTELLI FOURNI
GULF OF MERABELLO
Lato   AYIOS
                NIKOLAOS
KRITSA
                    Faneromeni
KALOKHORIO   PAKHIA AMMOS
        Gournia
        Vasiliki   STAVROKHORI
IERAPETRA

Psira
MOKHLOS   SITIA   Itanos
        SFAKA   ZOU   Palaiokastro
                TOURTOULA   Akhlada
                        KHANDRAS   Praisos   ZAKROS
                        ZIROS
L A S S I T H I

SIT A BAY
TOPLOU

N

90   100   110   120   130   140   150   160   Miles
140   150   160   170   180   190   200   210   220   230   240   250   260   Kilometres

ENER

zenia

RYERI

VO

YIA DH

M

VA

Vocabulary

	Pronunciation
Numbers	*(accents indicate stress)*
1	énas (masc.) mía (fem.) éna (neut.)
2	dhío
3	tris (masc.) tría (fem.)
4	tésseris (masc.) téssera (fem.)
5	pénde
6	éxi
7	eftá
8	októ
9	ennéa
10	dhéka
11	eńdheka
12	dhódheka
13	dhekatría
14	dhekatéssera
20	íkosi
21	íkosi éna
30	triańda
40	sarańda
50	penińda
60	exińda
70	evdhomińda
80	ogdhońda
90	enenińda
100	ekató
200	dhiakósi
1,000	khíli
2,000	dhío khiliádhes

Useful Expressions	
Sir	Kírie
Madame	Kiría
Yes	Nai
No	Oḱhi
Not	Dhen
Only	Móno
Please	Parakaló
Thank you	Evkharistó

English	*Pronunciation*
Good morning (good day)	Kaliméra
Good evening	Kalispéra
Hello	Khaírete
Goodbye	Adío
How are you?	Ti khánete?
May I (Can I) ...?	Boró na ...?
I want to ...	Thélo na ...
I must ...	Prépi ...
Do you speak English?	Miláte angliká?
Speak slowly.	Miláte sigá.
I do not understand.	Dhen katálava.
What is this called in Greek?	Pos to léne avto en elliniká?
What is your name?	Pos se léne?
Where is ...?	Pu ínai ...?
When?	Póte?
How much is it?	Póso káni avtó?
I am thirsty.	Dhipsó.
Street	Othoś
Square	Platía
Beach	Plaz
Mountain	Vunó
Sea	Thálassa

Food and Drink

restaurant	estiatórion
water	neró
oil	ládhi
salt	aláti
bread	psomí
milk	gála
tea	tsái
coffee	kafés
butter	vútiro
sugar	zákhari
egg	avgó
chicken	kotópulo
lamb	arní
veal	moskhári
beef	vodhinó
pork	khirinó

English	Pronunciation
fish	psári
cheese	tirí
honey	méli
ice cream	pagotó
grapes	stafília
watermelon	karpúzi
apple	mílo
fig	síko
beer	bíra
orangeade	portokaládha
wine	krasí
waiter	garsón
bill	logarisamós

Hotel

hotel	xenodhokhío
room	dhomátio
bath	bánio
key	klidhí
towel	petséta
soap	sapoúni
hot	zestó
cold	krío
bed	kreváti
blanket	kuveŕta
laundry	rúkha
toilet, lavatory	toméros

Travel

ship	vapóri
bus	leoforío
taxi	taxí
automobile	avtokínito
bus stop	stási
ticket	isitírio
map	khaŕtis
bags	bangázia
puncture	laśtiko
garage	garáz
petrol	venzína

English	*Pronunciation*
Post and Stationery	
post office	takhidhromío
stamp	grammatósimo
letter	grámma
by air mail	aeroporikós
telegram	tilegráfima
Facilities and Shops	
bank	trápeza
pharmacy	farmakío
doctor	yiatrós
newspaper	efimerídha
cigarettes	sigaréta
matches	spírta
torch	fakós
receipt	apódhixi
police	astinomikós
Time	
What time is it?	Ti óra ínai?
now	tóra
today	símera
tomorrow	avrio
morning	proí
afternoon	apóyevma
evening	vrádhi
Direction	
left	aristerá
right	dhexiá
near	kondá
far	makriá
behind	píso
beside	dhípla
Quantity	
few	líyi
many	pollí
enough	arketós
too much	pára polí

Index